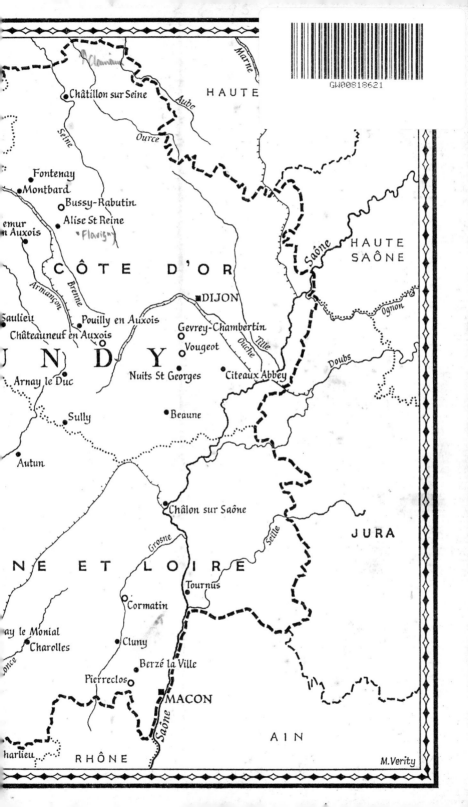

HAUTE

Châtillon sur Seine

Marne
Aube
Ource
Seine

Fontenay
Montbard
Bussy-Rabutin
Alise St Reine
"Flavigny"
emur
n Auxois

CÔTE D'OR

Saône

HAUTE
SAÔNE

Armançon
Brenne

DIJON

Ognon

Saulieu
Pouilly en Auxois
Châteauneuf en Auxois

Gevrey-Chambertin
Vougeot

Ouche
Tille

Doubs

UNDY

Nuits St Georges
Citeaux Abbey

Arnay le Duc

Sully
Beaune

Autun

Châlon sur Saône

JURA

Grosne
Seille

NE ET LOIRE

Tournus

Cormatin

ay le Monial
Charolles

Cluny

Berzé la Ville

Pierreclos

MACON

Saône

AIN

harlieu
RHÔNE

M.Verity

BURGUNDY
Landscape with Figures

BURGUNDY

LANDSCAPE WITH FIGURES

by

PETER GUNN

LONDON
VICTOR GOLLANCZ LTD
1976

ISBN 0 575 02123 3

Printed in Great Britain by
The Camelot Press Ltd, Southampton

Le style, c'est l'homme.
—Buffon of Montbard

CONTENTS

LIST OF ILLUSTRATIONS

The illustrations listed below are reproduced by kind permission of the French Government Tourist Office, unless otherwise specified.

PREFACE

THIS IS A book about the ancient French province of Burgundy. If the historical province may be seen as a tapestry, my intention has been to try to display something of the stuff of which it is woven—to represent, that is, a landscape with figures that stand out against the greens, old gold and blues of their background. It is a travel book, but a guidebook only in the extended use of the term—by courtesy, as it were. A guidebook proper—or a guide, for that matter—points to something and offers some relevant information about it. Guidebooks, then, like signposts, are essential to the traveller. Our grandparents travelled across Europe with *Murray* or *Baedeker* securely in their bags, for these books were as indispensable for their enlightenment as were the services of the enterprising Mr Thomas Cook for their comfort. Today the visitor to Burgundy has a choice of these necessary, indeed vital, concomitants: in French there is the excellent Michelin *Guide Vert, Bourgogne-Morvan*; published in both French and English is the volume *Burgundy* in the series of *Guides Bleus* of Hachette; and in English there is the invaluable Collins' *Companion Guide to Burgundy* by Robert Speight—to name but a few among them. By way of maps he would not do better than to equip himself with those published by Michelin in the series one centimetre to two kilometres, Nos 65, 66 and 69.

This book, then, is not intended to usurp the place of a guidebook; rather it is to supplement it. Or, if it did not sound pretentious, it might be called a meta-guide; a guide to guidebooks, in so far as it may suggest to the prospective visitor to Burgundy what he might look for in his guidebook. The chapters, which are in a broad sense complementary, need not be read in the order given, although this order is roughly chronological. They consist of self-contained essays which, if seemingly arbitrarily chosen, do in fact aim at conveying something of the characteristics of this generous and mellow countryside and of its people, who, even in their very down-to-earthiness, appear to have reflected their landscape, with its richness and variety. Burgundy was, after all, the heart of ancient Gaul, and it is therefore not surprising that its people should display those qualities which we recognize as quintessentially Gallic. It is to be hoped for this reason that the figures will appear placed fairly and squarely in the landscape. Because of the importance of Burgundian romanesque and gothic architecture, two chapters have been devoted to these periods, which, it is hoped, may serve as some sort of introduction to the enjoyment of the beauty of the abbeys, the crocketted cathedrals and those charming smaller churches, which are found in such profusion in the towns and countryside of Burgundy. And no book on the province would be complete without some reference to the world-famed *cuisine bourguignonne* and to those wines, particularly the reds of the Côte d'Or, whose reputation for excellence is rivalled only by those of the châteaux of Bordeaux.

I should like to take this occasion of offering my warmest thanks to those authors and publishers who have kindly allowed me to quote extracts from their books: Hamish Hamilton Ltd for Lucy Norton (editor and translator), *Historical Memoirs of the Duke de Saint-Simon*; Longman Group Ltd for Dr Richard Vaughan, *Philip the Good*; and Secker & Warburg for Colette, *My Apprenticeships*.

SWALEDALE, YORKSHIRE   PETER GUNN
SEPTEMBER 1975

BURGUNDY

CHAPTER I

Burgundy Known and Unknown

DOES THERE EXIST in the land of France such a place as the province of Burgundy? The question is not an idle one. If reference is made to the provinces of Normandy or Brittany, or Provence say, no one can fail to picture their clear-cut representations in his mind's eye. On the contrary, the Burgundy of the geographers and the topographers is an ambiguous region; no coastline, mountains or rivers bind it in; no geological formations distinguish it from its neighbours. Its shape is amorphous; so much so that, rather than fix with precision its boundaries, these scientific gentlemen have sometimes found it simpler, if not to deny, then at least to ignore its homogeneous existence. And the case of the Burgundy of the historians is not so very different. What is this Burgundy whose history they are relating? Is it the kingdom of Gundibald and his heirs, where ran the *Loi Gombette*, or the duchy of the Capets, or that of the Valois, or the hereditary governorship of the Condé family? For these princes ruled over territories that were by no means identical. And what relation does this historical Burgundy bear to the 'circumscription for the regional plan of economic and social development' of modern bureaucrats?

For that matter, are the art historians on firmer ground when they speak of a Burgundian style? On this last point, it has been ingeniously suggested that, with reference to the style of the Chartreuse de Champmol, it is perhaps called Burgundian because its artists were a Fleming and a Dutchman, a Spaniard and a sculptor from Avignon. And what about the redoubtable character of these so-called Burgundians—so 'sympathetic, fresh, smiling, colourful, frank, open . . .'? (It is a Burgundian, by the way, who is using these epithets to describe his fellow countrymen.) These are difficult matters.

Perhaps we should be wiser, then, to restrict our use of the name Burgundy simply to denote certain famous wines, seeking our refuge in the apparent security (only comparative these days) of an *appellation contrôlée*?

If one were to write a book, entitling it simply *Burgundy*, more people than not would imagine its subject to be that of wine, a study, popular or specialist, or a bit of both, primarily for the wine-lover. And in point of fact, a book could well be written on the ancient Burgundian province with precisely this as its central theme—the justly celebrated wines of Burgundy. The reader would discover how the ancient Gauls developed a strong liking for this suave, life-enhancing beverage, so much preferring it to their own meagre beers or vapid mead that they went to great lengths to obtain it from those Mediterranean peoples who then produced it. Diodorus Siculus, the Greek historian writing at the time of the Emperor Augustus, tells us that 'the natural cupidity of the Roman merchants exploits the Gauls' passion for wine. On the boats that follow the courses of the navigable rivers or on chariots that traverse the plains they transport their wine from which they gain unbelievable profits, going as far as to barter one amphora of wine for one slave, so that the purchaser hands over his servitor to pay for his drink.' A high price indeed. It may have been to remedy this unsatisfactory balance of payments that the Gallic Aedui began themselves to cultivate the vine, learning the secrets of Latin viticulture from such authorities as Cato and Varro, from Columella's *De re rustica* or Virgil's second *Georgic*—'*Nunc te, Bacche, canam* . . . Now of thee, Bacchus, I shall sing . . .'

By A.D. 312 vineyards were already established in the *Pagus Arebrignus*, that is, the district now known as the Côte d'Or, since in that year the authorities of Autun addressed their thanks to the Emperor Constantine for a reduction in excise duties. It would appear that the wine growers were suffering from a shortage of labour, consequent on the disruption caused already by the barbarian invasions. Among Roman connoisseurs the wines of the Côte gained a high reputation for their fineness and strength. Like the fourth-century Latin poet Ausonius, who, a native of Bordeaux, has left his name to the well-known Château Ausone, Roman administrators (or were they cultivators or simply *négociants*?) are recalled in Burgundy by the *Clos de la Romanée*.

With the coming of Christianity and the development of the monastic movement, it was the monks who cleared the forests and planted and tended the vines. Thus it came about that the Cistercians, the Order to which belonged St Bernard of Clairvaux, were in the forefront of the cultivators of the vineyards of the Côte d'Or. We learn that Duke Odo of Burgundy made a gift of his vineyard at Meursault to the newly founded abbey of Cîteaux at Christmas 1098. Some few years later one Guerric of Chamballe presented the land which was to become the justly celebrated Clos de Vougeot, and in the same century the Cistercian monks built the Great Cellar, in which today the Confrérie des Chevaliers du Tastevin hold their annual ceremonies.

In the Middle Ages the cultivation of the vine was dispersed over a much greater area of Burgundy than it is today. The Italian monk, the Franciscan Fra Salimbene, describing his travels in France about the middle of the thirteenth century, writes of the countryside around Auxerre: 'In the vast region that is included in the diocese of this city, the high ground, slopes, plains and fields are—as I have seen with my own eyes— covered with vines. The people of this countryside, in fact, do not sow, nor reap, nor gather into barns. All they have to do is to send their wine to Paris by the nearby river, which leads there direct. The sale of wine in this city yields handsome profits, which pay entirely for their livelihood and clothing.' Today the vineyards of this once extended region are for the most part restricted to those producing the famous growths of Chablis. But it was the wines of the Côte d'Or, those of the Côte de Nuits and the Côte de Beaune, that early won pride of place. Petrarch, writing in 1361 of the reasons which prolonged the Great Schism, made the pointed remark: 'The wines of Beaune, it is said, are not to be had so easily beyond the Alps.' In 1370 Jean de Bussières, abbot of Cîteaux, made a gift of thirty tuns of his monastery's wine from Beaune and Gevrey to Pope Gregory XI at Avignon. The Supreme Pontiff, in thanking the abbot for his generosity, promised that he would not forget him. Four years later he received the cardinal's hat. But it was in the

following century that the Valois dukes, who proudly asserted
that they were 'the Seigneurs of the best wines in Christendom',
put them to excellent effect by a judicious priming of political
gullets—the so-called 'wine diplomacy of the Grand-Dukes of
the West'.

The Cistercian Order, likewise, used their wines to good
effect. Dom Gervase, of the Strict Observance, complained that
it would be useless for his congregation to be represented at the
General Chapter in 1667, since the abbot of Cîteaux would get
his way 'by giving lavish hospitality to the abbots of Germany,
Switzerland, Poland and other countries, and by pouring out
for them in profusion the excellent wine of his Clos de Vougeot
—which on like occasions has worked so many miracles—he will
get them to do whatever he pleases'. Then ten years later, on
the evening of Sunday, 29th August 1677, Mme de Sévigné
partook of a memorable supper at an inn in Saulieu, which is
remembered today on the restaurant and inn signs of that
ancient town. She had been staying with the Comte de Guitaut
at his château of Epoisses, on her way to take the waters at
Vichy. On resuming her journey south she was accompanied
by the Count as far as Saulieu, where she was to spend the
night before going on the next day to meet her cousin, Comte
Roger de Bussy-Rabutin, with whom she was to stay at his
château of Chaseu on the Arroux, that 'place of enchantment',
as she called it. Whether it was the memory of Rabelais, who
had praised the good cheer of this part of Burgundy, and in
particular that of Saulieu, or whether it was simply the
excellence of the wines that their host offered them, the Count
and the Marquise sampled more than one bottle, each more
delicious and heady than the last. The result was that Mme de
Sévigné got tight for the first and only time in her life, and that
she and Guitaut, in the course of their repast, composed
alternately that *lettre-amébée* which has since become famous.

It was about this time that an enterprising Burgundian, a
M. Claude Brosse of Charnay-lès-Mâcon, decided that the
local wines needed a boost, a little national advertising.
Accordingly, he harnessed two massive white oxen, those
superlative specimens of the Charollais race, to a wagon, loaded
it with casks of his finest wines of the Mâconnais, and with

himself as drayman set out on the long trek northward, to make a present to his sovereign, King Louis XIV. His business acumen was rewarded and orders poured in from the court. This journey by bullock-wagon was repeated in 1965, when the mayor of Chasselas sent four barrels of Burgundy to the mayor of Versailles. Today, only ten years later, this would cost a pretty penny. Under Louis XV Mme de Pompadour favoured highly the delicate Romanée Conti; later still the Emperor Napoleon I declared his preference for the robust wine with the delicate bouquet from the 'Champ de Bertin', the modern Gevrey-Chambertin. But the wines of the Côte d'Or received their military apotheosis at the beginning of the nineteenth century. Stendhal tells us that a certain Colonel Bisson, marching his men north from the Italian campaign, drew up his regiment in front of the gates of the château of Clos de Vougeot. There he proceeded to pay the highest honour at his disposal. To the sound of solemn martial music he ordered the assembled troops to present arms.

Le jour de gloire est arrivé!

In the eighteenth century began the commercial exploitation of the *grands crus* of Burgundy, the formation of those *négociants*—proprietors whose names have won universal acclaim by the export of their wines in ever-growing quantities to England, Belgium, Germany, America—in fact, everywhere that good wine is sought and appreciated. Then in 1863 there appeared, first in the department of Gard, the little insect whose origin was in America, the *phylloxera*, which brought destruction to the vines. In 1878 the vineyards of Meursault were attacked and soon the whole of the Côte d'Or was ravaged, and the work of centuries lay in ruins. Fortunately, the country which produced the disease provided the cure. French grafts implanted on the hardier American stocks were proof against phylloxera, and gradually the vineyards of Burgundy were reconstituted, miraculously with no damage to the quality of the wines.

In 1934 a group of Burgundian *vignerons* and *négociants*, gathering in a cellar at Nuits-St-Georges, resolved, for the

greater publicity and sale of their wines, to inaugurate a society
with those estimable ends in view. In this way was founded the
now celebrated Confrérie des Chevaliers du Tastevin. Then
in 1944 the Confrérie bought the famous château of Clos de
Vougeot; and it is there, in the Grand Cellier, built some eight
centuries earlier by the monks of Cîteaux, that each year they
hold meetings of the chapter of their order. At the annual feast,
presided over by the Grand Master and Grand Chancellor,
the newly appointed chevaliers are installed in a ceremony,
religiously followed, which is based on the amusing conclusion
to Molière's *Le Malade Imaginaire*.

'Vivat, vivat, vivat, cent fois vivat!'

If, however, the name of Burgundy is clearly enough defined
when it is applied to its wines and circumscribed by an
appellation contrôlée, it is a very different matter when it is used
to delimit the historical province, to fix 'Burgundy' in space and
time. A recent writer, a Burgundian who lives on his property
in the wine-producing district of Meursault, M. Pierre Poupon,
has spoken of the 'three Burgundies': the Burgundy of the
vines, typified by the Côte d'Or; the Burgundy of the pastures,
the rich meadow where are raised the splendid race of
Charollais; and the Burgundy of the forests, especially those
that clothe the highlands of the Morvan. This description has
the advantage of drawing attention to the three sources which
have historically produced the wealth of Burgundy—wine,
beef and firewood, the last formerly floated down the rivers for
the hearths of Paris. But it does little more. However, by
common consent there are eight regions, '*pays*', which are
undeniably, indisputably Burgundy; it is when we cross their
boundaries that we find ourselves in no-man's-land—or in
another province. These '*pays*' are: the *Auxerrois*, the countryside around the town of Auxerre (pronounced 'Ausserre') on the
Yonne; the *Puisaye*, the damp region of ponds and streams
which centres on the little town of St-Fargeau, to the south-west
of Auxerre—the country of the writer Colette; the *Châtillonnais*,
the limestone hills of wheatfields, pasture and forest around

Châtillon-sur-Seine, to the north, where Burgundy borders on Champagne; south of this, the *Auxois*, whose principal town is picturesque, mediaeval Semur-en-Auxios, whose great round towers with their conical caps dominate the River Armançon; the *Côte d'Or*, where the escarpment of the 'Mountain', with its combes, forms a green trellis, an espalier of vines, that runs north from Chalon-sur-Saône almost to the gates of Dijon; further, there is the moist mountainous region of outcrops of granite which forms the *Morvan*, covered with its great forests; again, there is the *Charollais*, that district around Charolles which forms the south-western outpost of Burgundy, a country-side of lush meadows, where cattle are fattened—rich, too, in Romanesque churches; and bordering Charollais on the east, is the *Mâconnais*, a land of vineyards, whose chief towns are Mâcon, Tournus and Cluny, the last two with their masterpieces of Romanesque architecture.

All these '*pays*' are unquestionably in Burgundy. It is beyond them that the element of doubt enters. If, then, certain cities and towns are incontestably *in*—such, for example, as Dijon, Auxerre, Châtillon-sur-Seine, Autun, Beaune, Chalon-sur-Saône, Avallon, Charolles—what about certain others? What do we say of Mâcon, Charlieu, Nevers, Clamecy, Sens, St-Florentin, Auxonne? To achieve certainty, unambiguity, and unanimity, we can name other places still which are indisputably *out*—Troyes, Langres, Dôle, Bourg-en-Bresse, Lyons, Moulins, Sancerre, Montargis and Nemours—defining Burgundy thus by the method of exclusion. But also history may lend us here a helping hand. Today we have strong evidence—one would go as far as to say proof—that those princes and governors of the *Grand Siècle* were well aware of what they were about when they thought and acted on a recognition of the existence of the province of Burgundy. At the time of the Revolution, those progressive legislators who wished to re-draw the map of France, obliterating all traces of the *ancien régime* in their doctrinaire desire to re-shape and start afresh, showed them-selves to have retained something of the empiricism, the practicality, of a Vauban, as well as the analytic certitude, the mathematical precision of a Descartes. Fortunately for the future, the National Assembly narrowly defeated the proposal of the Citizen Thouret to divide France into a chessboard of eighty squares, each with sides of eighteen leagues, and adopted instead a system of departments, prosaically named after geographical features, for the most part rivers. Burgundy was then partitioned into the departments of the Côte d'Or and the Saône-et-Loire in their entirety, and into those of the Yonne for the greater part and of the Nièvre for a portion of its extent. Our contemporary administrators, however, have vindicated the territorial boundaries understood by their ancestors of the *Grand Siècle* and reverted to the use of the term 'Burgundy', as of greater administrative convenience to signify an area which lends itself to a plan of integral development. Among the twenty-one 'circumscriptions of regional action', the term used in the jargon of bureaucracy to apportion France for the purpose of centralized planning (how easily one falls into the language of politicians and bureaucrats), 'Burgundy' once more enjoys its former role, which indeed it had never ceased to perform. Consisting today of these four departments—Côte d'Or, Saône-et-Loire, Yonne and Nièvre— Burgundy has resumed, with this official cachet, at least something of its earlier political identity.

Burgundy, then, the ancient province, exists, with a life, a continuing vitality all its own; from the very beginnings of civilization in France it has been the focus of all those influences which have formed much that is of the very quintessence of French civilization. It is this *openness* to other cultures, the absence of geographically limited frontiers, and the political fluidity, which is reflected in the failure to find a strict and permanent demarcation of its borders, that have permitted Burgundy to absorb, to mould in its own fashion and then to transmit to Europe and the world something infinitely precious and *sui generis*, a life-style that is unmistakably Burgundian. Recently Bruce Allsopp in an admirable study, *Romanesque Architecture*, has picturesquely expressed the debt owed by the province to its central position: 'If we think of Paris as the face of France, because its eyes, ears and mouth seem to be there, Burgundy may well be its heart. This generous region, which produces some of the best wine of the world, is caressed in the south by the River Loire. The Seine rises there and the Saône flows through it to join the Rhône at Lyons. From the Mediterranean, from Italy through the Alpine passes, from Germany and Austria and the East, from the Moselle Valley, the Rhineland and the North Sea, all roads lead to Burgundy . . .'

This openness of the province has been facilitated by its natural features, which present no formidable obstacle to the movement of peoples. Geographically, on the other hand, there is nothing here which corresponds to more homogeneous regions like the Parisian basin, or even the Alps, lacking as Burgundy does any physical unity. In the north it is attached to the southern rim of the Parisian basin, bordered by the hills of the Puisaye and the limestone uplands of the Châtillonnais; and on the south-east and south-west Burgundy and the Nivernais are contained by the alluvial plains of the Saône and the Loire. If the nature of these plains and moderate hills has made the province easily accessible, nevertheless the region does present some distinctive, more mountainous, features in the Morvan, the Côte and the Mâconnais. These are part of the *massif central*, and reach in the Bois du Roi in the Morvan the height of some 2,960 feet. Distinct from the granite of the highlands of the Morvan, which were formed in the primary era and subsequently much eroded, are the limestone heights of the Côte and the Mâconnais, which constitute a prolonged escarpment to the west of the Rhodanian basin, that tongue of lowland stretching north from the Mediterranean, through which flows the Saône. Of particular interest is the Côte, which consists of a rectilinear ridge about 600 feet in height, running roughly north and south, a fault in the 'Mountain', caused by the sinking of the plain of the Saône. Here again erosion has brought about a number of indentations, known locally as 'combes'. These well-drained slopes present ideal conditions for the culture of the vine, and in more senses than one the Côte d'Or is the heart of Burgundy.

The historian of mediaeval France Professor Joan Evans had this to say of the province: 'If the vitality of Normandy flows through the channels of the seas, the life of Burgundy runs through the land. Michelet has said, "France has no element more binding than Burgundy, more capable of reconciling North and South." It lies at the centre of the river-system of France, and so has been from time immemorial a centre of trade. The fairs of Chalon, Autun, Dijon, Auxonne, Beaune, Châtillon and Tonnerre carried on a commercial tradition from Carolingian and even from Roman times. And besides being the home of commerce it was the home of religion; its abbeys —Cluny, Cîteaux, Clairvaux, Vézelay, Flavigny, Tournus, St-Pierre-de-Bèze, Pothières, St-Bénigne-de-Dijon, and the rest—were not only important in themselves but did much to bring religion into feudal life. Cluny made Burgundy the land of crusaders and pilgrims . . .'

This openness of Burgundy to foreign influences, particularly those coming from the Mediterranean basin—from traders, of whom we have evidence extending as far back as the sixth century B.C.; from its invaders, among whom the Romans and the *Burgundi* were by far the most significant; from those who spread Christianity or introduced new art forms—this accessibility has been of primary importance in tracing the historical development of Burgundy and in assessing the importance of its contribution to the civilization of Europe And here the traveller has a particular reason to be thankful; the history of the province could be written in stone, since Burgundy is unsurpassably rich in its monuments.

Rich it is, too, in the remains of prehistoric man. Between Auxerre and Avallon, in the charming, verdant valley of the River Cure, which is overlooked on its right bank by a bastion of limestone cliffs, is the village of Arcy-sur-Cure. The caves in these cliffs were inhabited in the early Stone Age by men who have left, engraved on the walls, representations of the animals they hunted—mammoths, bison, roebuck, reindeer— and a horse. Even more impressive still than this Burgundian Altamira are the discoveries made in 1866 in the Mâconnais, at the rock of Solutré, after which archaeologists have designated a period of the paleolithic age, falling between the Aurignacian and the Magdalenian—the Solutrian. Above the gently sloping hillside, covered with the green mantle of the vineyards of Pouilly-Fuissé, rises abrupt, sheer, the cliff face of Solutré, as if some geological storm had cast up and then petrified this breaking crest of a limestone wave. At the foot of this was unearthed last century a gigantic charnel house, the Cros du Charnier, containing, it is estimated, the skeletons of about a hundred thousand horses. The flesh from these slaughtered animals provided food for generations of paleolithic men. The spot is ideally suited for this monstrous holocaust. The rock of Solutré forms a promontory, joined to the plain behind by a mild declivity. Towards this spot from which there was no escape the Stone-Age men drove their whinnying prey, the horses becoming terrified into madness by the hunters' clamour and a cordon of fires. The scene of terror enacted on the cliffs of Solutré must have been fantastic in its dramatic inhumanity. There, with a thundering of hooves, the frenzied horses, their eyes and nostrils dilated, manes and tails flying, this aerial cavalry of Pegasus, plunged with a last shrieking neigh to their death on the rocks below. The paleolithic artist who drew the horse in the cave at Arcy-sur-Cure had an intimate knowledge of his subject.

The trading links of what was to become Burgundy with the Aegean world were forged very early. The evidence for this is incontrovertible. In January 1953 a young lecturer in philosophy at the *lycée* of Châtillon-sur-Seine, René Joffroy, had the rare fortune to discover near the village of Vix, at the foot of the ancient *oppidum* of Mount Lassois, a tomb of a Celtic princess, containing vases and jewellery of such rarity and value that it has become known as the 'treasure of Vix'. It is housed today in the museum at the Maison Philandrier in Châtillon. The most remarkable object is an immense *krater*, a bronze vase, standing four feet, nine inches in height and weighing some two hundred and fifty-eight pounds. This is not only the largest *krater* to have survived from antiquity, but is a perfect masterpiece of the bronze-worker's art. The beauty of the patina of the metal and the excellence of the vase's proportions, swelling as it does from its elegant base, decorated with a design of pearls and tongued fluting, to the two handles formed of Gorgon's busts, are in perfect harmony with the beautiful figured frieze of the vase's neck. This depicts a procession of warriors, with their high-crested helmets and their four-horse chariots, all in high relief, and suggests that the provenance of the *krater* was the Aegean world, the archaic civilization that flowered from Mycenae and Tiryns. Outstanding among the jewellery worn by the dead princess is an exquisitely worked diadem in the purest gold, seventeen ounces in weight, possibly of Graeco-Scythian workmanship. No equivalent to this diadem from the goldsmith's art of antiquity was known until 1970, when a bulldozer unearthed near La Rochepot, again in Burgundy, a gold bracelet, weighing more than forty-five ounces, today in the Musée Archéologique in Dijon. This is thought to be of indigenous workmanship, perhaps as early as the eighth century before Christ. On such an antique basis does the artistic heritage of Burgundy rest.

The Romans had long known, and had early cause to fear, the Gauls, those Celtic-speaking warriors of massive frame and long, fair hair, from beyond the Alps. In 390 B.C., Brennus, the chieftain of the Senones, who have left their name to the city of Sens, invaded Italy at the head of a Celtic army, and would have captured Rome itself, much of which they sacked, if it had not been, according to the tradition, for the timely conjunction of M. Furius Camillus and the Capitoline geese. Then, after 58 B.C., the Romans under Julius Caesar turned the tables on the Gauls, defeated the Helvetii at Bibracte in the lands of the Aedui, and finally, after the heroic resistance of the reformed Gallic league brought about by Vercingetorix, at Alesia completed the conquest of Gaul. The long process of the Romanizing of Gaul had begun. Between the years 15 and 10 B.C., the Emperor Augustus founded Autun (*Augustodunum Æduorum*) as the 'sister' and 'rival' of Rome, to replace the former capital of Bibracte. Here today in its gates and amphitheatre, which was capable of seating thirty-four thousand spectators, we can gain some impression of what this process meant. The Romans left their imprint deep in the soil—and one would like to say in the character of the inhabitants—of the future Burgundy. Burgundy is formed from Burgundian slips engrafted on sound Gallo-Roman stock—*pinot* or *chardonnay*, the resultant growth is unmistakably Burgundian.

In that richly coloured tapestry which is the *Nibelungenlied*, woven of myth and historical fact, of Norse and Teutonic saga perhaps inextricably intermingled, appear beside the familiar figures of Siegfried and Brunhild the Burgundian King Gundicar and his sister Kriemhild, the princess on account of whose beauty 'many a noble knight was doomed to perish'. Although handed down in oral tradition and not written until much later, these sagas deal with the *volkswanderung* of the northern peoples in the earlier centuries of our era, and in one version of great beauty record the defeat of the Burgundians of King Gundicar (Gunther, Gundahar, Gunnar) at the hands of the nomadic Huns in the year 436. The *Burgundi* or *Burgundiones*, a people of Scandinavia or Germanic origin, appear to have moved from their home on the Baltic in the general migrations, and under Gundicar found refuge about 411 in Gaul, where they were granted lands among the Sequani and Aedui and were accepted as 'allies' by the Gallo-Romans. After their defeat by the Huns and the death of their king, the Burgundians quickly re-established themselves and extended their power, which suggests a martial and political ability which would mark them as possessing a civilization superior to that of other barbarian races. This is shown also by the speed with which they assimilated the Gallo-Roman culture, and that included the Christian religion, which was already widespread. Under Gundicar's heirs the Burgundian dominion had progressed, by stages but inexorably, so that by the time of his great-grandson Gundibald, who died in 516, they occupied Langres, Autun, Dijon, Nevers, Mâcon, Lyons, Vienne, Besançon, Grenoble, Geneva, and most of Provence. It was this king who from his capital of Vienne promulgated a codification of law, combining both Roman and customary elements, known as the *Lex Burgundionum* or the *Lex Gundobada,* and in French the *Loi Gombette.* Throughout the middle ages the memory of this extensive, powerful and civilized Kingdom of Burgundy remained in the consciousness of the people and exerted a profound influence in forming a *Burgundian* mentality and character—what has recently been described by Canon Maurice Chaume as a 'truly national Burgundian sentiment'.

But Gundibald and his Burgundians had rivals in the struggle for power in the lands that were to be France—such formidable competitors as the Visigoths, the Ostrogoths and the Franks. To safeguard his kingdom Gundibald sought an alliance with Clovis, King of the Franks, and signed a treaty with him in 506 on the banks of the Cure. However, his successors were unable to maintain their position against these Merovingian kings, and in 534, with the fall of the former Aeduan capital Autun, the dynasty failed in the person of Gundimar and their kingdom passed to the Merovingians. In 561 the former kingdom of Burgundy was revived under members of the French royal family, the first of the new dynasty being Guntram, who ruled from his capital at Chalon-sur-Saône. From 613 Burgundy reverted to the status of province of France, and so it remained until the troubles and break-up of the empire of Charlemagne after his death in 814. At the Treaty of Verdun in 843, which followed the defeat two years earlier of Lothair by his brother Charles the Bald at Fontenoy-en-Puisaye, the *county* of Burgundy —that is Lyons, with the lands to the east of the Saône (the later Franche-Comté)—became part of the Empire, while those territories to the west of the river, which were to form the nucleus of the *duchy* of Burgundy, remained as a province of the France of Charles the Bald.

The pertinacity with which men held to the conception of the 'kingdom' of Burgundy is reflected by the events which followed. In 879 Boso founded the kingdom of 'Cisjuran' Burgundy, which embraced Provence and extended north to Lyons, and even for a time to Mâcon. With some territorial losses and additions (in Savoy and what is now Switzerland), this kingdom of Burgundy became in the thirteenth century the kingdom of Arles. The Carolingians, to oppose Boso's pretensions, granted the duchy of Burgundy (the lands remaining under the French crown) to his brother, Richard the Justiciar, Count of Autun. The duchy comprised at first the countships of Autun, Mâcon, Chalon-sur-Saône, Langres, Nevers, Auxerre and Sens, but its boundaries fluctuated during the tenth and eleventh centuries. In 1032, the duchy, having been once more joined to the French crown, was granted by King Henry I to his brother, Richard, from whom sprang the first Capetian ducal house of Burgundy, which continued until 1361.

With Duke Richard and his eleven successors there thus came into being that state within a state, having its capital now in Dijon, a compact Burgundy based firmly on the developed feudal system, administered by a competent body of officials, with an almost royal court, paralleling that of the dukes' overlords, the kings of France, and with its own Parlement, the '*Jours-Généraux*', which met in Beaune—a shadow, no doubt, of the ancient *regnum Burgundiae*, but a state ready-made to achieve greatness under the succeeding dynasty of Valois dukes. Evidence of the material and spiritual condition of the duchy is seen in the fact that it was in Burgundy that there rose the great revival of the monastic movement at Cluny, Cîteaux, and the Clairvaux of St Bernard—it became indeed 'the land of crusaders and pilgrims'. Related as they were by birth and intermarriage with the royal house of France, the hereditary dukes of Burgundy were among the greatest nobles in the feudal hierarchy. At the coronation of Philip Augustus in 1180 the 'twelve peers of France' were six laymen: the Dukes of Burgundy, Normandy and Guienne, and the Counts of Champagne, Flanders and Toulouse—and six ecclesiastics: the Bishops of Laon, Noyon, Châlons, Beauvais and Langres.

In 1361 on the failure of the Capetian line with the death from the plague of the seventeen-year-old Duke Philippe de Rouvres, the duchy of Burgundy was annexed once again to the crown of France, King John the Good promising the Estates gathered at Cîteaux to maintain inviolate its ancient rights. Then, secretly in 1363 and officially in the following year, the King bestowed the duchy as an hereditary appanage on his fourth son Philip, who as a boy of fourteen had fought valiantly at his father's side on the disastrous field of Poitiers. Where the Capetians had sown the Valois dukes were now to reap a rich harvest. Under the four princes of that dynasty—Philip the Bold (1364–1404), John the Fearless (1404–19), Philip the Good (1419–67) and Charles the Rash (1467–77)—the duchy of Burgundy was to reach its apogee, becoming the most splendid, powerful and civilized state in Europe. It has been said that beside these Valois dukes of Burgundy, their cousins the kings of France—Charles VI, Charles VII and Louis XI— appeared but simple provincial lords. The ruling passion with the Valois dynasty was ambition, everything was bent to their aggrandizement—the protocol and fastidious luxury of their more than regal court, the employment of the finest artists, their dynastic marriages, the increase of territory by purchase, arms and chicanery—nothing was lacking, save a crown, and this only narrowly escaped Charles the Rash. The marriage of Philip the Bold to Marguerite, daughter of Louis de Maele, Count of Flanders, brought them on the latter's death in 1384 the counties of Flanders, Artois, Burgundy (the later Franche-Comté), Nevers and Rethel, the provinces in the Low Countries, at that time hardly equalled in Europe for their industrious inhabitants and their commercial riches. Philip attracted to his court artists, painters, sculptors, goldsmiths, miniaturists, musicians. He built as a family mausoleum the Chartreuse de Champmol, employing such artists as Jean de Marville, Jean de Beaumetz, Jean le Malouel, Klaus Sluter and Melchior Broederlam. If one wanted to describe what was meant by the Burgundian style, one could state simply that it was what appealed to the discriminating taste of Philip the Bold and his successors. The ostentatious refinement of their court—for artistic taste was but the handmaid of political prestige—did much to earn them the title of the 'Grand-Dukes of the West'.

Political ambition brought the Dukes into opposition to their feudal overlords, and as princely rulers of a virtually independent state they allied themselves with the kings of England against the kings of France. The overweening ambition of Charles the Rash at length overreached itself. Brave, as were all his family, intelligent, well read in the ancient authors, he was blinded by his own megalomania; as the son of a Philip, he sought to play the role of an Alexander. But in the political game he was no match for Louis XI, and militarily his forces were inferior to the Swiss peasants he so despised, with whom he found himself at war. 'And what was the cause of this war?' asks Philippe de Commynes, who, forseeing the outcome, had left Charles' service for that of King Louis: 'A cartload of sheepskins which my lord of Romont had taken from a Swiss passing through his lands!' Then followed the resounding defeats of Grandson and Morat in the spring and summer of

1476; and finally in the succeeding year the death of Charles the Rash, the last duke of Burgundy, under the walls of Nancy, his body, stripped of arms, jewels, even clothes, being discovered, covered with wounds, on the muddy edge of a pond. The duchy of Burgundy, after more than a century of glorious history, sank irrevocably to the level of a French province, and the Valois possessions in the Low Countries and the Franche-Comté passed by way of Charles' only child Mary into the patrimony of the Habsburgs.

But Burgundy, with the loss of its independence, was too close to the heart of France, too much of an integral entity in French civilization supinely to succumb when the glory of the dukes departed. It was not until July 1479 that King Louis XI dared enter the city of Dijon, where in the church of St-Bénigne he swore 'to preserve the franchises, liberties, immunities, rights and privileges' enjoyed hitherto by the duchy of Burgundy. Thereafter, particularly in the wars of France against the Empire of Charles V and his successors, the duchy became a frontier region, bristling with fortifications. The Emperor Charles V failed to wrest Burgundy from France, although he expressed his wish, should he have succeeded in this, to be buried in the Chartreuse of Champmol among his maternal Burgundian ancestors. In the wars with Spain and the Empire Louis XIV by the Treaty of Nijmegen in 1678 gained for France the ancient county of Burgundy, now Franche-Comté. Even after the passing of the Valois dukes the primacy of the duke of Burgundy as the premier peer of the realm was maintained at the coronation of the kings of France, the duke being always represented by the first prince of the blood, who carried the royal crown and buckled on the king's sword. From the time of François Ier the government of Burgundy was accorded to the princes of the house of Guise, but from 1595, following the victory of Henry IV over the Leaguers at Fontaine-Française, members of the family of Condé were appointed hereditary governors, and as such they remained until the Revolution.

In the seventeenth and eighteenth centuries the Burgundian aristocracy and rich bourgeoisie, particularly that of Dijon, which retained its Parlement and Estates, contributed much to the civilization of their province and of France. Burgundy could still boast of remarkable men—statesmen in the tradition of the Chancellor Rolin and Philippe Pot, like Pierre Jeannin, Nicholas Brûlart and the cultivated President Charles de Brosses; in literature and the arts, such celebrities as Bossuet, Bussy-Rabutin, his cousin, the Marquise de Sévigné, the Crébillons and Alexis Piron; the musician Jean Tabourot was succeeded by the more famous Rameau; and among men of science, there were the great naturalist Buffon of Montbard, the engineer Vauban, and the inventor of descriptive geometry, Gaspard Monge—these, to name but a few. From the time of Colbert increasing attention was paid to economic matters, especially in the encouragement of agriculture and manufactures. To facilitate the circulation of goods, roads were built and the two great canal systems of Burgundy and the Centre were constructed in conjunction with the navigable rivers, formidable engineering feats for the times, necessitating the building of impressive series of locks. These waterways, as easy means of access, were only superseded with the advent of the railways in the last century, which transformed Dijon into an important centre of communications between northern and southern France.

Perhaps typical of the practicality, the sound common sense combined with intellectual acuity, that is said to characterize the Burgundian, is the career of Sébastien le Prestre de Vauban, Marshal of France (1633–1707). Rising from humble circumstances by the force of his talents and character, his experience of the conditions of the poor led him to present to Louis XIV his ideas on social amelioration in the *Project d'une dîme royale*. Snubbed by the King, and his book suppressed, Vauban is said to have died of a broken heart. The ideas, however, were prophetic; eighty-two years later they burst out in the French Revolution, which stripped the remnants of autonomy from the historical duchy of Burgundy. The identity of a province that for long had meant so much to the civilization of France was obliterated by the stroke of an administrative pen. By order of the National Assembly its Parlements were suspended on 3rd November 1789, then suppressed on 16th August of the following year, a month after its Estates had been abolished. The very

name of Burgundy was erased from the map of France. Easier
to decree than to achieve; Burgundy lived on in the minds and
hearts of Burgundians, even when, like the great Carnot and
Prieur de la Côte d'Or, they rallied to the defence of the
imperilled Republic. Throughout the tumultuous changes of
the nineteenth century Burgundy remained a provincial back-
water, although it contributed its share of the better type of
statesmen, in Lamartine and Sadi Carnot, to the successively
resuscitated Republics. The idea of Burgundy was fostered,
fondly nurtured by its writers: by Romain Rolland in his
Colas Breugnon, by Gaston Roupnel in *Nono*, above all perhaps
by the incomparable Colette, in her *Claudine* series, *Sido* and
My Mother's House. The world was not allowed to forget the
ever-present reality of the ancient province.

Then, on 3rd January 1964, that which in truth had never
ceased to exist was officially revived. A decree from the same
central authority that had ordered the demise of the duchy
sanctioned with its approval 'the regional plan for the economic
and social development and for the administration of the
territory of the circumscription "Burgundy" (the departments
of the Côte d'Or, of Nièvre, of Saône-et-Loire and of Yonne)'.
The wheel had come full circle. There is no longer any doubt,
even to officialdom, of the existence of Burgundy.

B

CHAPTER II

Dijon

THE GREAT NORTH road (today the N.6) that very early
ran from Provence by way of the Rhône Valley to what became
the capital of *Gallia Lugudunensis*, *Lugudunum* (Lyons), was then
by the Romans continued on up the Saône to serve Belgica
and the Upper and Lower Germanies, to connect the capital
with *Durocortorum* (Rheims), *Augusta Treverorum* (Trier) and
Moguntiacum (Mainz). On this road were built at strategic
points fortified staging posts; one such was the important
junction of *Cabillonum* (Chalon-sur-Saône); another, in the
lands of the Gallic Lingones, was established where the river
now known as the Ouche is joined by its tributaries, the
Raines and the Suzon. This last, which the Romans named
Castrum Divionense or simply *Divio*, was the forerunner of Dijon.
At the period of the Emperor Aurelian, about A.D. 273, the
growing town was encircled with walls, some twelve hundred
metres in circuit; at intervals thirty-three towers were raised,
and access was provided by four gates. These were the walls
described by Gregory of Tours in the second half of the sixth
century. Within, the inhabitants had grouped their dwellings
for the greater part around the ancient abbey of St-Etienne.
Outside the walls, and in view of the hillsides planted with
vines, there grew up another settlement in the vicinity of the
shrine of St-Bénigne, the apostle to the Dijonnais, who was
put to death there late in the second century, at the time of the
philosopher-emperor Marcus Aurelius. About 525 an abbey was
founded, in honour of the martyr, the town's patron saint,
which, surviving the destructions of Saracens in 737 and
Normans in 888, achieved considerable celebrity at the beginning of the eleventh century under its great building abbot,
William of Volpiano. This quarter, known simply as the
Bourg, was gradually joined during the early Middle Ages by a

warren of narrow streets to the other part of the town around
St-Etienne, but it always retained its country flavour. It was
here in the seventeenth and eighteenth centuries that the
vignerons came to make their purchases, as their ancestors had
for generations, and their gathering-places and taverns
resounded in the evenings to the *Noëls* of Aimé Piron and
Bernard de la Monnoye, those songs in the people's *patois*, so
humanly down-to-earth, so robustly sane, and well sprinkled
with their native Burgundian salt.

Dijon's life as the capital of the province of Burgundy only
began after King Robert the Pious in 1015 bought the town
from the Bishop of Langres and, joining it to the duchy, gave
it as an appanage to his son Henry. The latter, becoming himself
King of France in 1032, bestowed the duchy on his brother
Robert and his heirs, thus creating the line of Capetian dukes
which continued uninterrupted for three centuries, until the
failure of the house with the heirless Philippe de Rouvres in
1361. After a fire in 1137, which destroyed many buildings,
Duke Hugues II rebuilt the town, encompassing it with new
walls, which now enclosed St-Bénigne and the habitations that
surrounded the abbey. It was to this church that the dukes
repaired on their first official entry to Dijon, and there they
swore to respect faithfully the rights, privileges and franchises
of the province and city; in symbolic recognition of the sanctity
of this oath the abbot of St-Bénigne then placed on the duke's
finger a consecrated ruby ring. In 1187 the existence of the
commune was formally recognized by Duke Hugues III, the
Maieur, later to become the Viscount-Mayor, being elected
from among the town's notables. King John the Good came to
Dijon in 1364 and took the customary oath in St-Bénigne, but
in the same year he made over the duchy of Burgundy to his
fourth son Philip the Bold and his heirs male in perpetuity.
With the four dukes of the house of Valois, Dijon, as the chief
city of the 'Grand-Dukes of the West', became the capital of the
richest state and of the most powerful princes in contemporary
Europe, the outward and visible sign of which was the creation
by Philip the Good in 1429 of a body of chivalry, the celebrated
Sovereign Order of the Golden Fleece, with its headquarters in
the Sainte-Chapelle of Dijon.

Henri Quatre is said to have referred to Dijon as '*la ville aux beaux clochers*', and if he did so, he must have been unwittingly responsible for one of those tasteless descriptive epithets given to towns in France (and states in America) which are so flattering to popular local pride. Both Dijon and Rouen share the doubtful distinction of being described as 'the city of a hundred belfries'. From the time of the Middle Ages drawings and prints of Dijon do indeed show the skyline above the town to have been punctuated by the high silhouettes of church gables, towers and steeples, of the prominent features of the Tours de Bar and de la Terrasse, rising above the palace of the dukes, and the lofty ramparts of the now demolished citadel. In 1460, when the number of inhabitants had grown to twelve or thirteen thousand persons, and the modest House of the Monkeys, decorated by Claus de Werve, still did office as the town hall, it is reported that there existed seven parish churches, the Sainte-Chapelle of Monseigneur le Duc, the towers of the many abbeys and convents, and the *flèches* of some twenty well-built chapels. And so it remained until the Revolution, as we see from the drawing of J.-B. Lallemand, whose beautiful engravings illustrated the *Voyages Pittoresques de France*, which was published in 1787.

The damage done to Dijon's architectural and artistic heritage by the fanatical iconoclasm of the first revolutionaries can never be too much regretted. The ancient rotunda, which contained the shrine of St-Bénigne, was wantonly destroyed; the abbeys and convents were secularized, their communities dispersed and their buildings taken over for institutional use or sold; the beautiful Sainte-Chapelle, a repository of precious objects of art, had its treasures put up for public auction, the fabric being later pulled down to make way for a theatre; the mausoleum of the Valois dukes at the Charterhouse of Champmol, was, with the conventual buildings, confiscated by the State, the magnificent tombs of Philip the Bold and of John the Fearless and his wife having been most fortunately transferred to a crypt under St-Bénigne, until the first fury of ignorant prejudice had abated; the equestrian statue of Louis XIV by Le Hongre was melted down for cannon, and the Place Royale, in the centre of which it stood, more appropriately renamed the Place d'Armes; and with all these, so much else of priceless value, the work of Burgundian and Flemish artists over the centuries, vanished for ever. An incident representative of the Revolution is provided by the freethinking chemist Bernard, who day after day, furnished with hammer and chisel, betook himself to the church of Notre-Dame, where he patiently set to work, hammering away before a crowd of onlookers as callous as himself, obliterating all the faces of saints and angels on the doorways, statues and archivolts. He made an excellent job of it, superior—at least in respect of the amount achieved—to the *citoyen* who smashed the fifteenth-century figures of the saints on the central *trumeau* and niches of the western doorway of the church of St-Michel, said to have been 'the most beautiful in Burgundy'.

But if much was destroyed, much still remains. Unlike Rouen, which before the last War was considered, with Dijon, to be the most remarkable of French provincial capitals, Dijon suffered little in the oldest, the most central parts, from wartime bombing. If at first sight Dijon seems so architecturally homogeneous, belonging to the *Grand Siècle* and to the ages of the Louis's Quinze and Seize, in out-of-the way corners or behind the imperturbable façades that look out over its narrow streets the curious stroller may come upon many relics and reminders of the Middle Ages. This feeling of historical continuity and survival, which impresses itself so strongly on the traveller in Burgundy, and especially in Dijon, has been well expressed by the learned authority on St Bernard of Clairvaux, my friend Monseigneur Bruno Scott James: 'There are many other parts of France that have a more direct and dramatic appeal but no one with any historical sense at all can fail to be moved as he wanders through the old townships of Burgundy, and no one with any sense of beauty can travel through the gracious and fertile countryside with its rich fields, famous vineyards, and old red-roofed manor houses, and remain insensible to its charm. Something of the past certainly lingers here amongst these quiet woods and fields. All this is as true of Dijon, the rich capital of the province, as it is of the small walled towns of the hills and valleys. Much of Dijon is quite modern. Motors and buses fill the gay and crowded streets with their din. But an atmosphere of the Middle Ages still seems to hover and eddy around her old courtyards, dim alleys and solemn buildings, where the noise and bustle of the busy streets is muted and only the church bells stir the silence.' And this evocative part of old Dijon is conveniently compact, so that it may be, without any great exertion or peripatetic powers, accomplished on foot; a trapezoid marked out by the churches of Notre-Dame and St-Michel, the Ecole de Droit and St-Bénigne roughly comprehends most of what no visitor would willingly miss. As Huysmans wrote in *L'Oblat*: 'Despite everything, this town is still one of the only ones that one can, in the provinces, amiably stroll round.' And 'amiable' is the perfect word to describe Dijon.

The reason for the presence here of this undeniable quality, which suggests at one and the same time states of mind induced by a generous and a civilized style of living, derives from a happy conjunction of circumstances—the richness of the countryside and the nearby Côte d'Or conjoined with the civil history of Burgundian Dijon. 'It is well known,' said the mayor and corporation of Dijon as early as 1452, 'that this town is based upon the culture of vines, and that wine, through which the greater part of the inhabitants make their living, is its chief merchandise.' When, precisely a quarter of a century later, the death of Charles the Rash at Nancy brought the extinction of the house of Valois, the resumption of royal rule did not entail the loss in entirety of provincial autonomy. Alongside of the hereditary Governors (the Guise and the Condé) and the later Intendants there persisted instruments of administration—of taxation and justice—of the utmost importance in preserving the idea of Burgundy—the triennial Estates, the Parlement and the Chambre des Comptes. From this there arose a patriciate of the robe; enriched bourgeois and the lesser territorial nobility, by means of the legal profession, came to the forefront in charge of affairs. Burgundian civility owes everything to lawyers; but to lawyers whose feet remained firm on the soil of the vineyards, when their fingers leafed through lucrative briefs and their well-covered frames reposed comfortably in the chairs of high office. Burgundy produced, as a province, more than its share of distinguished men and, looking into their backgrounds, we will find, almost without exception, a lawyer forebear—if the man himself was not trained in the law. Stendhal in his most entertaining *Mémoires d'un touriste* has this to remark: 'Dijon, a small city of thirty-thousand souls, has given France Bossuet, Buffon, Crébillon, Piron, Guiton-Morveau, Rameau, the President de Brosses, author of the *Lettres sur l'Italie*; and in our days Madame Ancelot: while Lyons, a city of seventy thousand inhabitants, has produced only two men—Ampère and Lémontey.' (I am at a bit of a loss about Stendhal's Madame Ancelot; perhaps she was an actress or of an allied profession.) Add to this formidable list the Fremyot forebears of Madame de Sévigné, the great Carnot, whose father and elder brother were magistrates and judges, and the ancestors of the poet Lamartine, and it will be seen what a cultural debt Burgundy owes the legal profession. And by the tolerance of fortune, in Dijon these parliamentarian families have left their material mark in the architecture and interior furnishing of their magnificent town houses.

In the *Voyages pittoresques* the artist Lallemand has depicted the Place Royale de Dijon as it appeared in the closing years of the *ancien régime*. From a raised booth placed directly under the plinth of Le Hongre's huge statue of the *roi soleil*, mounted on his charger in the garb of a Roman imperator, a mountebank harangues a small group of townsfolk. Nearby is another group of the better sort of citizen, the ladies in the silk panniered dresses of the period with their short trains and wearing the high coiffure for which the court of Versailles had set the style. Towards the foreground moves a tall figure, his cloak flung back over the left shoulder, his high walking stick poised, in the fashion of some *hidalgo* of Goya. A single vehicle, a four-wheel coach drawn by two horses, passes the iron railings of the Logis du Roi and Palais des Etats de Bourgogne. In the background, to the right, is the single-storey arcade in pale stonework, with its shapely balustrade, which we see today—except that another storey has been added, and a roof of grey slates. In the left background, however, beyond the triumphal entrance gateway, the buildings are dominated by the high nave of the Sainte-Chapelle, and above it the single tower of its façade and its substantial tapering *flèche*. Here only a corner of the Tour de Bar of the still existing edifices is to be discerned. Place Royale, Place d'Armes, Place de la Libération—the changes in nomenclature giving some indication of its history—the vast open semi-circle, with the buildings that surround it in such perfect architectural harmony, remains as it was laid out, a magnificent monumental centrepiece to the city of Dijon.

After the passing of the Valois dukes, the palace rebuilt in the fourteenth century by Philip the Bold had for long gone neglected, until it was partly adapted and much added to as a lodging, both for the Princes of Condé and for the King—the Logis du Roi. The Etats de Bourgogne and the Chambres des Comptes then met in what is today the Palais de Justice. King Louis XIV, his Queen and the court had paid state visits to Dijon, notably in 1658 and 1674. About this latter time, perhaps with some prompting by the Intendant, the municipal authorities, in conjunction with the Estates, had come to the resolution that 'in order to add to the embellishment of the city and the decoration of the *Logis* of His Majesty, which is very large and magnificent, it would be necessary to make a *place* in front of the aforesaid *Logis*, in order to render the entrance more accessible and more beautiful'.

The proposal won the powerful support of Colbert, who had the superintendence of the finances of the kingdom, and kept a careful eye on those of the chief provincial cities, as well as on the King's buildings. In 1680 steps were set in train with this end in view, and plans drawn up under the care of Jules-Hardouin Mansart, the architect of Versailles, with the assistance of his pupil Martin de Noinville, the work being put in the skilful hands of the Burgundian Pierre Lambert. By 1692 the Palace Royale was finished and ready to receive the great bronze statue of King Louis that had been wrought in Paris and was to complete this outstanding example of intelligent town-planning. Alas, it was taken by barge as far as Auxerre, but there it stuck, no means being conceived of how to convey it further. It was not until some thirty-three years later that all difficulties—which included demolishing houses and widening streets—were overcome, and the Grand Monarque in imperial effigy surveyed the Place Royale and his royal palace.

Since 1674 the gothic Palais des Ducs and its later annexes had housed the chambers of the Etats de Bourgogne, as well as the Logis du Roi and the apartments of the Princes of Condé. It was eventually resolved by the Prince of Condé and the Estates that the palace should be rebuilt in a manner more consonant with their prestige (and the King's majesty) and as a worthy companion to the new *place*. Again, Mansart and his pupils and collaborators, Noinville and Gittard, drew up the plans and Lambert was given the contract for the building. Between 1681 and 1689 were constructed the Salle des Etats, with its vestibule and grand staircase, and the central façade, which blocked out from the Cour d'Honneur the view of the ancient Salle des Gardes of the Valois palace. Today, from the Place de la Libération this *corps de logis*, which is high outtopped by the fifteenth-century Tour de la Terrasse (or de Philippe le Bon, from its original builder), is in part occupied by the Hôtel de la Ville, the rooms of which should be visited for the splendour of their decoration of the seventeenth and eighteenth centuries. Particularly impressive are the carved chimney-pieces in three adjoining salons, the work of the Dijonnais Jean Dubois (1624–94), the verve and florid vigour of whose carvings in high-relief are reminiscent of Bernini. In the first room is the well-known *cheminée de la Renommée*, in which a buxom (anything but ethereal) angel, billowed on a nugget of cloud, sounds a triumphant trumpet call to the hero whose fame is about to be rewarded with a wreath of laurel. In the third salon the allegories are no less clearly pointed: Jason gains possession of the Golden Fleece and King Louis XIV triumphs over troublesome heresy. By 1720 Noinville's plan for a monumental access from the west was achieved by the cutting through of the Rue Condé (now de la Liberté), and work was well under way on the Cour de Flore, whose buildings, which were not completed until 1787, impart all the charm and elegance of the age of Louis Quinze.

At the entrance to the Cour de Flore from the Rue de la Liberté, eighteenth-century carved doors open to a spacious porch, presided over by a genial bust of the goddess Flora. To the right is the most impressive entrance by which the representatives of the Estates of Burgundy ascended to their meeting-place. In 1733 it was decided to replace Mansart's grand stairway by something even grander. The beautiful flight of stairs, with its magnificent wrought ironwork, which we now see, was designed by Jacques-Jules Gabriel, the father of the architect of the Petit Trianon. From Gabriel's staircase, which has been described as 'one of the most beautiful monumental conceptions of the eighteenth century', Mansart's vestibule leads to the Salle d'Etats, where the Princes of Condé once summoned the Estates of Burgundy. These rooms, with the adjoining Salle de Flore, are lavishly decorated; in fact, the Salle d'Etats underwent an over-restoration in 1895, at which time was hung the vast composition by H. Lévy, representing the *Glories of Burgundy*. This rhetorical painting evoked the sly comment of the late P. Huguenin, by way of explanation: 'It was placed there at the command of the Government . . .' Of the same period as Gabriel's stairs is the Chapelle des Elus, which was built to the plans of Le Mousseux, with sculpture by the Burgundian Claude Saint-Père and the finely carved Louis Quinze panelling of Jacques Verbeckt. Somewhat later, in 1783, the east wing of the Cour d'Honneur was constructed to the design of the architect Le Jolivet; this contains the Salle Condé, with its beautiful period *décor* by the Dijonnais Jerome Marlet, and the Salle des Statues, the decoration of which was designed by Bellu. The doors of the latter room were carved also by Marlet in the purest style of Louis Seize. These rooms now form part of the Musée des Beaux-Arts. The rebuilding and extension of the Palais des Ducs were completed by the execution of Le Jolivet's plans for the façade on the Rue Rameau, the part today occupied by the Beaux-Arts; and finally by the east wing. This faces on to the Place de la Sainte-Chapelle, where stands the statue of the musician Rameau, and overlooks the west side of the Théâtre Municipal (1810). This eastern portion of the Palais, which houses the Museum (the entrance is in the Place de la Sainte-Chapelle), is, as its style reveals, of the Second Empire (1852).

Three passages lead from the Cour d'Honneur: the first connects it on the west with the Cour de Flore; the second, passing under the Hôtel de Ville, comes out into the charming Place des Ducs de Bourgogne, from which there is an excellent view of the gothic Salle des Gardes, with its high dormer windows, and the Tour de Philippe le Bon; the third, on the east side of the court, leads to the Cour de Bar, the oldest remaining part of the Valois palace. The court is overshadowed in its north-eastern corner by the severe and angular mass of the Tour de Bar, built by Philip the Bold at the end of the fourteenth century, and so called from its having been the place of imprisonment of 'the good king' René of Anjou, who was also at one time Duke of Bar and of Lorraine. René was captured by Philip the Good at the battle of Bulgnéville in 1431, and spent the next four years, on and off, in prison here. Beside it is an elegant external stairway leading to a gallery, constructed in 1614 by the Duc de Bellegarde, the Governor of Burgundy at the time, and the godfather of Roger de Bussy-Rabutin. At the foot of the stairs has been placed the modern statue of Claus Sluter by the Dijonnais sculptor Henri Bourchard (1875–1960). On the south side of the court are the external walls of the famous ducal kitchen, in front of which stands an ancient well. On the lion that supports the pulley appear the flint and tinder-box, one of the favourite devices of Philip the Good, which he also employed as links in the chain of the insignia of his Order of the Golden Fleece. The Cour de Bar is flanked on the east by the Second-Empire building which is occupied by the Museum.

The Musée des Beaux-Arts of Dijon is perhaps the most outstanding of all French provincial museums. Here there have been brought together, and displayed in a manner worthy of their aesthetic value, those masterpieces of artists whose work reflects the patronage and cultivated taste of the 'Grand-Dukes of the West'—those, that is, which have been saved from the ignorant fury of revolutionaries. (Important additions to the notable exhibits here are Sluter's *Head of Christ* in the Musée Archéologique, and his *Prophets* and figures of *Philippe le Hardi and Marguerite de Flandres with attendant Saints* still *in situ* at the Charterhouse of Champmol.) The Salle des Gardes, which was originally built by Philip the Good and restored after a fire in 1502, has been the setting for those scenes of gorgeous mediaeval pageantry, when the courtiers, dressed in

all the bizarre splendour of Valois Burgundy, waited, while
voices and instruments were raised triumphant in the marvellous
music of Dufay or Binchois, to greet the arrival of their Duke, as
at the 'joyous entry' of Charles the Rash into Dijon in 1474.
The room, although not grand in extent, is beautifully proportioned, being well lit by high windows on the north. At the
further end is a great fireplace of flamboyant open stonework,
whose lambent flames and quatrefoils decorated with *fleurs de
lis* were carved by Jean d'Angers in 1504. Here have been
gathered in one place the surviving treasures from the Charterhouse of Champmol and the Sainte-Chapelle, and the sixteenth-
century Flemish tapestry, representing the *Siege of Dijon by the
Swiss in 1513*, from the church of Notre-Dame. The two
monumental tombs, those of Philip the Bold and of John the
Fearless and his wife Margaret of Bavaria, these masterpieces
of the Flemish-Burgundian school of sculptors, have been
placed, to be clearly visible in their detail, in the centre of the
room.

During his lifetime Philip the Bold ordered his tomb from Jean
de Marville, who was aided in the carving by Claus de Hain. This
was as early as 1385; later the work was taken up by Claus
Sluter. On Philip's death in 1404, his successor, John the
Fearless, contracted with Sluter to finish the sculpture of the
figures, but the latter, too, died in 1406 and it was his nephew
Claus de Werve who completed the work in 1411. The theme is
well known, and set a fashion; as we can see, for example, in
the magnificent tomb of the Burgundian Philippe le Pot, now
in the Louvre. The effigy of the defunct lies, his hands joined in
prayer, on a great slab of black Dinant marble, his head resting
on a cushion, behind which two kneeling angels support his
elaborate helm; at his feet is a couchant lion. But it is the figures
of the mourners (*'ymaiges pleurant'*, *'deuillants'*) which, within
twin-arched arcades, move in procession around the four sides
of the tomb, that call forth our profoundest admiration. These
choirboys, clergy, monks, relations of the deceased, great
officers of state and loyal retainers, all dressed in a heavy
mantle of grief, some with cowl drawn forward, as if to meditate
alone with their sorrow, some pausing and turning towards us,
so absorbed in their thoughts that they seem unaware of the

passing cortège—Sluter's *pleurants* are of a mastery that passes beyond realism into the reality of highest art. The tomb of John the Fearless and his wife resembles his father's in general design, but the figures, being more highly wrought, although of great beauty, are considered by some to lack the power of the earlier *pleurants*. The tomb was commissioned first from Claus de Werve; the work was continued in 1443 by the Aragonese Jean de la Heurta, and only finally completed twenty-seven years later by the sculptor from Avignon, Antoine le Moiturier.

These tombs did indeed suffer damage at the Revolution, but they have been reconstituted, following the discovery of accurate drawings executed in the eighteenth century, so that much that was missing or injured has now been made good. It may come as a surprise to learn that of the figure of Philip the Bold the beautiful hands alone are original. These were happily preserved by an art collector. The rest of the body and (presumably) the angels have been copied from the drawings, and with reference to other contemporary tombs. Similarly with his son's tomb, only the faces and hands survived, the bodies having been remade in the last century. Most of the *pleurants* have been retraced and replaced in their correct order. A pair of choirboys is still missing from the tomb of Philip the Bold, and an aspergent from that of John the Fearless. Three mourners from the former's monument and one from the latter's are still in other collections, but it is to be hoped that one day they too will be restored to their rightful place.

Also in the Salle des Gardes, and also coming from the Charterhouse of Champmol, are three retables ordered by Philip the Bold to decorate the altars of his family mausoleum. These exquisite pieces were carved in wood and gilded; two were commissioned in 1391 from Jacques de Baërze—those representing the *Crucifixion* and the *Saints and Martyrs*. On the reverse of the wings of the former are the famous paintings in the international gothic style carried out between 1393 and 1399 by Melchior Broederlam—the *Annunciation* and *Visitation* and the *Presentation in the Temple* and *Flight into Egypt*. In the last named, Broederlam has most arrestingly depicted Mary with a youthful grace and an almost wistful fragility, qualities which are peculiarly French, while he had represented Joseph as a

Netherlandish boor, who unseeingly leads the donkey, as with his head thrown back he swigs from a wine-bottle. Could it have been that the painter intended in this way to symbolize the disparate parts that made up Philip's duchy of Burgundy? In the same room is the well-known portrait by Rogier van der Weyden of Philip the Good, wearing his Order of the Golden Fleece.

With collections so rich as those in the Beaux-Arts of Dijon and so admirably housed, it is impossible in this place to do more than to refer, in passing, to the magnificent ducal kitchens, the chapterhouse of the destroyed Sainte-Chapelle, the richly decorated Salle des Statues and the Salle Condé, with their *décor* of the eighteenth century; to the works of Burgundian sculptors from the gothic age and the school of Sluter, to Boudrillet, Sambin, Dubois, Saint-Père, Marlet, Attiret, Rude, Piron, Yencesse, Bourchard and the animal-sculptor Pompon; to the rooms devoted to paintings both by native Burgundians and from the principal schools of Europe. However, the visitor's attention should perhaps be drawn to a room dedicated to the memory of François Devosge. Born in Gray in 1732, Devosge was trained as an artist. In 1766, with the support of the Estates of Burgundy, he established a free art school in Dijon, which grew into the Ecole des Beaux-Arts. Devosge was essentially a teacher rather than a practising artist, and numerous pupils passed through his hands, of whom the painter Pierre-Paul Prud'hon (1758–1823) and the sculptor François Rude (1784–1855) were the most famous. During the Revolution he was instrumental in saving many works of art from destruction or from dispersal, and it was he whose far-seeing enthusiasm preserved them for the state, founding in the year VII the Musée des Beaux-Arts de Dijon. He died in 1811.

Furthermore, for a closer understanding of the architecture of the town-houses, those hotels of the sixteenth and the two succeeding centuries, of which Dijon is so justly proud—and of the wood-carving with which many of them, as well as public buildings, were so magnificently furnished—one should not miss seeing the doors carved by Hugues Sambin, which have been brought into the protection of the Musée as a safeguard against time and weather. The role of Maecenas to Burgundian artists and craftsmen once played by the Valois dukes was taken up and continued in Dijon by rich churchmen and members of the parliamentary patriciate. One such person was the first commendatory abbot of St-Bénigne, the Italian Cardinal Frederico Fregoso, whose family were doges of Genoa. (His brother, Octavian, was a luminary of the celebrated court of Montefeltro and appears as one of the distinguished speakers in *The Courtier* of Castiglione.) It was Cardinal Fregoso who called from Troyes the sculptor Jean Boudrillet in 1527, to carve the choir stalls for his abbey church. (These masterpieces of the wood-carver's art—contemporary with the stalls of the Rigoley brothers at Montréal—were destroyed in the Revolution.) To Boudrillet's studio in Dijon came the young apprentice Hugues Sambin from Franche-Comté, who was to become in turn master, son-in-law of Boudrillet and heir to the tradition of his school. Sambin has been described as architect, engineer, wood-carver and sculptor in stone. Moreover, in his maturity, in 1572, he published a well-known treatise on architectural design, *Œuvre de la diversité des terms en architecture*, following the example in France of Serlio and Philippe de l'Orme. To appreciate fully the work of Sambin one must bear in mind the age in which he lived—the age when Pierre Lescot and Jean Goujon were working on the Louvre of Henri II, that exuberant age which found its expression in the *Gargantua and Pantagruel* of Rabelais and, closer at home in Burgundy, in the rumbustious tales of the *Ecraignes* and the *Bigarrures et Touches du Seigneur des Accords* of the fantastic Etienne Tabourot. As happened throughout its history, Dijon was then the centre of those currents, those filiations of innovating art forms, which criss-crossed throughout Europe; in sculpture the native tradition of romanesque and gothic carvers and the powerful heritage of the school of Sluter were played on and modified by northern Italian, particularly Lombard, styles and those prevailing in the contemporary school of Fontainebleau.

If Sambin was trained under Boudrillet on the stalls in St-Bénigne, he had a wealth of other models before his eyes in Dijon: the west doors of St-Michel, for example, which were carved in 1537 and 1540, and suggest a northern Italian hand; and in the archivolts (almost ceilings) of the deep rounded bays of these same portals, where gothic gives way to the Italianate in the portrayal of the angel musicians, figures of great formal beauty. These were carved between 1529 and 1537. Further, there was the decorative sculpture on such town houses as the hôtel de Rochefort (1547) at 56 Rue des Forges, where a frieze shows the influence of the antique; and the same influence six years earlier inspired the fluted pilasters, decorative arabesques and mythological medallions in the pavilion at 39/41 Rue Vannerie. Or, again, the decoration of the two wells, the *Puits d'Amour* and *de la Samaritaine* (1524) which have now been placed in the court of the Bibliothèque Municipale. But if the sources of Sambin's style are clear, there is, in the existing works that we have good reason to believe his, a stylistic discrepancy, which is puzzling. The two doors in the Musée des Beaux-Arts, which come from the Palais de Justice, reveal a mastery of controlled design in the bold torsos, the trophies, the heads of grotesques and lions, the swags of fruits and flowers, and the panels of palmettes (popularly known as '*choux bourguignons*'), with a crisp delicacy of carving in the exquisite arabesques of tendrils and leaves. A similar technical mastery of the art of the wood-carver and of the principles of design is even more evident in the most beautiful doorways executed by Sambin for the Chapel of the Saint-Esprit in the Palais de Justice. When, however, one is then confronted with the street façade of the so-called Maison Milsand, No. 38 Rue des Forges, it is with some sense of loss, a feeling that this heavy over-decoration, with little apparent regard for the demands of structure or of taste, could not be by the same master's hand. One answer to this enigma is that Sambin, as the architect and the designer of the ornamentation, could hardly in a long lifetime have been responsible personally for all the works that have been attributed to him. He gave the plans, which others carried out; and these builders and carvers, being Burgundians, were carried away with the vigour of their inventive chisels, leaving us something of themselves in these Dijon town-houses, something which, if not in accordance with the strictest canons of architectural taste, is marvellously imaginative, Rabelaisianly robust, and wholly charming.

Dijon is, as Huysmans remarked, the ideal city for the leisurely *flâneur*; and strolling through those narrow, winding streets and sheltered courtyards is the only way possible to discover it, in the richness of its historical and architectural past. If it is not possible in this place to do justice to the treasures of the Musée des Beaux-Arts, it is equally impossible to give but the briefest indication of some of the beauties of Old Dijon, which is itself, as has often been said, *une musée lapidaire*, a museum in stone. For the convenience of the visitor on foot who sets out from the Place de la Libération, which is taken as the centre of the city, the area to the north is here considered as one, and in a similar manner is treated the whole district to the south and south-west, around the ancient Bourg. In this way each visitor may cover the same ground by following any particular itinerary of his own choosing.

From the Place de la Libération the passage under the Hôtel de Ville brings one out in the Place des Ducs, overlooked at the corner of Rue Longepierre by the oriel window of the renaissance hôtel de Berbis. As the street names recall, this part of the mediaeval city was largely given over to the trades: Rue des Forges, de Vannerie, de Chaudonnerie, de Verrerie—the streets of the blacksmiths, basket-makers, coppersmiths and glass-makers. From the Place des Ducs we may take the Rue des Forges, passing behind the Palais des Etats and leaving on the right the Place Ernest-Renan. At Nos. 34–36 is the beautiful hôtel Chambellan, built in 1490 in the flamboyant gothic style, with its corridor from the street and its inner court. The hôtel is remarkable for its stairway, known as the *Escalier du Jardinier* from the figure of a man with a basket on his back, supporting the ribs of the vaulting. Today the building contains the main office of the *Syndicat d'Initiative*. At No. 38 is Sambin's hôtel de Milsand (1561), noticed above. Next door, at No. 40, is the thirteenth-century façade of the hôtel Aubriot (or du Présidial), where early in the next century was born Hugues Aubriot, the celebrated Provost of Paris under Charles V and builder of the Bastille. The portal with its seated statues of Force and Justice, is of the sixteenth century. In the hôtel has been arranged the Musée Perrin de Puycousin, a most interesting folk museum, with, among the dresses and utensils of the past, a fascinating reconstitution of a traditional Burgundian inn. At No. 56 is the hôtel Rochefort, which we have already referred to; and attached to it, Nos. 52–56, which formed one establishment when built in 1435, is the hôtel Morel-Sauvegrain, where once lived the nurse of Charles the Rash, Simone Sauvegrain. From here we come out on the irregularly shaped Place Rude, with its conglomeration of roofs and old houses, in one of which, at No. 5 Rue François-Rude (the house with a bust on the façade) was the birthplace of the sculptor (1784–1855).

North of the Place Rude, in the direction of the Covered Market, the Rue François-Rude is crossed by the Rue Musette, which brings one back to the Place Ernest-Renan. Between the houses of the narrow Rue Musette can be seen the west front of the church of Notre-Dame. At certain times of day, or of the evening, the visitor may be surprised at this spot with the feeling that he is in Venice; looking up at the arcades formed by their slender columns, he may be momentarily reminded of the gothic front of a Venetian palace. High above the south-western angle of the façade of Notre-Dame is the famous Jacquemart brought from Courtai by Philip the Bold after the victory of Roosebeke in 1382. The name 'Jacquemart' originally designated the single figure of the man who struck the hours. About 1610 the kind Dijonnais, considering celibacy a somewhat unsatisfactory state, gave him a female companion. Then, in 1714, the poet of the Noëls, Aimé Piron, pitying the plight of the couple, who seemed to have taken a vow of perpetual chastity, suggested that they should be given a son, Jacquelinet. Finally, in 1881, they were blessed with a daughter, Jacquelinette, who strikes the quarter-hours. Notre-Dame, besides the beauty of its architecture, has much to interest the visitor: its mediaeval glass and frescoes, the carved head of the 'Vieux Dijonnais' in the south transept, and the much-venerated 'Black Virgin', Notre-Dame du Bon Espoir. The tapestry dedicated to her at the time of the lifting of the siege of Dijon by the Swiss (bought off with the heady wines of Burgundy) on 11th September 1513 is today in the Musée des Beaux-Arts; but the Gobelins tapestry offered to the Virgin to commemorate the liberation of the city from the Germans, which fell on the same date, 11th September, in 1944, is in her chapel on the right of the choir.

From the north of Place Renan (note, by the way, the façade of No. 7 in the renaissance style of Sambin) run the Rue de la Préfecture and, flanking Notre-Dame, the Rue de la Chouette (formerly Babeuf). In the latter street, at No. 8, stands the hôtel de Vogüé, originally hôtel Bouhier de Versalieu, built in 1614 and (it is said) designed by a counsellor to Parlement, Étienne Bouhier. This most beautiful house, in the style of Burgundian renaissance tempered by an Italian taste, is constructed on a familiar plan of a main *corps de logis* flanked by two pavilions, forming thus a court of honour, which has from the street a handsome carriage entrance in the manner of Sambin. On the east of the court is the *salle des gardes*, with a fine chimneypiece composed of caryatids. Next door stands a fifteenth-century house, the hôtel Millière, its façade in curiously carved wood. The Rue de la Préfecture has all the appearance of the eighteenth century, with its hotels of the age of Louis Seize: Nos. 2, 15, 22, 37, 38, 45, and, at No. 40, the Hôtel de Dampierre, built to the plans of the architect Saint-Père. This house, both without and within, bears witness to the elegance and taste of those parliamentary families of the Dijon of the *ancien régime*. At No. 49, preceded by its monumental gateway, rises the palatial façade of the Prefecture, once the hôtel de Lantenay. This magnificent structure, contemporaneous with the Petit Trianon, was built in 1759 by the architect Philibert Lenoir for Benigne Bouhier, a soldier in the royal army, and sold by Président Bouhier de Lantenay to the Estates of Burgundy as a residence for the Intendants.

Opposite the Prefecture opens the Rue d'Assas, where at the corner of the Rue Verrerie is the hôtel which was occupied by the Academy of Dijon from 1741 to 1773, and where this distinguished body awarded in 1750 its essay prize to Jean-Jacques Rousseau. At the crossing of the street with the Rue J.-J.-Rousseau rises the monument to Garibaldi, who in 1870 fought successfully outside Dijon with his force of volunteers against the Prussians. Beyond this, one comes to the Rue Vannerie and may turn right (south). Nos. 39 and 41, the hôtel Chartraire de Montigny (note the beautiful carved doorway) and the ancient hôtel of the Military Commandant, are today occupied by the Ecole-François-de-Sales. The saint was here in 1604, when he preached the Lenten sermons and met 'Sainte Chantal', the relative of Roger de Bussy-Rabutin. We have commented earlier on the antique style of the renaissance decoration on the pavilion which is now incorporated in the school chapel. The hôtel Le Compasseur, No. 66, was built to the designs of Hugues Sambin, and possibly carved by him, about 1570. Further on, Nos. 41 to 45 present a pleasant line of eighteenth-century houses; at No. 43 resided the famous Dominican preacher and thinker, Henri-Dominique Lacordaire, from 1815 to 1822, moving from no. 36, where he had lived since 1809.

We may retrace our steps at this point and turn left in the Rue Jeannin. On the other side of the street from the interesting seventeenth-century hôtel at No. 19 and the little renaissance gem at No. 13 are the Departmental Archives, which occupy the ancient Hôtel de Ville, originally built by the Chancellor Rolin in the fifteenth century (the 'House of Monkeys'), and reconstituted in 1708. One can visit some of its rooms, one of which, the *Grand Salle des Séances* has a fine ceiling, carved by Rancurelle in 1628, and a caryatid chimney-piece. Continuing in Rue Jeannin, the visitor may turn right in the Rue Verrerie and pause before the stone and frame façade of the ancient hostelry of the Croix d'Or. There is a most fascinating collection of mediaeval houses about this spot: the frame houses at Nos. 8–12; the façade of No. 21, which has the mark of the school of Sambin; and at No. 29, the hôtel de Saint-Seine of 1664. In the Rue Chaudonnerie, which crosses the Rue Verrerie, are grouped another series of most interesting hôtels, particularly noteworthy being the thirteenth-century Maison des Griffons (No. 4), and at No. 28, the so-called Maison des Cariatides, formerly the hôtel Pouffier, constructed in 1603, most likely by a pupil of Sambin. From there the visitor may turn right in the Rue Vannerie, which leads into the Place Edgar-Quinet and to the north side of the church of St-Michel.

St-Michel is remarkable in being a late flamboyant gothic edifice (begun 1495) on to which has been grafted a renaissance façade (completed 1537). We have already had occasion to notice the carving on the doors. Above the rounded arches of the entrances six busts of prophets in medallions are surmounted by a finely executed frieze in the manner of the antique. Over the central doorway the tympanum representing the Last Judgement in low-relief is by the Flemish sculptor Nicolas de la Cour. The figure of St Michael on the *trumeau*, a reconstituted work of the end of the fifteenth century, replacing that broken at the Revolution, is supported on a console, where pagan figures assort curiously with the Christian. Noteworthy are the most beautiful angels of the coffered porches.

The west front of St-Michel faces the Rue Vaillant, and this may be taken as the starting-point of an exploration of the south and south-western portions of Dijon. But first a detour may be made. The Rue Buffon runs roughly south from the Place Edgar-Quinet, and there, at No. 34, is the stately hôtel where the great naturalist Buffon passed some years of his youth. On the south side of the Rue Vaillant is the secularized church of the ancient abbey of St-Etienne, the city's cathedral when the see of Dijon was separated from that of Langres in the eighteenth century. Today it houses the Bourse and the Musée Rude, a museum dedicated to the work of the Dijonnais sculptor. At the Place du Théâtre the visitor may turn left into the Rue Chabot-Charnay, the street being called after Léonor de Chabot, Comte de Charnay. It was in the hôtel de la Sénéchaussée, No. 65, that Charnay, who was the King's Lieutenant, decided, in agreement with the Président Jeannin, to ignore the royal commands and thus saved the Protestants of Dijon from the massacre of St Bartholomew. Almost immediately on the left stands what remains of the fourteenth-century gothic doorway of the abbey. The Rue Chabot-Charnay possesses some fine hôtels: No. 18, the hôtel de Vesvrotte, contemporary with the hôtel de Vogüé; No. 32, the fifteenth-century hôtel of one of Burgundy's most distinguished families, the Vienne; and at No. 45, the hôtel des Barres, another typical parliamentarian town-house. The Rue Chabot-Charnay debouches in the Place Wilson, from which the tree-lined Cours Général-de-Gaulle and then the Cours du Parc lead to the Parc de la Columbière, part of the magnificent park laid out in the seventeenth century by the celebrated Le Nôtre for the Princes of Condé.

But we are anticipating. First, on the right of the street, the Rue des Bons-Enfants runs back to the Place de la Libération. Here, at No. 4, is the ancient hôtel Lantin, begun in 1652, and containing a magnificent stairway. The hôtel today is occupied by the Musée Magnin, an important collection of paintings of some well- and some lesser-known artists of French and foreign schools. Retracing our steps, we take the short narrow Rue Philippe-Pot to the Rue de Palais, where, at No. 5, was born in 1572 Jeanne-Françoise Fremyot, who later became 'Sainte Chantal'. Nearby is the high gabled façade of the Palais de Justice, raised by the architect Hugues Brouhée in 1572. The doors at the top of the steps are copies of those by Hugues Sambin, today in the Beaux-Arts. This building, which was the early meeting-place of the Parlement de Bourgogne and the Chambre des Comptes, was begun by Louis XII. It should not be missed by any visitor to Dijon, for the beauty of the decoration in the Salle des Pas Perdus and adjoining rooms, the ceilings in the Chambre Dorée and the Salle des Assises, and the doors to the Chapel of the Holy Spirit, the master-piece of Hugues Sambin. Noteworthy, too, are the seventeenth-century Gobelins tapestry and the three windows in grisaille representing *Faith, Hope* and *Charity*, the gift of François Ier. The door to the Advocates' Library flaunts the joint emblems of Henri II and Diane de Poitiers. The Burgundian Parlement and Chambres des Comptes met here, until they moved to the Palais des Ducs in 1674. The Rue du Palais terminates in the Rue de l'Ecole-de-Droit, where the Bibliothèque Municipale occupies the ancient College des Godrans, founded in 1581 by the Président de Parlement, Odinet Godran. It was another Président, Pierre Fevret, who in presenting his fine library to the Collège in 1701, established the nucleus of the municipal library. This contains, among other precious works, manuscripts of the early thirteenth century, illuminated by the monks of Cîteaux. It is to a courtyard here that has been recently brought the renaissance Puits d'Amour, formerly in a house which is now demolished.

The Rue de l'Ecole-de-Droit is continued to the west in the

Rue Amiral-Roussin, where, at No. 23, is one of Sambin's best-known houses, the hôtel Fyot de Mimeure (1562). Opposite, with its monumental entrance at No. 21 Rue de Vauban and its rear on Rue J.-B.-Liégeard, is the hôtel de Chissey-Varanges, begun in 1535 (the rear façade), added to in the eighteenth century by Legouz de Gerland, the naturalist and founder of the Botanical Gardens, and lived in early this century by the poet Stéphen Liégeard, who restored this typical parliamentary family residence in 1909, and after whom the hôtel is now usually named. Another such town-house is No. 12, where lived in the mid-eighteenth century a member of a distinguished Dijonnais family, the Président Bouhier, member of the French Academy. The Rue Amiral-Roussin comes out in the Place Jean-Macé, the centre of the popular mediaeval district of the Bourg. On the corner of the Rue du Bourg (where, at No. 70, Bernard de la Monnoye, the author of the '*Noëls bourguignons*' was born in 1641) and of the Rue Piron, once stood the apothecary's shop of Aimé Piron, the dialect poet of other '*Noëls*' and friend of La Monnoye. His famous son, the witty Alexis, was born here in 1689.

There is a well-known story about Alexis Piron, which is repeated by Stendhal. Piron had not a good word to say for the townsfolk of Autun, whom he abused in prose and verse, declaring them to be so stupid that it was but natural that they should grow asses' ears. One day Piron was rash enough to go to Autun, where he took himself to the theatre. On his being recognized, the hubbub, the challenges and insults hurled at him were such that the words of the piece were quite drowned. At last some irate member in the audience shouted, 'Quiet! One can't hear a word!' 'It's not for want of ears,' remarked Piron audibly. Swords were drawn, Piron fled, and he was only saved from physical harm by a citizen's taking him into his house and slamming the door in the face of his pursuers.

In the Place Jean-Macé five streets converge. The Rue Charrue leads to one of the most characteristic squares of Old Dijon, the Place des Cordeliers, where the charming old houses are roofed with typical Burgundian tiles, some with their patterns of colour-glaze. The Rue Berbisey is lined with fine

old hôtels, among them two of the seventeenth century; at
No. 3, the hôtel de Sassenay, which has a beautiful staircase;
and at No. 6. Nos. 19 and 21 are of the sixteenth century, and
both belonged to the Berbisey family. Another good example of
a parliamentary town-house of the eighteenth century is at
No. 33 which was lived in by the Président de Ruffey, the second
founder of the Dijon Academy. Opposite this hôtel opens the
Rue Crébillon. Here, in the ancient hôtel des Pringles, which
was reconstructed at the end of the seventeenth century by the
architect Noinville, the Academy of Dijon met, after it moved
from the other side of the town in 1773. Taken over by the
State at the Revolution, the hôtel became the residence of the
Rector of the University. Within, the Salle des Actes de
l'Académie has a magnificently rich seventeenth-century
décor by Boichot, the busts of celebrated Burgundians being the
work of the eighteenth-century sculptor Attiret. Continuing
and turning right in the Rue Monge, the stroller passes, at
No. 32, the birthplace of the elder Crébillon (1674) and
arrives in the Place Bossuet, formerly Saint-Jean, which is
surrounded by hôtels of some of the oldest and most distinguished Dijonnais families. At one time a reference to 'the society
of Place Saint-Jean' conveyed the same meaning as we attach
to 'Bloomsbury'.

Against the wall of the truncated apse of the fifteenth-century
edifice dedicated to St John is the modern statue of the great
Bossuet, who was baptized in the church, having been born
nearby, at Nos. 10/12, in 1627. At No. 17 lived the celebrated
lawyer and chemist Guyton de Morveau (Stendhal's Guiton-
Morveau). No. 19 is the seventeenth-century hôtel de Migieu,
with a handsome doorway and *cour d'honneur*. The hôtel Perreney
de Balleure, No. 21, is of about a century earlier. At 27/29 was
born in 1627 Nicolas Brulart, the Président of Parlement who
defied Louis XIV; and at the corner of the Rue Monge stands
the splendid hôtel d'Esterno (1643). Of great historic and
literary interest is the hôtel de Brosses (No. 4), where the famous
Président de Brosses of the *Lettres sur l'Italie* was born in 1709.
The original house, or rather the land, was given by Philip the
Good to the Prince of Orange, and afterwards (it was reconstituted in 1697) came into the possession of the Févret

family, one of whom, Pierre, was the founder of the Municipal Library.

From the west front of St-Jean it is but a step by the Rue Danton to the secularized church of St-Philibert, built in the twelfth century by the Order of Cluny. In the Middle Ages this was the popular church of the *vignerons*, and the Viscount-Mayor of Dijon was elected beneath its early thirteenth-century porch. Afterwards he went in solemn procession to the church of Notre-Dame to take the oath of office. Next to St-Philibert rises the mass, crowned by its multi-coloured Burgundian roof of glazed tiles, of the cathedral of St-Bénigne, with its rotunda-crypt adjoining its apse. To the north of the church are ranged the most impressive buildings of its ancient monastery, with the splendid thirteenth-century dormitory of the monks raised on the vast underground vaults of two centuries earlier. Here today has been established the Musée Archéologique, without doubt one of the most outstanding collections of Gallo-Roman antiquities and gothic sculpture in France.

From this point a continuation of the walk, beyond the railway station, will bring the more energetic visitor to the Promenade de l'Arquebus, so-called from its being in the Middle Ages the practice-ground for the city's trained bands— and next to it the delightful Botanic Gardens, established by Legouz de Gerland in 1772. Somewhat further west is all that remains of the celebrated Chartreuse de Champmol, founded by Philip the Bold in 1383 on ground then outside the town walls. It is perhaps an ironic comment on the eclipse of so much striving for earthly greatness that today the stone effigies of the founder of the Valois ducal house and his wife, who brought him the Low Countries as dowry, kneel, surrounded by the distracted inmates of the mental hospital.

CHAPTER III

Roman Gaul

ABOUT 411, UNDER their king Gundicar, the Burgundians finally gained possession of that part of Roman Gaul which afterwards bore their name, their forcible seizure of these lands long inhabited by the Aedui and other ancient Gallic tribes being given a shadowy form of legal title by the Emperor Honorius, when he recognized the new-comers as 'friends and allies of Rome'. He was powerless to do otherwise. By this conquest, for it was that, a new direction was given to such Gallo-Roman cities as *Augustodunum* (Autun), the rich and populous capital of the Aedui; to the busy river-ports of *Cabillonum* (Chalon), their commercial capital, and *Matisco* (Mâcon), on the Saône; likewise to *Belna* (Beaune), and *Alesia*, on Mont Auxois. All these principally Aeduan towns, with their *pagi*, became part thenceforth of the new Burgundian state. Other Gallic peoples were drawn in to the developing kingdom; for example, the Senones, who were centred on *Autissiodunum* (Auxerre), and the Lingones, with their important town of *Dibio* or *Divio* (Dijon)—although a Gallic origin of this last has been sometimes denied. These first Burgundians revealed the same remarkable powers of cultural assimilation as their descendants (derived from their intermarriage with the Gallo-Romans) were to show throughout their history; they rapidly absorbed much of both the Roman and the Gallic characteristics of the preceding civilization, qualities which were to remain, and remain today, quintessentially Burgundian.

It is difficult to give a precise date to that *volkswanderung*, when the first Celtic peoples from east of the Rhine began to move into the lands which the Romans knew as *Gallia* (Gaul); but it would appear to have been at the period of the Early Iron Age, known as that of the Hallstatt culture—in the centuries after 900 B.C. The culture usually associated with this Celtic or

Gallic civilization is that of the next, the La Tène, period (after 450 B.C.). Excavations at Fontaines-Salées, under the hill of Vézelay, have brought to light a vast Gallic sanctuary, built at a very early date around some medicinal springs. In the museum, in the *place* opposite the entrance to the gothic church at nearby St-Père, is a section of the spring's piping, thought to be of the Hallstatt period (possibly 600–500 B.C.?). This is formed from a trunk of oak, hollowed out by fire, and preserved by the action of the salts contained in the spring water. Certainly by the beginning of the sixth century B.C., the Bituriges were established in Gaul under their king Ambigatus, and seem to have exercised a hegemony over the other tribes. The nephews of Ambigatus, Segovisus and Bellovisus, led an army of Celts into Italy, and we hear at that time the names of those tribes that Caesar was later to find in Gaul: besides the Bituriges, the Arverni, Aedui, Senones, Carnutes and Aulerci. About 400 B.C., waves of these barbarians (in Roman eyes) swept down from the Alps, overran northern Italy, extinguished what remained of Etruscan culture, and settled in the territory that became known as *Gallia Cisalpina*. In 390, their army, including the Senones under their chieftain Brennus, took Rome, and ultimately had to be bought off. Movements among the peoples to the north of the Alps always constituted a threat to Rome, even after the conquest of *Gallia Cisalpina* (by 222 B.C.) and that of *Gallia Transalpina* (*Narbonensis*, 'the Province', Provence) in 121 B.C.

As a rule, the native Gaul greatly excelled in physique the somewhat short-statured, stocky Roman. His colouring was lighter, his complexion being mostly fair or ruddy; the hair, which was worn long, was of a light brown shade, auburn or, occasionally, red. He delighted in bright colours and the wearing of ornaments: torques, buckles, bracelets and brooches of gold by the richer classes, or of bronze and coloured enamels. The Gauls lived by agriculture, carried out by the menial classes and by slaves; or by stock-raising—cattle, sheep, pigs—and by the rearing of horses. The Gallic cavalry was famous, and later made up the greater part of the horse attached to the Roman legions, the Romans themselves, after

the Marian reforms of the army, preferring to serve as traditional
legionary infantrymen. Politically, by the first century B.C.,
although the power of the druids remained, the earlier rule of
kings had given way to a form of feudal aristocracy, of chieftains
and their freeman warrior dependants, jealous of their liberty
and of rivals, and ready to take up arms at any attempts at
ascendancy. As a consequence, within the tribe factionalism
and mutual suspicion were rife, while inter-tribal enmity was
endemic, the warring tribes always prepared to seek allies
among other Gallic peoples, or to call to their assistance the
Germanic races from across the Rhine, and at a later period the
Romans. It is clear, from archaeological finds, that there was
in those last centuries B.C. a quite considerable trade up the
Rhone and Saône valleys between Massilia and the Province
and the North, an exchange of necessary goods—of amber,
British tin and Gallic corn, timber, iron and skins for southern
wine, Campanian pottery and even articles of luxury.

Shortly before 100 B.C., not only the peoples of Gaul but the
Romans as well were seriously threatened by the invasions of the
Germanic Cimbri and Teutoni, foes far fiercer and more
militarily formidable than the Celts. The Gallic tribes, including
the Aedui, were powerless against their Teutonic opponents;
all, save the Belgic races in the far north, saw their lands
devastated, their livestock carried off and many of their own
peoples reduced to slavery. Nor did the Romans fare better, the
consul Cassius Longinus being defeated near Bordeaux in 107
and his army forced to pass beneath the yoke; and two years
later, near Orange in the Province, two consular armies were
overwhelmed by the joined forces of the Cimbri and Teutoni.
It was not until Gaius Marius was recalled from Africa, and
had thoroughly reconstituted the Roman armies, that the
Teutoni suffered a crushing defeat at Aquae Sextiae in Provence
in 102, and in the following year the Cimbri also were destroyed
by Marius in Cisalpina Gaul. But Rome had had good cause to
fear these northern tribesmen.

While the severe rule of the propraetor Marcus Fonteius
(76–74 B.C.) brought order, if discontent, to Gallia Transalpina,
the tribes further to the north in what was then termed *Gallia
Comata*, 'Long-haired Gaul', continued their inter-tribal

warfare, looking for possible allies beyond their frontiers. Such a Gallic quarrel was one which broke out between the Aedui and their neighbours to the east, the Sequani, over matters to do with tolls on the Saône. When the Aedui sought Roman help, the Sequani, with a singular lack of political foresight, invited Ariovistus, king of the German Suebi, to intervene on their behalf. This he did, and claimed as a reward large slices of territory both from the Aedui and Sequani—that is, in the future Burgundy and Franche-Comté. Soon more Germans followed from across the Rhine and occupied Gallic lands, Caesar in his Commentaries putting their numbers in excess of 100,000. The Aedui appealed for a second time to Rome for assistance. Ariovistus likewise had taken the precaution of sending envoys to the Roman Senate, which acknowledged him as king and as 'friend and ally of Rome'. This was in 59 B.C.; the consul of that year was Gaius Julius Caesar.

At the expiry of his term of office, Caesar was appointed governor, as proconsul, of Gallia Cisalpina, Gallia Narbonensis and Illyricum for five years. This command was prolonged in 56 for a further term of five years—that is, until the end of February 49 B.C. In 60 B.C. Caesar had formed with Pompey and Crassus the First Triumvirate. It is clear that he had in mind, by his proconsular appointment, to emulate the feats of Pompey in the East—the conquering of fresh territory for Rome in the West, and the creation of a highly trained force of legions, devoted above all to himself. At the time of taking up his command, news reached Rome that the Helvetii, a Gallic tribe living near Lake Geneva, feeling themselves threatened by the Germans, were preparing to migrate, to seek new lands in the west of Gaul, and pass through the Province on their march. The occasion which thus presented itself for interfering effectively in Gaul was not lost on Caesar.

In the spring of 58 B.C., with one sole legion, Caesar denied the Helvetian host (numbering, it is said, more than 300,000 men, women and children) the crossing of the Rhône as it issued from Lake Geneva, and by this action saved Provence. Moving north, then west, the Helvetii rounded the Jura, passed through the lands of the Sequani and into those of the latter's enemies, the Aedui. Hastily enrolling two fresh legions, and reinforced by three legions of trained troops, Caesar marched north, out of Provence into Gallia Comata, to the aid of Rome's Aeduan allies. He came up with the Helvetii as they were crossing the Saône above Lyons, and administered a sharp defeat on part of their army which was still on the east bank. Caesar's first major battle in his campaign for the conquest of Gaul was fought at the end of June 58 B.C., near the hamlet of Armecy in Burgundy, some two miles north-north-west of Toulon-sur-Arroux and about fifteen miles almost due south of Bibracte, the Aeduan capital on Mont Beuvray, in the southern Morvan. The site of the Roman camp on the night preceding the battle was in what is now the village of Toulon-sur-Arroux, astride the Luzy road, a curve in the River Arroux defending his right and rear. On the hillside just to the west of Armecy was located the embankment thrown up by the two untried legions to protect their own and the veterans' packs. This was discovered in 1853 by Colonel Stoffel, who was surveying the sites of Caesar's Gallic campaigns on the command of the Emperor Napoleon III.

After his resounding victory over the Helvetii, whose survivors he repatriated to Switzerland, Caesar called a gathering of Gallic chiefs at Bibracte, and there, listening to the pleas of the Aedui, he formulated his plans for decisive Roman intervention in the affairs of Gaul. First, he marched out of Burgundy into Alsace, where he met and defeated Ariovistus at Müllhausen, before taking up winter quarters at Besançon. The following year Caesar spent campaigning against the warlike Belgae and, in alliance with the Remi, overthrew a combined army of the Nervii, Viromandui and Atrebates on the River Sambre. In the meantime his lieutenant Publius Crassus, son of the triumvir, was subjecting the maritime tribes on the Atlantic seaboard. In 57 and 56 Caesar and his lieutenants continued their operations against the maritime Gauls, building a fleet with which the Romans overcame the Veneti in Brittany. In 55 Caesar made a show of force among the Germans, constructing his famous bridge by which he crossed the Rhine. In the autumn of that year, and again in 54, Caesar, having secured the coast around Boulogne, was in Britain, where in the latter year he defeated the native chief

Cassivellaunus. The lateness of the season, however, and the news of unrest among the Belgic tribes caused him hastily to return to the continent. No sooner had the five legions begun to prepare winter quarters—separated from each other but all within a radius of one hundred miles—than the signal for revolt was given by the Eburones, under their chieftain Ambiorix, who attacked the legion commanded by Quintus Sabinus and Lucius Cotta. By an act of treachery the Eburones seized the person of Sabinus and slew him; then rushing the unfinished camp, they overwhelmed Cotta and the legionaries; few survived the slaughter. Immediately other tribes of the Belgae were up in arms; the Nervii attacked the legion of Quintus Cicero, and simultaneously the Treveri, under their leader Indutiomarus, who was the chief instigator of the revolt, threatened the camp of Labienus. Caesar, at the head of two legions quickly came by forced marches to the relief of Cicero, and administered a crushing defeat to the Nervii; whereupon Indutiomarus withdrew. Early in the following spring the latter, after vainly trying to raise the mass of Germanic tribes from across the Rhine, was pursued by Labienus and slain. On this the revolt of the Belgae collapsed; but their defeat left a smouldering resentment among the tribes; and Ambiorix was still abroad, urging on others among the Gauls to fresh resistance.

The year 53 B.C. was spent by Caesar in extinguishing such embers of revolt as remained among the Belgic tribes, unsuccessfully attempting to apprehend Ambiorix, and devastating in reprisal the lands of the Eburones. He recrossed the Rhine to impress by his military presence those Germans who had assisted in the recent disturbances. At this time the news of the defeat and death of Crassus at the hands of the Parthians brought nearer what now appeared to most thinking men the inevitable struggle for power in Rome between the two leaders in command of armies, Caesar and Pompey. The latter, with the support of a majority of the Senate, had not set out for Spain, where he had been appointed in command, but remained in Italy, ostensibly raising troops for use against the Parthians. In the winter of 53–52 Caesar was in Cisalpine Gaul, also engaged in recruiting and training fresh legions.

The leaders among the Gauls, aware of the political storm gathering in Italy, were preparing to seize any occasion that might offer for a final, and supreme effort, to defeat and expel the Romans. The execution of the rebellious chief of the Carnutes, Acco, who was publicly flogged to death at Caesar's order, was a reminder to other Gallic chieftains of the penalty of failure. Rumours were heard from time to time of secret meetings of the tribal leaders in remote places. Everyone, Romans and Gauls alike, waited apprehensively on the turn of events.

It is something more than a rhetorical expression to say that for modern Frenchmen the legendary figure of the young Gallic chieftain Vercingetorix, the leader of the tribe of Arverni, represents the true founder of the Gallic nation. With him, rather than with Clovis and the Salian Franks, springs the true Gallic spirit, the spirit of France. This was clear to the Emperor Napoleon III, when in 1865 he had erected on Mont Auxois above Alise-Ste-Reine the colossal statue of Vercingetorix, rising triumphant over the scene of his final defeat. The Arverni held lands in Auvergne, one of their *oppida*, Gergovia, being not far distant from Clermont-Ferrand. Vercingetorix was the son of Celtillus, who had been put to death by an aristocratic faction, headed by his brother Gobannitio, when he had tried to revive the kingship hereditary in his family. As a young man, rich, of a handsome presence and with considerable persuasive powers, Vercingetorix had put himself in the forefront of the national Gallic party opposed to his appeasing uncle Gobannitio, who had come to an arrangement with Caesar, as a result of which the Arverni had remained neutral in the recent fighting.

In January 52 B.C., while Caesar was in Gallia Cisalpina and the legions in winter quarters at Sens or among the Belgae, the signal for a general revolt among the Gauls, long planned at meetings among their chiefs, was suddenly given by the massacre of all the Romans and their sympathizers in Orléans. This was the revenge taken by the Carnutes for the death of their chieftain Acco. Before evening the news of the uprising, transmitted by a kind of bush-telegraph, reached Gergovia, a hundred and sixty miles away. Immediately Vercingetorix

called on the Arverni to rise, cast off the Roman yoke and
regain their ancient liberties. Driven from the town by the
supporters of Gobannitio, Vercingetorix retired to his estates;
gathering around him a strong force, he returned and captured
Gergovia, where he was immediately proclaimed king. For the
first time the Gauls had found a natural leader, who by
eloquence, bribes and ruthless punishment of waverers (he cut
off their hands, gouged out their eyes or burned them alive),
placed himself at the head of an almost universal rebellion of
the Gallic peoples. The Aedui and the recently chastised Belgae
alone among the principal tribes held aloof. Caesar, informed
of the revolt, hurried to Narbo, set in motion the defence of the
Province, then, with the troops he had raised in Italy, crossed
the Cevennes, which was covered with snow to the depth of
six feet in places, and slipped past Vercingetorix to rejoin his
legions at Sens. As usual, divided counsels, disunion and
inevitable procrastination had prevented Vercingetorix from
fulfilling the first part of his plan—to separate Caesar from his
army. But henceforth Vercingetorix was determined to raise the
whole of Gaul and to impose his will on the contentious Gallic
chieftains. Having a great superiority over the Romans in
cavalry, he saw that the way to a Gallic victory lay in refusing
to be drawn into fighting an infantry battle, in cutting off
Caesar from his sources of supply by a scorched-earth policy,
and in continually harassing the legions and their baggage
train, thus driving them to retreat and take ignominious refuge
in Provence.

The first setback to the Gallic cause was at Bourges. Vercingetorix reluctantly had allowed himself to be persuaded by the
Bituriges, whose capital it was, not to destroy this flourishing
city, as he had all other towns and villages. After a short siege
Caesar took Bourges and burnt it. He was able thus to revictual
his army. Determined to carry the war into the territories of his
enemies, Caesar split his army, sending Labienus with four
legions north against the Parisians and the tribes around the
Seine, while he led six legions and auxiliaries (some 28,000
men) south into Arvernian country, and encamped below
Gergovia. Vercingetorix, consistently refusing a battle, followed,
dogging the Romans' every move and harassing their scouts

C

and forage parties. It was in the difficult situation around Gergovia (for the strength of the place and the disparate numbers of the opposed armies made it impossible for it to be taken by storm) that Caesar heard that the Aedui, hitherto his allies, were wavering in their loyalty, won over by the arguments (and bribes) of Vercingetorix. Immediate and decisive action was imperative. Caesar did not hesitate. Hurriedly alerting two legions he set out and covered the twenty-three miles which separated him from the Aeduan army of 10,000 men, who were marching to join Vercingetorix. These he persuaded, or rather compelled, to accompany him against Gergovia. Then, without allowing his legions more than three hours rest, as hurriedly he returned to meet a powerful Gallic attack. Shortly afterwards, an attempt to storm the heights, which failed, cost the Romans some seven hundred dead, among them many seasoned centurions. Such losses could not be sustained in the face of Gallic superiority in numbers. In dividing his forces Caesar had over-reached himself, and he now found it necessary to retreat and concentrate his army.

Vercingetorix had thus justified his policy, and his leadership was thenceforth acknowledged throughout Gaul. His success finally brought the Aedui over to the Gallic side. The Aeduan force with Caesar had retired, and on their homeward march they crossed the Loire at Nevers, which Caesar had constituted a depot for his Spanish remounts, his public chest and vital stores. Observing that the place was weakly held, the Aedui attacked Nevers, and killing the Roman garrison, destroyed the town and what they could not carry off of the provisions. At a council of the Gauls held in Bibracte, Vercingetorix was appointed commander-in-chief of the combined armies of Gaul, his strategy accepted, and fresh orders were sent to the tribes.

With Labienus also things had not gone well. The Belgae rose behind him, as he withdrew his legions and marched south to meet Caesar, who was moving northwards into Burgundy, followed closely by the Gallic army. Reinforced by cavalry, for which he had sent across the Rhine from among the German tribes, Caesar administered a sharp reverse near Dijon to the hitherto preponderant Gallic horse. Awaiting the general rising among the tribes, which had been ordered at the council in Bibracte, Vercingetorix in turn retreated and took up a strong position on Mont Auxois in the *oppidum* of Alesia. Caesar turned and followed. The last act in the drama of Vercingetorix and Gallic independence was about to be played out. Caesar, with an army of some 40,000 legionaries, supported by his Germanic and Gallic cavalry, set to work to throw up ditches and walls of circumvallation to contain Vercingetorix within Alesia, at the same time as he constructed a vast system of defences facing outwards, in anticipation of the Gallic army of relief. These works of fortification carried out by Caesar, which extended twelve miles in circumference, have been described as the greatest of their kind to have been constructed until modern times. The excavations of Colonel Stoffel in the 'sixties of the last century show them to have been very accurately described by Caesar in his *De Bello Gallico*.

Vercingetorix seized an opportunity of sending out his cavalry, which managed to slip through the Roman lines, to urge on the converging forces to hasten to his relief. Thereupon he expelled the unfortunate Mandubii, whose town Alesia was, rationed the provisions of his troops and, after some costly but vain sorties, sat down to wait. The vast army collected from all the tribes of Gaul is said to have numbered more than 200,000 effectives, a large portion being cavalry, since the Gallic foot-soldier, indifferently armed, was loath to engage the well-trained and equipped legionary. Arriving at Alesia, the Gauls flung themselves, without proper reconnaissance, against the Roman works, hoping to overcome by sheer weight of numbers, while the troops of Vercingetorix attacked the Romans in their rear. Repulsed with great loss on the first day, the Gauls paused for an interval during daylight on that following, then the fighting was resumed at midnight, with an attack on the perimeter defences, and went on until nearly dawn. Again they were driven off, leaving the ditches filled with their dead. Vercassivellaunus, the general in command of the relief army, next attempted a surprise attack by infiltrating around Mont Réa, which rises to the north-west of Alise-Ste-Reine. This was the last, the supreme effort, the Gauls throwing in men desperately to replace their huge losses, while Vercingetorix simultaneously launched wave after wave in furious attacks against the inner perimeter. Everywhere the Gauls failed to penetrate the Roman positions. Finally, when they began to waver, Caesar ordered Labienus to counter-attack, and the Gauls' failure turned suddenly into a panic-stricken rout. The Germanic cavalry completed the carnage; the battle was irretrievably lost.

Vercingetorix called a last council inside Alesia, and proposed to the gathered chieftains either that he be put to death by his own people or that he give himself up to Caesar in an attempt to save their lives. The chiefs accepted the latter course, and in a moving ceremony in the sight of both armies Vercingetorix, mounted on a beautiful charger and in his magnificent panoply of war, rode down the hillside and surrendered. For six years he languished in prison, while the Civil War raged, until he was brought out at length to adorn Caesar's triumph. That evening, as was the Roman custom, he was strangled in his cell at Tullianum. Of the prisoners taken at Alesia, Caesar allowed the Aedui and Arverni to go free, since he required them as allies in the future; the remainder he gave as booty to his victorious troops, one Gaul to each legionary.

Although the spirit of the Gauls had been broken at Alesia, Caesar wintered uneasily at Bibracte in Burgundy. Thereafter he spent the two following years, first in repulsing the last desperate revolts of the Belgic Bellovaci and of Lucterius in Aquitania, and finally in settling Gallia Comata, where he sought by wisdom and clemency to obliterate his past acts of calculated cruelty and to reconcile the Gallic peoples to the rule of Rome. When Caesar left Gaul in 49 B.C., he installed Decimus Junius Brutus in command of the province. Under Decimus Brutus and his successors, Tiberius Claudius Nero, father of the Emperor Tiberius, and Aulus Hirtius, peace was maintained during the period of the Civil War, when the legions trained in Gaul and his Gallic recruited cavalry proved Caesar's most invaluable assets in his final victory over Pompey. These, and the forty million sesterces of tribute that he had imposed on conquered Gaul. Caesar's legate-designate at the time of his death, Lucius Munatius Plancus, founded in 44 B.C. Lugudunum (Lyons), the future capital of the Gallia

Lugudunensis of the Augustan settlement of Gaul; and his firm governorship of the province preserved the peace during the civil wars between Octavian and Anthony.

In the settlement of the Empire the 'three Gauls' of *Gallia Comata* (*Belgica*, *Lugudunensis* and *Aquitania*) came directly under Augustus, and the importance in which the Emperor held the province is shown by the eminence of the governors he appointed—as, for example, Agrippa, who was governor in 39–37 and again in 19–17 B.C. Augustus himself was in Gaul in 27 B.C., and for a long sojourn from 26 to 13 B.C., when on his departure he left as governor his stepson Drusus. It was the latter who inaugurated the new state religion by dedicating an altar to Rome and Augustus outside Lyons, and decreeing an annual assembly of representation of the Gallic tribes, with a festival and games. The province was administered according to the old tribal divisions (*civitates*), which were subdivided into *pagi*. (From the Latin *pagus* is derived the French *pays*.) Augustus thought it politic to destroy Bibracte, the ancient capital of the Aedui on Mont Beuvray, and to transfer elsewhere its inhabitants; and with this end in view he founded in about 12 B.C. *Augustodunum Aedorum* (Autun) on the great north road from Lyons to Boulogne. It is interesting that in building their magnificent network of roads the Romans retained the old Celtic measure of distance in leagues on their milestones, the use of which remained in France until the metric system was introduced after the fall of the *ancien régime*. In Roman Gaul Dijon (*Divio* or *Castrum Divionense*) was a town of only secondary importance in the *civitas* of the Lingones, their capital being Langres (*Andematunum*); and this subordinate relation of Dijon is shown, even at the time of the Grand-Dukes of the West, by its being included in the diocese of the Bishops of Langres. In the *pagi* the great Gallic estates became Roman *villae*, and these were known, for the purpose of the Roman *fiscus* (taxation), by the names of their owners, with the suffix *-iacum* or *-iacus*. Thus the domain of Paul was called *Pauliacus*, and this usage appears today in place names, becoming Paulhac in Aquitaine, Paulliac in the claret-producing country of the Gironde, and Pouilly in Burgundy.

Autun of the Aedui rapidly developed in the peaceful era of the early Empire into one of the richest and fairest of the Roman cities of Gaul, second in extent only to Nîmes and Trèves (Trier)—'the sister and rival' of Rome, as its inhabitants proudly claimed. Its famous school, the *Maenianum*, did much to educate the Gallic youth of the better-off families in Latin culture. It seems to have survived the destruction of the city in A.D. 272 by lawless troops, masquerading as the army of the last Gallic Emperor, Tetricus, since an impassioned plea for its restoration was addressed to the Emperor Constantius Chlorus. In the re-building of Autun workmen, among them masons, were brought from Britain. At the height of its greatness the city, its water supplied by aqueducts, possessed fine walls, with four main gates, a temple of Apollo, the schools, the Capitol, a colonnaded forum, basilicas, baths, amphitheatre and a theatre capable of seating 16,000 spectators. Part of the ancient walls and two of its gates, the Porte d'Arroux and the Porte Saint-André, remain today, in addition to the excavated theatre, placed in a beautiful site with a background of wooded hills. Outside the Port d'Arroux—across the bridge over the River Arroux, then, turning left and crossing the two arms of the stream of the Ternin—the visitor comes to the ruins of an imposing Roman structure, known since the sixteenth century as the Temple of Janus, possibly the sanctuary of a Gallo-Roman deity. The Musée Rolin and the Musée Lapidaire contain many remains of the sumptuous town houses and public buildings: mosaics, statues of Roman and Gallic gods and goddesses, stelai, funerary sculpture, and articles of domestic use and personal adornment. Noteworthy are the head of *Venus* (or *Diana*) in the Musée Rolin, and the beautiful, although mutilated, statue of *Arroux* at the nearby château of Montjeu.

The excavations that are still proceeding on the site of Alesia (Alise-Ste-Reine) have revealed early Gallic dwellings, as well as those of the Roman period. The famous *Vase* of Alesia, a splendid example of the work of Graeco-Alexandrine silver-smiths, is today at the museum of St-Germain-en-Laye. In 1933 at the Sources de la Seine were discovered, besides numerous votive offerings to the river goddess, the fine bronze figures of a *Faun with a crab* and the *Dea Sequana* herself, the goddess standing on a boat shaped in the form of an aquatic bird, which holds a marble in its beak. These are now in the Musée Archéologique in Dijon, a magnificent collection representative of the high excellence of Gallo-Roman civilization in Burgundy. Other good collections of local finds are possessed by the museums of Chalon, Mâcon and Beaune, as well as by those of smaller towns and even villages. After Provence, Burgundy surpasses all other provinces of France in the richness of the archaeological material of this period, which will amply justify the high claims made by historians and connoisseurs for the art and culture of Roman Gaul. But nothing can possibly rival in magnificence and quality of workmanship the celebrated *Treasure of Vix* in the museum of Châtillon-sur-Seine.

As elsewhere, Christianity spread throughout the Roman world by means of the legionaries and traders. Along the great roads north from Provence, following the Rhône and Saône, and then branching east and west at Chalon, were established communities of converts to the new faith; at Autun there exists Christian inscriptions from as early as the third century. The religious hold of the druids over the Gauls appears gradually to have diminished, as the natives assimilated their ancient tribal gods to those of their Roman conquerors. Caesar tells us that Mercury was the god most worshipped in Gaul, where he was identified with the ferocious Celtic Teutates and Esus, to whom human sacrifices were once made. But similarly these two gods were also reverenced as Mars. The Celtic Taranis, the greatest celestial deity, could easily be equated with Jupiter, as well as Dis Pater. But older Celtic deities remained: from near Autun comes a statuette of a cross-legged god, with antlers and holding two ram-headed serpents; and some thirty similar statuettes have been found, mostly in Burgundy. Three curious neckless, headed divinities, discovered at Chorey near Beaune, show the persistence of Celtic traditions. Many Celtic goddesses became associated with the consorts of Roman gods; but Epona, the Gallic goddess of horses, is perhaps unique in that her cult spread over the Empire. Beside her we find a boar-goddess, Dea Artio. Perhaps the most strange animal-god, however, is the boar-god Baco, who had a temple at Chalon-sur-Saône. Baco, by way of Old French, seems to have been the etymological source of the English *bacon*.

When in 407 the Burgundians began their invasion of Gaul they found Christianity well established in the towns, even if it had not penetrated into the remotest parts of the countryside, where lived the *pagani*—pagans or *paysans*. It seems that, following the missionary activities of St Martin of Tours (*c.* 337), directed against these religious observances of earlier ages, something very like a crusade was undertaken to overthrow the ancient gods. Two recently observed cases would appear to be evidence of this: at Entrain-sur-Nohain (Nièvre) a colossal statue of Apollo was found head down, as if it had been thrown into a marsh. Nearby in Burgundy, at Fontaines-Salées, a mutilated bas-relief from a temple has been discovered lying in the bed of a neighbouring stream, where apparently these early iconoclasts had cast it.

CHAPTER IV

The Cluniac Empire

In 1098, when the future St Bernard of Clairvaux was a boy of eight, Pope Urban II wrote to the great Abbot Hugh of Cluny in praise of the monastery where he, the Pope, had served his noviciate: 'The community of Cluny, more plentifully endowed with the divine charisma than others, shines as another sun over the earth, so that in these our days it is more fitting to apply to it the words of our Lord: "You are the light of the world"—*Vos estis lux mundi.*' Emile Mâle, the distinguished historian of religious art, once declared unequivocally that Cluny was the grandest creation of the whole Middle Ages. Again, more recently, Professor Wolfgang Braunfels in his most informative *Monasteries in Western Europe* wrote, 'One monastery of the tenth and eleventh centuries towered above all others, and resolutely raised itself to become the capital of a monastic empire—Cluny in Burgundy.' From this remote corner of Burgundy, then somewhat off the beaten track, radiated such powerful impulses in art and architecture that a history of romanesque architecture and sculpture in France could be written around Cluny and its dependencies. And Cluny's influence extended beyond this period into the twelfth century—the great century of monastic building—by way of Cistercian architecture, which, although that Order was in reaction to Cluniac ideals, was nevertheless imbued with its principles. It will be recalled that in point of time the great abbeys preceded the great cathedrals. From Burgundy the structural canons of Cluny entered the Ile de France, when Abbot Suger employed Cluniac architects in the royal monastery of St Denis, and there the romanesque developed into the full glory of the gothic style. By way of these channels the constructive genius of the Romans was transmitted through Gaul, where it was resuscitated in Burgundy, to find a magnificently fresh expression, first in the cathedrals and churches of the Ile de France, and thence throughout Europe. These Burgundian builders were not conscious of creating anything new, but imagined that they were but perpetuating the traditions of Roman and Carolingian Gaul.

Broadly speaking, monasticism in the East, where it arose, was individualistic, eremitical, fired by the desire of individual men and women to seek God in solitude by the practice of the severest asceticism. The type of these was St Anthony and the Egyptian anchorites of the Thebaid at the beginning of the fourth century. Under the influence of St Pachomius (*c.* 320) this marked individualism became directed towards a rudimentary form of coenobitical living, which was further developed and given coherent shape by St Basil the Great (*c.* 330–79), whose Rule was thenceforth the basis of monastic life both in the East and the West. When the Romans began to form religious communities their gifts for administration led them away from this earlier preoccupation with the individual's salvation and towards a stressing of the life shared in common by the members of the monastery, the *vita communis*—thence to the regulation of that corporate life. The Rules of St Augustine (354–430) are the earliest known of such regulations in the West; but it was St Benedict of Nursia who in founding the monastery of Monte Cassino (*c.* 529) gave the shape to Latin monasticism, and through it may be said to have inaugurated the Latin Middle Ages. When in the early ninth century Charlemagne ordered the reconstruction of the monasteries of his empire, it was to the Rule of St Benedict that he turned, and not to that, more eremitically inclined, of St Colomban.

In Gaul monasticism arrived very early, the first monastery (of the rather primitive eremitical kind) being formed between 350 and 370 by St Martin of Tours and his disciples, who built a village around his cell on the banks of the Loire—it has indeed been called a 'monastic kraal'. Martin, who was the son of a Roman soldier, and who was serving in the legion stationed at Amiens when he performed his famous act of charity by dividing his cloak with the beggar, became the patron saint of the Franks. As legend embroidered on Martin's holiness and miracles, many daughter houses were found in emulation of his monastery at

Marmoutier-lès-Tours. Of similar type was the monastery that grew up between 400 and 410 on the island of Lérins opposite Cannes, founded by St Honoratius, who was believed to have also been a Roman, a refugee from Britain. These hermitages and chapels, and others on the islands and mainland, were constituted as monasteries, the monks, who lived under the Rule of Macarius, numbering at the beginning of the seventh century some 3,700 souls. When an attempt was made in 677 to introduce the Benedictine Rule, the monks revolted and killed their abbot. In 732, five hundred of them, with their abbot, were slain by the Saracens. It was only after the tenth century that the Lérins communities became Benedictine.

Professor Evans, in her *Life in Medieval France*, describes the drift of this monastic movement northwards: 'But French monasticism only really became rational when the centre of its spiritual life shifted from Provence to Burgundy. From the ninth century until the end of the Middle Ages, Burgundy was the source of monastic inspiration of France. It is there, after the reforms of Columbanus had been effected, that the Rules of Benedict of Nursia were first practised in France; and it is thence that the French form of Benedictism spread through the land. Benedict of Aniane, who took the monastic vow and remained for some time in the monastery of St Seine near Dijon, was the instrument of reform.' It was Charlemagne who, on the advice of the Englishman Alcuin, set Benedict of Aniane the task of reforming the monasteries of France on the model of the Rule of St Benedict. Earlier, it has been conjectured, although it is difficult to be certain in these matters, ascetic monasticism of a distinctly eremitical character had spread to Ireland from 'British roots, probably under Burgundian influence' (W. Braunfels). St Patrick, (*c.* 389–461), escaping from his Irish captivity, was for several years a monk on Lérins, and afterwards attended the famous schools at Auxerre —Burgundy was at that time in close connection with Britain and Ireland. Patrick seems to have spent some fourteen years in Auxerre, where he was ordained deacon by Bishop Amator, before he set out in 432 on his evangelical mission among the Irish.

Two early French monastic foundations were Fontenelle

(St-Wandrille) and Jumièges in the valley of the Seine, in what was later Normandy; these were founded in 649 and 655 respectively, the Rule of St Columban, modified by that of St Benedict, being that first adopted, until in the Carolingian revival the latter Rule was universally prescribed. At the time of the destruction of these monasteries at the hands of the Normans, many monks fled for safety, bearing with them their sacred relics, and found a refuge in Burgundy. There in 909 or 910 Duke William of Aquitaine, drawing to the close of a long life, gave a farm and a chapel in the valley of the Grosne, a small tributary of the Saône, with the purpose of founding a monastery. This foundation was to be subject neither to the local bishop nor duke, but to the Pope alone; and Duke William journeyed to Rome to enfeoff Cluny to the Holy See. It is for this reason that so many of the churches of the daughters of this Benedictine foundation of Cluny are dedicated to St Peter—the mother-church itself being consecrated in the names of Sts Peter and Paul. From its inception Cluny was thus foreseen as a 'monastic kingdom exempt from civil powers'.

This early tenth century in France, when Cluny was founded, of all the centuries before and since has most justifiably earned the title of a Dark Age, largely from the social chaos brought about by the incursions of Hungarians, Norsemen and Saracens. Cluny was to become the beacon whose light shed over the land heralded the triumphs of the French Middle Ages. The founding father, Abbot Berno of Baume (910–26), who appears to have made his profession at the abbey of St-Savin-sur-Gartempe in Poitou and to have been for a time at St-Martin d'Autun, took over the chapel and farm buildings and built the first abbey church, now known to art historians as Cluny I. Duke William in his deed of gift ordained that 'our foundation shall serve for ever as a refuge for those who, having renounced the world as poor men, bring nothing with them but their good will, and we desire that our superfluity shall become their abundance'. Berno's successor, Abbot Odo (926–44), raised his monastery to such an eminence as to receive from the Emperor Henry I the privilege of subordinating other monasteries to Cluny, the first step to the formation of an independent Cluniac Order within the Benedictine movement. The election of Majolus (Mayeul) as abbot in 954 marked the beginning of a succession of four great abbots whose rule over a period of two hundred years brought Cluny to its recognized position as the greatest monastery in Christendom. The buildings at the time of Abbot Mayeul were most likely of wood or an adaptation of the original farmhouse and offices, but he began the construction of a larger abbey church (distinguished as Cluny II), which was consecrated in 981. His successor, Odilo, who was abbot for fifty-five years (994–1049), completely rebuilt the monastic buildings, with a splendour that amazed contemporaries. We have an account of Odilo's Cluny, written by a Roman cleric in the retinue of Peter Damian, who as a cardinal visited France in 1063.

The unknown author relates: 'how all the stone-built offices are disposed in monastic order; how the great and vaulted church is furnished with numerous altars, endowed with no ordinary number of relics and most richly adorned with various precious things; how vast the cloister is and by its very beauty seems to invite the monks to dwell there; how spacious the dorter is, and how the light from three lamps kept constantly burning virtually precludes anything evil being done there; how the refectory, painted not with any superstition but with the Last Judgement, is built large enough for all the brethren to eat together; how in all the offices and wherever water is necessary, it marvellously flows at once and of its own accord from hidden channels; these and other things I might relate of the said monastery . . .' Benefactions to this abbey already so famous had followed rapidly after the visit of the Emperor Henry II in 1114, when he dedicated to Cluny his coronation sceptre, orb and crown and a great cross of gold, as well as the revenues from estates in Alsace. Odilo's biographer, Jotsaldus, wrote of his building: '. . . in his last years he constructed a cloister, admirably decorated with marble columns from the furthermost parts of the province, transported not without great labour by the powerful currents of the Durande and Rhône. Of this he was wont to boast in a joking way, saying that "he had found it wood and left it marble", following in this the Emperor Augustus . . .' Cluny, under Abbot Odilo, began to play its part in the development of feudal France, assisting with its counsel the King, as it had already Popes and Emperors. Its authority was such that it could lend its powerful weight to the acceptance of two contemporary institutions which did much to mitigate the horrors of feudal anarchy—the *Pax Dei* and the *Truga Dei*, the Peace and Truce of God. It was at this time that the Customs (*Consuetudines*) of Cluny were drawn up, to serve as a model for those increasingly numerous Benedictine monasteries that submitted to its Order. Still today, nearly a thousand years after the death of Odilo, the church bells of the Charollais ring out from vespers into the night of All Saint's Day in commemoration of the dead, as instituted by the Abbot of Cluny for his monasteries in 998.

The observances of the Order of Cluny differed from those followed by other Benedictine houses chiefly in their attitude to manual labour. St Benedict in his Rule had laid down that the monks were to work with their hands for seven hours daily, '*quia virtus est animae et corporis*', because virtue is of the mind as well as of the body. This rule had been relaxed over the years; latterly only a token gesture to its observance was made on the orders of the Prior, when the monks went in procession to the monastic gardens, where, after hearing a homily on the dignity of labour, and to the accompaniment of chanted psalms, they weeded the vegetable beds. In place of field work, which was performed by laymen (paid hands or serfs), Cluny became—besides its primary devotion to the *Opus Dei*, the almost continuous service in choir—an intellectual monastery; and as such it had a widespread and beneficial influence on the arts—on architecture, sculpture, music, and literature, even poetry. The writing and copying of books were favoured at Cluny, and so highly was the art of the illuminator held that the most skilled scribes were excused certain of the regular hours in order to devote the time to their manuscripts. Peter the Venerable expressed the Cluniac point of view explicitly: 'It is more noble to set one's hand to the pen than to the plough, to trace divine letters on the page than furrows on the fields. Sow on the page the seed of the word of God, and when the harvest is ripe, when your books are finished, the hungry readers shall be satisfied by the abundant harvest.' The library at Cluny possessed the works of many classical authors, including Ovid's *De arte amatoria*, although some abbots had qualms about such intellectual fare. Abbot Mayeul, we are told, had studied the classics at Lyons before making his profession; but as librarian at Cluny, 'having read the philosophers of old and the lies of Virgil, he no longer desired to read them himself or to let others do so'. Abbot Odo also read Virgil, until his scruples were aroused on dreaming of a vase beautiful in form but filled with serpents; and the great Abbot Hugh likewise turned resolutely from profane to sacred literature.

Cluny, then, was essentially a learned Order; daily a chapter of the Rule of St Benedict was read and discussed in the chapter-house (hence its name); besides the communal reading in the refectory, certain hours also each day were given over to solitary reading, and in Lent the monks were prescribed the study of some book, which was issued to each from the library. In fact, the Cistercians complained that the Cluniacs read too much. In the twelfth-century *Dialogue between a Cluniac and a Cistercian* the Cistercian says: 'By your speech, by your quotations from the poets, I recognize the Cluniac, for you and your brethren take so much pleasure in the lies of the poets, that you read, study and teach them even in the hours which St Benedict has definitely reserved for the reading of Scriptures and for manual labour.' The Cluniac's reply would perhaps only convince one of his own Order: 'If we read the books of the pagans, it is to make ourselves perfect in their language, and thus to fit us to understand the Scriptures.' The strict Cistercian rebukes the monk of Cluny for the time spent in these 'idle occupations', especially in the beautiful illumination of their books: 'I will say no more of the others, but will ask, Is it not useless to grind gold to powder, and therewith to paint great capital letters?' (This is somewhat ironic, since the illumination done at Cîteaux itself greatly influenced subsequent sculpture.) The full force of the Cistercian attack on the 'aestheticism' of Cluny was left to St Bernard of Clairvaux. Nevertheless, the contribution of Cluniac culture to that flowering of French art in the early Middle Ages is inestimable—and not only to art in France, but in Italy, England and Spain.

The influence of Cluny reached its highest point under the

great Abbot St Hugh of Semur-en-Brionnais, that little
hilltop town, where today not far from its beautiful romanesque
church may still be seen the keep of his family's castle. As a
boy Hugh studied at the Cluniac house of St-Marcel-lès-
Chalon; from there, against the wishes of his martial family, he
entered the noviciate, and after professing, was appointed at
an early age to the office of Grand Prior of Cluny. For sixty
years, from 1049 to 1109, he was abbot of Cluny, becoming one
of the leading statesmen of Europe. Called to the counsel of
the Kings of France, Emperors and Popes (he was present at
Canossa when the Emperor Henry IV humbled himself before
Pope Gregory VII), he still had time to watch over his
monastery and the entire Cluniac Order, which was finally
established at this time. By papal deed, Abbot Hugh was given
the same legislative, judicial and administrative powers over
the other houses as over Cluny itself, some 1,400 abbeys and
priories being thus subordinated to one man. The superiors of
all houses were of his own choice, and the profession of every
member of the Cluniac Order, however distant his abbey or
priory lay, was with his personal approval; most monks, if
they were able, journeying to Cluny to make their profession.
During the lifetime of Abbot Hugh there were founded
or, as older foundations, were incorporated in the Order
such famous monasteries and churches as: La Charité-sur-
Loire, St-Etienne-de-Nevers, St-Pierre-de-Moissac, St-Germain
d'Auxerre, Vézelay, and St-Martin-des-Champs in Paris, this
last the gift of King Philip I. In 1056 the earliest Cluniac
nunnery was founded at Marcigny in Burgundy, at the
instigation of St Hugh's brother, Geoffroy II of Semur; and
their sister Ermengarde was appointed as its first Prioress.
Houses were established in Italy, England and Spain. In this
last country the Order had already under Odilo played some
part in the Burgundian crusades for the *reconquista* of the land
from the Moors, but now Abbot Hugh, who twice visited
Spain, became one of the most honoured of the counsellors of
King Alonzo VI of Castille, who presented the Order with the
monasteries of S. Isodoro de Duegna, S. Jaime de Campomondo,
St Colomba de Burgos, and the hermitage below Montserrat.

It was with the 10,000 pieces of gold, part of the booty at the capture of Toledo in 1085, and the annual tribute of 2,000 pieces granted to Cluny by King Alonzo that Abbot Hugh began in 1088 the building of his great basilican church, when he was then sixty-five, having already been abbot for nearly forty years. Other benefactors of Cluny were King Henry I of England, who also gave an annual tribute, raised on the revenues of London and Lincoln, and his daughter, the Empress Matilda, who presented the monastery with its bells, cast in England of a metal different from that employed in France. There is a legend concerning the events that led to the creation of Hugh's abbey. The paralysed Abbot of Baume, Gunzo, had been brought to end his days at Cluny. One night, lying on his pallet, he was visited in a dream by St Peter, St Paul and St Stephen. St Peter spoke to him, bidding him go to Abbot Hugh and command him to build the church, regardless of cost, and marking out for Gunzo its dimensions with ropes. To vouch for the reality of the vision, St Peter promised Gunzo that he would be cured of his paralysis. Abbot Hugh, when he saw the aged Gunzo hale and hearty again, was persuaded by the inescapability of the apostolic command, as well as by the necessity to expand his overcrowded monastery, which then numbered more than four hundred and sixty monks; and the immense work was started. With the narthex, which was added in 1220, Hugh's abbey church of Cluny III, which was finally consecrated by Pope Innocent II in 1130, was the largest in Christendom, measuring in length 525 feet; and it remained so until the building of the new St Peter's, whose overall length exceeded it by some 150 feet.

Hugh's plan was for a basilican church with two transepts, a broad nave flanked by double aisles, and a rounded apsidal end with an ambulatory, off which opened five radial chapels. The nave, consisting of eleven bays with pointed arches, surmounted by two arcades of rounded arches, was 260 feet long; together with the apse it measured 415 feet. The barrel vaulting, 92 feet from the floor, was supported by great piers, with fluted classical pilasters towards the nave and engaged columns on the other three sides. Of this huge edifice only the southern arm of the first or great transept, with its soaring tower, the 'Clocher de l'Eau Bénite', remains; this, together

with some of the marvellously carved capitals of the ambulatory (*c.* 1095)—certainly among the finest examples of any
romanesque sculpture, whose survival only serves to heighten
our sense of the loss of so much else. These capitals are housed
today in the Musée Lapidaire, and were preserved in the last
century by the care of a M. Ochier, who as a boy saw the abbey
before the vandals had begun their work of destruction. Today,
the church at Paray-le-Monial may give the visitor some
small idea of how Cluny once appeared, but the scale here is
one much reduced, and Paray has nothing comparable by way
of decoration. (Some conception, perhaps, of the choir and apse
at Cluny may be gained from those, smaller but very beautiful,
of La Charité-sur-Loire.) Many of the capitals and much of
the walls of Cluny were originally painted; in the apse was a
large painting of Christ in Glory, supported by angels and
accompanied by the four evangelists. The impression given by
the immensity of the church and the richness of its decoration
must have been one of the utmost splendour and magnificence
when it was seen lit by hundreds of candles in candelabra,
whose light gleamed on the gold of crucifixes and reliquaries,
played on the mosaics of the pavement, and revealed the
marvel of all these colours—sienna-green, ultramarine-blue and
cinnabar-red. St Hugh, when wearied from his multifarious
activities and cares, he sought to refresh and restore himself by a
country retreat, used to retire to a grange, which was in the
possession of the monastery, at nearby Berzé-la-Ville. There in
the chapel that he built we can still see the frescoes, which must
have been similar to those in his abbey church. The style of
these figures of Christ and his saints is hieratic, Byzantine, and
is clearly derived from the same tradition as those of San
Vitale in Ravenna, most probably by way of Abbot Desiderius'
Monte Cassino, which Abbot Hugh visited.

The remaining eight capitals, which are now in the Musée,
many much damaged, came from the lofty columns of the
ambulatory, and seem to have represented the 'quaternities'
of Radulphus Glaber, those symbolic groupings of four which
the Cluniac monk describes in his *Historiarum liber V*: such
groups as the Four Ages, the Four Rivers and Trees of Paradise,
the Four Virtues, the Four Gospels, the 'double quaternity'

of the eight tones of Gregorian plainsong, and the rest. It seems unlikely that these Corinthian-styled capitals were pigmented; the carving is of the highest quality, crisp and elegant, and beautiful in the rhythmic movement of the designs. It was a crime against civilization that this monastery of Cluny, the painful creation of men, should have been wantonly destroyed, part blown up with gun-powder, by the fanaticism and cupidity of the men of the Revolution of 1789. Much of what we now know of its appearance, when it rose in all the grandeur of its conception and the beauty of its execution, is owed to the life-work of the American architect, Professor K. J. Conant. What we should give today to have seen it, as Mabillon saw it, still standing complete after six centuries, when it called from him the amazed comment, 'If you were to see it a hundred times, you will still be astounded by its majesty.'

One of the major reasons for the high place that Cluny held in the mediaeval world was its peculiar and intimate relationship with the Papacy. This was clearly evident at the time of Abbot Hugh, whose counsel was sought by several Popes. Although Pope Gregory VII was not, as some have claimed, a Cluniac monk, he strongly supported the Order, and Abbot Hugh in return backed the Pope in his quarrel with the Emperor Henry IV on the question of investiture. Both Pope Urban II, who consecrated the high altar in Hugh's new but unfinished church in 1095, and his successor Pascal II, who also visited the abbey in 1106, had served their noviciates at Cluny and were lavish in their favours. Ten years after the passing from the scene of the great Hugh of Semur in 1109, the abbey church provided a curious death-chamber for Pope Gelasius II, when a bed of ashes was placed for him in the choir, where he died, surrounded by the monks of Cluny. After his burial in the nave, the conclave present elected as his successor the Burgundian Pope Calixtus II, who renewed the abbey's privileges and made Pons de Melgueil, who had succeeded Hugh as abbot, cardinal priest of Ste Cecilia. So many lords had come to enter Cluny, to end their days as simple monks— men like Hugh II of Burgundy, Simon of Crépy and Eustace III of Boulogne—that Pope Gregory had on a particular occasion complained to Abbot Hugh: 'You have taken or you have received in your peaceful retreat of Cluny the Duke of Burgundy and you have thus left a hundred thousand Christians without a protector. . . .' Some years later, in 1140, Cluny received a still more distinguished visitor in the dying Peter Abelard.

The Abbot, Peter the Venerable, moved the invalid to the more comfortable priory of St-Marcel-lès-Chalon, to be cared for by the monks, and after Abelard's death two years later he wrote a moving letter to Heloïse, informing her of it, and consoling her: '. . . What more can I say? His mind, his speech, his actions, were ever meditated, and taught and bore witness to holiness, philosophy and learning. Such among us was this man, simple and righteous, fearing God and shunning evil; such among us for a little while, consecrating the last days of his life to God. For the sake of the rest—for he was more than usually troubled with the itch and other weaknesses of the body —I sent him to Chalon, for the mildness of the climate, which is the best in our part of Burgundy; and to a house well fitted for him, near the town, but yet with the Saône flowing between. There, as much as his infirmities permitted, returning to his former studies, he was ever bent over his books . . . In the midst of such labours Death, the bearer of good tidings, found him— not, like so many, asleep, but awake. . . .' Abelard was buried in the monks' cemetery at the priory of St-Marcel, but a few months later, at Heloïse's request, Abbot Peter had the body removed, and himself accompanied it to the grave prepared by Heloïse at her convent of the Paraclete.

The Cardinal-Abbot Pons de Melgeuil, a barbarian baron masquerading as a priest, was compelled by Pope Calixtus, on complaints by the monks of scandal and extravagance, to resign his charge in 1122. His successor, Hugh II, having died within three months of his election, the monks chose as abbot Pierre Maurice de Montboissier, known usually as Peter the Venerable. In 1125, during Abbot Peter's absence on a visita-tion to Cluniac houses in Aquitaine, Pons at the head of a band of soldiers, citizens of Cluny, whom he had bribed, and dissident monks, seized the monastery and, to pay his ill-assorted supporters, melted down the treasures—the gold crosses, candlesticks and censers; nor were the chalices and reliquaries spared. The Pope summoned Peter and Pons, whom he had excommunicated along with the rebel monks, to Rome. The verdict going against the unrepentant Pons, he was thrown into prison, where he died. The great days of Cluny were already over, although Peter the Venerable strove to restore order and discipline and to replenish the exhausted treasury. In this last work he was greatly helped by a former monk, Henry de Blois, Bishop of Winchester (St Bernard's 'old whore of Winchester'), who in all gave 7,000 marks of silver to the monastery. Formerly the abbots of Cluny had played a large part in the world of European politics, taking a lead in the Burgundian crusades against the Spanish Moors, but now it was St Bernard who preached the Second Crusade at Vézelay, in the absence of Abbot Peter. The building continued, but the earlier dynamism had departed from Cluny, although the decline was gradual. One hundred years later, in 1245, the monks could proudly relate how the monastery had at one time accommodated Pope Innocent IV, with his retinue of twelve cardinals and twenty bishops, Saint Louis and the French court, as well as the King's mother and brother and their entourages, to say nothing of the Byzantine Emperor and his train, without the monks themselves having had to give up their dorter, refectory, chapter-house, or indeed any of the principal offices. It was not only St Bernard of Clairvaux who inveighed against abuses and relaxation of St Benedict's Rule: Peter the Venerable attempted to stem the tide, replying magnanimously to St Bernard's strictures and calling his own monks to order in a circular letter to the Cluniac Priors, which reveals a pleasant irony of tone. He rebukes the monks for their unspiritual interest in their food:

'Like hawks and vultures, they gathered wherever they saw smoke from a kitchen, wherever they smelt meat cooking. . . . Beans, cheese, eggs and fish disgusted them; they only found savoury the flesh-pots of Egypt. Roast or boiled pork, a well-fatted heifer, rabbit, hare, a goose chosen with care, chicken, in fact every kind of meat and fowl appears on the table of these holy monks. But soon such food in its turn ceases to be good enough; satiety brings fastidiousness; rare and royal luxuries must be provided. Today a monk cannot stay his hunger but on the flesh of kids, of stags, of boars, of wild bear. Huntsmen, range the forests! Fowlers, catch partridges, pheasants, pigeons! Let not the servant of God die of hunger!...'

Although St Bernard of Clairvaux and Peter the Venerable greatly admired each other and exchanged friendly letters, the Cistercian reform was directed chiefly against their Burgundian neighbours at Cluny. St Bernard's spirited *Apologia* and his ascetic mysticism were winning the day and drawing recruits to the growing Cistercian Order. With the death of Peter the Venerable in 1157, the days of Cluniac supremacy were past, its civilizing mission was taken up by more vigorous hands. Important monasteries were removed from its spiritual juris-diction; in 1162 Pope Alexander II freed Vézelay from Cluny, saying that the latter had fallen away from its earlier virtues. Reforms were of no avail. In 1518 the monks lost the right of electing their abbot, when King François Ier appointed the first commendatory abbot, Armand de Boissy. Finally came the Revolution. On 25th October 1791, the anniversary of the consecration of the abbey church, the last high mass was said at Cluny, before the monks were dispersed. In the summer of the same year the Empress Matilda's great bells were melted down to forge into cannon; in November the monastery was profaned and sacked by the revolutionary mob. Then on 21st April 1798 the buildings were sold to three citizens of Mâcon, one of them the ex-priest Génillon, for something in excess of two million francs. The destruction went on until 1811, the apse and narthex being blown up to expedite the process. At length, all that was left of what was the glory of Burgundy and of France was the single arm of the south transept, that the visitor sees today. What civilized man had created over centuries was cancelled out by other men in an act of wanton barbarity. All men are equal.

CHAPTER V

Burgundian Romanesque

THE PROVINCES OF France are immeasurably rich in architecture of the romanesque period. If its gothic cathedrals constitute one of the chief glories of France, there is something no less rewarding in the architecture of the earlier age, something perhaps not so immediately apparent, but which none-theless appeals with an interest and a beauty all its own. We have only to think of those ruins of once great abbeys or of those churches, solid, four-square, that have defied the passage of time and today serve the same purpose for which they were built eight or nine centuries ago. Normandy, Poitou, Guyenne, Auvergne, Languedoc, Provence—every province possesses its variations on a common architectural theme, its characteristic nuances of style. Nor is Burgundy an exception; indeed the visitor is likely to be embarrassed by the richness of its romanesque. In the department of Saône-et-Loire alone there exist today no fewer than two hundred and fifty romanesque or part-romanesque churches. Here in this focus that is Burgundy all roads met; and it was the fusion of the many influences that came from outside with what had been inherited from its own past—in this again, the native genius working on the foreign elements to make them its own—that has allowed art historians to speak of a Burgundian romanesque style, or rather of a family likeness that is unmistakably Burgundian. Many have seen in the abbey or collegial church of Ste-Madeleine of Vézelay the grandest and most beautiful of all romanesque churches surviving in France. And in the sculptor Gislebertus of Autun we have not only one of the few known masters of the period, but also an artist of the very highest rank.

Romanesque, as its name indicates, is derived from the art of classical Rome, more particularly from Roman architec-tural principles and practice, taken in their widest sense of constructional design and technique, together with the attendant sculptural decoration. Very early the Roman basilican form and the use of domed vaulting had been adopted for Christian churches. In Roman Gaul the employment of ashlar, of dressed stone set in mortar, was widespread. Despite barbarian invasions—not only those that put an end to Roman rule in Gaul, but the many others throughout the centuries—and the destruction wrought by Frenchmen themselves in the Wars of Religion, the Fronde and the Revolution, much Roman work has survived, especially in southern France. To the uninitiated French museums are surprisingly profuse in Roman sculpture. And building in stone did not cease in Burgundy even during the Dark Ages—the material was plentifully at hand and easily worked. The Roman tradition lived on; and then in the Carolingian and again in the Ottonian periods there came about a very considerable architectural renaissance in France, although this suffered severely in the invasions of Saracens, Normans and Hungarians. It was in the latter period that, with the foundation of Cluny (910), a new age of construction began in Burgundy, ecclesiastical rather than secular: the founding of monasteries and priories and the building of parish churches.

This renewal was marked by the ubiquitous presence of masons from northern Italy, who were known universally as Lombards, and in particular the so-called *magistri comacini*. It is unlikely that we shall learn much more than the little we already know of these stone-workers from around Lake Como; but what is well established is the existence of itinerant *ateliers*, workshops of masons and sculptors, that moved freely from place to place, thus diffusing and developing their technique, and evolving fresh styles under influences derived from sources as disparate as Byzantium and Moorish Spain. By about the year 1000, in Burgundy the nascent feudalism and the increasing riches of the Church had brought about the social conditions necessary for that extraordinary growth of architecture and sculpture that burgeoned and flowered in the Burgundian romanesque. It is a common error to assume that the building of monasteries and churches was the work primarily of monks; in the Cluniac Order, which was the originator in so much, this was certainly not the case. With the Cistercians, monks may indeed have worked by the side of their professional brethren; and in both Orders it was the abbots and their monastic advisers—men like Abbot Hugh of Cluny and his architect Hézelon of Liège, or St Bernard of Clairvaux—who most often ordered and drew up the plans, as well as provided the iconography for the carvings on capitals or in such decorative, and frequently didactic, features as tympana, corbels and doorways. But the masons and sculptors who created the masterpieces of Burgundian romanesque were for by far the greatest part anonymous lay craftsmen.

As Carolingian architecture grew naturally out of the Roman, so romanesque developed, with many a backward glance at the earliest models, from Carolingian building. The studies of M. Jean Hubert have shown that all the methods of vaulting employed by the Carolingian architects were taken over into Burgundian romanesque. Long-established monastic foundations, many of them brought into existence by the munificence of the Carolingians, became centres of expansion—such ancient abbeys as St-Martin d'Autun, St-Bénigne de Dijon, St-Germain d'Auxerre, St-Pierre de Flavigny-sur-Ozerain, St-Pierre-le-Vif de Sens and St-Philibert de Tournus. And, towering above all, the great abbey of Cluny, the most powerful and influential monastery in contemporary Christendom. The renewed activity in the reconstruction of existing edifices and the widespread building of others, a revival unprecedented in its *élan* and intensity, was vividly described by the Benedictine Radulphus Glaber, who had been a monk at St-Bénigne de Dijon and ended his days at Cluny: 'A little after the year one thousand it came about that basilican churches were rebuilt throughout the known world, principally in Italy and Gaul; and although most of them were very adequate and in need of almost nothing, a great spirit of emulation took hold of each Christian people to exceed others in magnificence. One might have said that the world, shaking off and casting aside its old age, everywhere clothed itself anew in the white finery of churches.' Radulphus Glaber doubtless had in mind the rebuilding of the abbey church of Cluny under Abbot Mayeul, and the arrival of William of Volpiano at St-Bénigne, where he had been sent by Mayeul to reform the Dijon monastery, which was indeed Benedictine, along Cluniac lines.

William was no simple monk, being a scion of the Counts of Volpiano, a northern Italian family connected with those Marquises of Ivrea who were claimants to the ancient Lombard throne; he was also godson to Adelaide, wife of the Emperor Otto the Great, as well as being related to the Count of Burgundy, the Bishop of Langres, Brun de Roucy, and Richard II, Duke of Normandy. The new Abbot found his monastery in a poor state of repair, his abbey church in a ruinous condition, as likewise was the complex of buildings next to it—the circular Carolingian mausoleum of the second-century martyr Bénigne, the apostle to Dijon, and the adjacent chapel dedicated to the Virgin. Furnished with ample funds by his relative, the Bishop of Langres (Dijon was in his diocese), William of Volpiano resolved on a magnificent reconstruction, summoning Lombard masons and sculptors from Italy and elsewhere, as well as craftsmen trained in the *chantiers* of Cluny. Work began on 14th February 1001. Some years later, when the church and the rebuilt rotunda were completed, Duke Richard, visiting Dijon, was so impressed with his kinsman's work that he called him to Normandy to introduce the Cluniac reforms at his new abbey at Fécamp.

The crypt of St-Bénigne, which one visits today, is but the lowest of the three floors of William's famous building, the rest having been destroyed in the Revolution, the material from the upper floors being then used to fill in the crypt. The latter was discovered and excavated between 1843 and 1858, when the work of restoration was carried out imaginatively, but with perhaps insufficient care in the completely accurate replacement of the masonry. Nevertheless, the crypt of St-Bénigne de Dijon is most important in tracing the development of Burgundian romanesque. Beyond this, the visitor, on descending the stairway and coming in the semi-darkness upon this subterranean forest of pillars, is moved by a sense of the impressiveness of the place, something at once solemn, mysterious, outside of time. These columns constitute two concentric deambulatories encircling other columns that form an octagon enclosing the central space, which was once occupied by the shrine of the saint. Drawings of the rotunda made before the destruction of the upper floors show it to have been Lombard work, superimposed on presumably Carolingian foundations. Groined and barrel vaulting is supported by some interesting capitals, one of which is very curious, being rudely carved (perhaps Carolingian?) with a man's face between his arms and hands raised in supplication. The rotunda communicated in the east with the *cella* (today closed), which was the original sanctuary dedicated to the Virgin. This feature of an eastern prolongation of the deambulatory had an interesting future, since it and other similar extensions in Carolingian churches—such as those at St-Androche in Saulieu—led to the radiating apsidal chapels of Cluny and Anzy-le-Duc, and their many followers. Further, the rotunda of William of Volpiano was of a design fairly common among Carolingian buildings, which were sometimes preceded by a two-storeyed porch, a form which became developed into the familiar romanesque narthex (with its first-floor chapel, often dedicated to St Michael)—as we see at Cluny, Tournus and elsewhere.

William's patron, Bishop Brun de Roucy of Langres, also undertook the reconstruction in the Lombard style of the ancient church of St-Vorles at Châtillon-sur-Seine (which is today being restored), where at the end of the century St Bernard of Clairvaux was to go to school. One of the most perfect examples existing of this style in Burgundy is the beautiful little church of Chapaize, near Tournus, which was built about this time—at the end of the tenth century or beginning of the eleventh. It possesses in its tall tapering tower (a familiar feature) vertical raised bands, blind arcading, rounded window-openings and triple apse, elements which are everywhere associated with the Lombard builders, examples of whose work are found scattered over a wide area—in Italy, France and Catalonia.

One of the most imposing of these early romanesque churches in Burgundy is undoubtedly St-Philibert of Tournus, the construction of which has furnished art historians with matter for endless debate. It is not inappropriate, therefore, that part of the ancient abbey buildings should today be occupied by

the International Centre for Romanesque Studies, the learned
society which was inaugurated in 1953. Leaving behind the
unending roar of traffic on the N.6, the visitor passes between
the two round towers of the mediaeval Porte des Champs into
the other-world tranquillity of the Place de l'Abbaye. Ahead of
him rises the sober façade of St-Philibert, the crenellation which
joins the massive square towers suggesting something of the
impregnability of a military stronghold. (This battlement and
the central porch are additions made by the last-century restorer,
Questel.) The decorative elements that relieve the flat stonework—the blind arcading, the raised vertical bands and the
horizontal saw-edge mouldings—immediately declare the
presence of Lombard workmen. On the left-hand tower,
beneath the pyramid which caps the topmost storey, are visible
some elongated sculptured figures in the mullions and at the
angle, which are some of the earliest examples of this use of the
human figure, and suggest that the date of this part of the
structure was before 1150.

On this site the apostle to Tournus, Valerian, was martyred
in 179, and the early shrine which was raised on the spot was
later transformed into a monastery. Then in 875 the community
was joined by monks from the Ile de Noirmoutier, fleeing with
the relics of their patron, St Philibert, from the raids of North-
men. This earliest Carolingian church and monastery was
destroyed in the terrible Hungarian invasion of 937. It is the
dates of the subsequent stages of rebuilding that are open to
question. We are informed that Abbot Stephen in 979 placed
the relics of St Valerian under the altar of the crypt. This may
well be the crypt we see, with its deambulatory of slim columns
and beautiful capitals and, off it, the five rectangular chapels;
but here Abbot Stephen could have based his design on the
pre-existing Carolingian structure. In 1006 a fire destroyed or
very seriously damaged the church, only sparing the crypt. We
hear of a dedication in 1019, but of what we are left ignorant.
Finally in 1120, under Abbot Francon de Rouzay, the church
was solemnly consecrated by Pope Calixtus II. The dates, then, of
937 and 1120 seem to register the span of time for the building of
St-Philibert—but this leaves many questions unanswered.

The visitor, on entering the great narthex (a splendid

development of the Carolingian two-storeyed porch), may well find himself taken momentarily off-guard, firstly by the massiveness of the construction, with its huge round pillars supporting ribbed arches and groined vaults—and secondly, perhaps, by the seeming clumsiness, not to say extreme primitiveness, of the stonework, of shallow, almost brick-like courses set in thick layers of mortar. It is not until he has ascended to the St-Michael chapel above that he realizes in all its impressiveness the skill, the mastery, of those early eleventh-century architects and builders. Here he will be astonished at the unexpected daring of the barrel vaulting (tied on high by wooden beams) over the central nave and this vast disposition of thrusts and buttressed supports. And in St-Philibert the visitor to St-Bénigne de Dijon will recognize some similar sculpture, inset in the wall of what is known as the 'arch of Gerlannus'. Two carvings are of rudimentary capitals; two others show representations of a human face, one depicted front view, and the second of a man, seen in profile, his right hand raised in apparent benediction. Near this very primitive Carolingian or early romanesque work is a mysterious inscription, referring perhaps to the sculptor or to the abbot.

GERLANNUS

ABATE ISTE MO

NETERIUM E

ILE

This effect of massiveness, of solemn majesty, is retained when we enter the church; but any sense of heaviness is relieved, redeemed by the presence of abundant light from on high. The same great rotund pillars of the narthex here rise up unbroken to where two overlapping narrow courses serve as imposts from which spring the rounded arches of the five bays that form the nave. These imposts, on the nave side, carry short engaged columns, that in turn support the double ribs of the central vaults and their diaphragm-walls, so as to constitute bays above the nave arcades. These bays are covered by transverse barrel vaults, thus permitting the opening of windows high in the external walls, hence the unimpeded entry of light. This early form of solving the problem of covering the large span of the nave, by the use of barrel vaults at right angles to the axis of the church, is very rare, the only other example perhaps in Burgundy being in the little church of Mont-St-Vincent, some distance to the west of Tournus.

In addition to the recognition of Carolingian and Lombard elements in St-Philibert, it must come as a surprise to see a purely classical treatment of columns and capitals above the crossing, where arches and squinches are thus supported in the passage from the square formed by the nave, choir and transepts to the dome beneath the central tower. This is most elegant in its classical simplicity. Whatever the stages were in the building of St-Philibert, there is indubitably a remarkable homogeneity in the whole construction, as if the design were conceived in one piece and drafted on one drawing-board.

Doubtless both the churches of St-Philibert of Tournus and of St-Bénigne of Dijon (as distinct from the rotunda) had many points in common with the great church the Abbot Mayeul had created at Cluny, which was dedicated to Saints Peter and Paul in 985. But these were abbey churches; others more humble—priories and parish churches—were to spring up, particularly in southern Burgundy, in the eleventh and twelfth centuries. Many of these have the central Lombard tower, square or octagonal, capped with a pyramid roofing, as well as the characteristic external decoration. Some also in the internal walls of their semi-circular apses were decorated with the Lombard vertical raised bands and blind, round-headed arcading. This form of decoration developed at the end of the eleventh and beginning of the twelfth century into a system of recessed arcades separated by slim columns or pilasters. We can see the transitional stage at Anzy-le-Duc or St-Germain-en-Brionnais and the full development at Berzé-la-Ville or Mazille.

Furthermore, some of the earliest churches of Burgundian romanesque are of a type known as 'blind-nave'—that is, with no windows opening in the nave itself; instead, the lighting comes from windows in the aisles or in the east and west ends.

Not far from Tournus, the church at Farges is an early example of this type of church. Here we find also a three-storeyed central tower, with the usual Lombard ornamentation. Built in the first third of the eleventh century (the nave is a little later), Farges not only has the somewhat squat but massive pillars of St-Philibert and a blind nave, but the usual early barrel vaulting is replaced by the first timid, tentative attempts at the broken or pointed barrel vault (*berceau brisé*). At Malay the church, which dates from the beginning of the twelfth century, has both the blind nave and the pointed barrel, but already the vaulting is much more surely conceived. The way is thus set, *via* Cluny and Fontenay, for the magnificent Cistercian arches and vaulting, the precursors of the soaring lancet of developed Gothic. It is to be noticed that Farges and Malay, and other churches of the blind-nave type—those, for example, of St-Julien-de-Sennecy, Brancion, Varennes-l'Arconce, Iguerande and Sigy-le-Châtel—are within easy range of Cluny. Usually the aisles of these churches are covered by groined vaulting, although we find barrel vaults at St-Julien-de-Sennecy and Brancion. In the naves the central arch and those of the lateral arcades illustrate both barrel and pointed barrel, the latter becoming more usual as we approach the twelfth century.

Of the influences that flowed outwards from the building of the successive great abbey churches of Cluny, culminating in that of Abbot Hugh of Semur, which, began in 1088, was consecrated in 1130 by Pope Innocent III, much has been written. T. W. West in his *History of Architecture in France* claimed that any study of the 'regional expressions of the Romanesque style in France' must begin 'with the ancient Kingdom of Burgundy, which proved to be one of the most varied, inventive and influential: Cluny is evidence of that'. The construction of this magnificent edifice of Cluny III, completed in considerably less than a single man's lifetime, has never ceased to amaze posterity, as it astonished contemporaries. It was as if a powerful beacon shone forth from its topmost pinnacle, shedding its beams over Burgundy and penetrating far beyond its confines. St Hugh, who had visited the rebuilt monastery of Abbot Desiderius at Monte Cassino only a few

years before he began work on his own abbey church, gathered
together in his mason's yard the best workmen available; all
the then practised styles were brought to bear on the creation of
'this magnificent hybrid with its exotic scents', as Professor
Conant described Cluny—'it is a summation of romanesque
architecture and of its sources of influence, made in Burgundy
for the old Benedictine institution of Burgundy, and under a
Burgundian abbot'. Apart from its grandeur, the immensity of
its conception and the quality of its execution, Cluny has
bequeathed many of its architectural features to other
Burgundian churches, as well as providing in its *atelier* of
sculptors the finest and most influential school of romanesque
carving. At Paray-le-Monial, founded personally by St Hugh;
at the Charité-sur-Loire, consecrated by Pope Paschal in 1107,
two years before the death of St Hugh; and in the village church
at Semur-en-Brionnais, his birthplace and the nursery of his
family, we can see today, if on a reduced scale, the immediate
influence of Cluny III and of its creator, St Hugh.

The vast dimensions and decorative splendour of the abbey
church—if now they may only with difficulty be envisaged
from the woefully truncated and mutilated remains—can
be gauged and better appreciated from several eighteenth-
century drawings made before its destruction in the Revolution.
The arches of the nave openings on to the first of its double
aisles were of the earliest pointed barrel type, the outline being
very effectively picked out by an ornamental moulding. The
nave piers were cruciform, consisting of three engaged columns
and (on the nave side) a pilaster, which was fluted, after the
antique. Above the nave arches was a blind triforium of three
bays, with rounded arches; and above these again opened three
windows, also circular-headed, from which the light flooded
the building. The old drawings show that a barrel vault
covered the nave and choir. Remarkable, and of great beauty,
were the choir and apsidal end. In the dome was a great fresco
of Christ in Glory, similar most likely to those seen today at
Paray-le-Monial or Berzé-la-Ville. Eight tall columns with
exquisitely carved capitals, supporting high rounded arches,
formed the semi-circular end of the choir, separating it from
the deambulatory and the five radial chapels. The space above

the choir arches and the round-headed windows beneath the dome was divided by pilasters, again fluted, forming shallow bays. A similar arrangement survives today at La Charité-sur-Loire, except that here the lowest arches are pointed barrel. Raising their great height above this huge building (the most vast at that time in the West), the four main towers, which were both square and octagonal, had their window-openings, as well as their decoration, in the characteristic Lombard style. The destruction by the Revolutionaries and their mercenary successors of this magnificent fabric and its marvellous sculpture cannot be sufficiently deplored. In what little has survived of the carving of the choir capitals of Cluny we may see the source of the masterpieces of romanesque sculpture which are found today at Saulieu, Vézelay and Autun, and in the churches of the Brionnais.

In addition to the churches that we have noticed as being intimately associated with Hugh of Semur, there remain three other great Burgundian churches whose building reveals unmistakably the Cluniac stamp—St-Andoche of Saulieu, St-Lazare of Autun and Notre-Dame of Beaune. The extraordinary prestige of Cluny, and in particular its direct relation with the Papacy, which, by maintaining its immunity from local episcopal jurisdiction and administration—to say nothing of permitting its encroachments on the revenues normally due to the bishops—brought the abbey into collision with neighbouring sees, especially that of Autun. In 1112, however, Bishop Norgaud, Cluny's implacable enemy, was succeeded in the see of Autun by Etienne de Bagé, its friend and sincere admirer. Relations between the abbey and the Bishop improved —for a time. Bishop Etienne was stirred by the example of Hugh of Semur to reconstruct the abbeys and churches of his diocese, beginning with the ancient Carolingian foundation of St-Andoche of Saulieu, the rebuilt collegial church being consecrated in 1119 by Pope Calixtus II. More sober and restrained in its architecture than its model, Cluny, it is remarkable for the excellence of the carving of its capitals, the work of sculptors of the Cluniac school, the beauty of which is today perhaps only rivalled by those of Vézelay and the masterpieces of Gislebertus of Autun. And it was Bishop

D

Etienne de Bagé who employed Gislebertus in his own new cathedral of St-Lazare d'Autun, begun about 1120 and dedicated on 28th December 1130 by Pope Innocent II. Although the grandeur of Cluny was again the model, St-Lazare appeals by its restrained elegance. The fineness of its structure has, in fact, revealed serious weaknesses, which have required constant attention and intermittent rebuilding. Flying buttresses were added in the thirteenth century; and later the gothic raised choir and apsidal windows (executed by Cardinal Jean Rolin about the middle of the fifteenth century); finally, in the last century, the pillars of the crossing were strengthened. Happily, the reconstituted apse is in perfect keeping with the body of the church. Here, in its triforium, an atavistic element has appeared, since the model for its arches derives from antiquity, from the Porte d'Arroux of Roman Autun. With the work of Gislebertus, which makes St-Lazare a venerated shrine for all connoisseurs of romanesque sculpture, we deal elsewhere (Chapter VI, page 106). A further example of Cluniac influence in the building of major churches, from this same diocese of Autun, is the collegial Notre-Dame of Beaune, constructed also by Bishop Etienne between 1120 and 1140; but the church has been much rebuilt, and, although Notre-Dame has its individual beauties (for example, the formal arrangement of the apse, seen from the exterior), subsequent alterations have somewhat obscured its original Cluniac form.

In addition to the 'pure' Lombard, the blind-nave and the Cluniac types of romanesque church in Burgundy, there is another important type, which has been known as 'Martinian', from the fact that many priories and parish churches were built by or under the influence of the famous, now demolished, abbey of St-Martin in Autun. Alternatively, and more appropriately, this architectural style has taken the name of the district in which some of the best known examples of these churches are to be found—the Brionnais. In general, the Brionnais churches may be described as consisting of two storeys, the nave walls being characteristically pierced by windows above the aisle arcading; both nave and aisles are covered by groined vaulting; and the choir and apse are separated from the nave by the crossing of the transepts. In the purest examples of the type we find, as a rule, the use of both rounded arches and of piers formed by engaged columns—not pilasters, whether plain or fluted in the Cluniac manner. But the powerful influence of Cluny has in places modified the purity and aesthetic logicality of this Brionnais style of romanesque, which, adopted and adapted by gothic builders, was to spread over Christian Europe. In the two beautiful churches of Avallon, St-Lazare and St-Martin-du-Bourg, pointed barrel arches have replaced the rounded barrel; a blind triforium has been added to the churches of Toulon-sur-Arroux and Gourdon-en-Charollais; and in St-Philibert of Dijon simple bays are placed above the nave arches and below the upper windows.

No amateur of Burgundian romanesque architecture and sculpture should fail to make the tour of the churches of this district of the Brionnais; it, in the words of Michelin, *vaut le voyage*. They are found within easy distance of each other in this gentle yet fecund countryside; some simple country churches, others serving the parishes of the small towns. Built mostly in the local limestone, whose colours pass through shades of straw and warm yellow to yellow-gold, these little *paroissiales* harmonize with the browns of the earth, or the greens of orchards, meadows and scattered vineyards; or in the sunburnt *places* of the town they stand out against the warm siennas of walls and the red-browns of the roof tiles. Anzy-le-Duc, Montceaux-l'Etoile, Semur-en-Brionnais, St-Julien-de-Jonzy, Iguerande, Charlieu, Châteauneuf-sur-Sornin, Bois-Ste-Marie, Marcigny, St-Germain-en-Brionnais, Varenne-l'Arconce, St-Laurent-en-Brionnais, St-Bonnet-de-Cray, St-Martin-la-Vallée, Vareilles—the list could be easily extended. And by way of contrast, the visitor to Charlieu (itself simply not to be missed) should drive out to nearby La Bénisson-Dieu, the Cistercian monastery founded in 1138 by St Bernard of Clairvaux, with its typical Burgundian roof of glazed slates, in colours and design suggesting an oriental prayer-rug.

The eleventh-century church of St-Fortunat of Charlieu was almost entirely destroyed at the Revolution, so that today the priory church of Anzy-le-Duc, which was very similar in design, best exemplifies the Brionnais type of Burgundian romanesque.

The priory of Anzy was founded about 878 as a dependency of St-Martin d'Autun. It owed its fame as a place of pilgrimage to the tomb of its first prior, the saintly Hugh of Poitiers, who was the contemporary and friend of Berno of Baume, the founder of Cluny. At the beginning of the eleventh century Anzy became part of the Cluniac world; and it was Abbot Odilo, who had previously ordered the rebuilding of the Carolingian church at Charlieu, who now set in train the reconstruction of Anzy-le-Duc, using St-Fortunat as his model. Both churches had small apses grafted on to the central apse. At Anzy there were two periods of building: the choir, transept and five apses in echelon belong to the first half of the eleventh century; the nave, with its five bays and the accompanying aisles, to early in the second half. The architect of Anzy understood thoroughly the value of light; this is seen not only in the interior of the church, where it brilliantly reveals the disposition of forms; but also externally, where the octagonal central tower in three storeys, each stepped back slightly from the preceding, has openings divided by a slender column on each of its faces. This method of fenestration allows us glimpses of sky, which add a lightness and grace to the sturdy tower, which itself gives an equilibrium to the whole structure. The restored frescoes, which may be of the twelfth century, are different in style from those at Berzé-la-Ville and may have been influenced by Poitevin artists. However, besides the excellence of the architecture, it is the sculpture of Anzy-le-Duc that excites our profoundest admiration.

In writing of the sculptured portals of the Brionnais in his most informative *Bourgogne Romane*, M. Raymond Oursel expresses the view that the region allows us to follow in close detail the development of its sculpture. From the first tentative beginnings there is seen a steady gathering of experience, an advance both in surety of touch and power of expression, which led in course of time to a splendid flourishing; this in turn was only too quickly succeeded by a distinct decline, and finally ended in utter exhaustion. This evolution of style (which on occasions presents difficulties of chronology) extended from early in the eleventh century to its extinction at the end of the twelfth; in fact, at Anzy-le-Duc the visitor may trace a progression in the carving of capitals, corbels and doorways over a period of a half-century from sometime before 1050. M. Oursel cites as the earliest example of those sculptured *Christs in Glory*, which were to appear in many variations throughout the Brionnais, that of the west door of Charlieu's St-Fortunat (*c.* 1070). The *Ascension* of the western doorway at Anzy-le-Duc was carved about fifteen years later and already shows the ripening experience. The magnificent capitals at Anzy illustrate the progress from the more primitive at the east end (first half of eleventh century) to the later thirty-two capitals of the nave, where the artists reveal an ever-increasing skill, and a sensibility and power hitherto unachieved. These would appear to have been executed over a period—from about 1050 to about 1090.

It will be recalled that the main period of the building of Abbot Hugh's Cluny fell between the years 1088 and 1130. From this *atelier* the refinement of the sculptor's art radiated outwards over the Brionnais. M. Oursel gives as among the finest examples of carving in the region the tympana at Varenne-l'Arconce (*The Paschal Lamb, c.* 1100?) and at Montceaux-l'Etoile (*c.* 1120–5); the tympanum which once stood over the main gateway to the priory of Anzy-le-Duc (*c.* 1125–30—known as that of d'Arcy from its being bought at the Revolution by the owner of the château of d'Arcy; now in the Hiéron museum at Paray-le-Monial); and the two doorways on the north side of the remains of the narthex at Charlieu (*c.* 1130). In the beautiful *Ascension* at Julien-le-Jonzy we can see again the same hand of the master of the Charlieu narthex. At Perrecy-les-Forges the tympanum (*c.* 1120) shows how the influence of the Brionnais sculptors passed beyond the confines of the region. The period of decline is illustrated by the third of the Anzy-le-Duc doorways (*c.* 1145–55); that at Neuilly-en-Donjon, beyond the Loire (*c.* 1140); at Fleury-la-Montagne, and at Semur-en-Brionnais. In this last named exhaustion is reached, when the sense of design fails in jejune anecdote. Fleury and Semur are both of the second half of the twelfth century.

Away in the north, but still in the diocese of Autun, these humble churches of the Brionnais can claim a close relative——a rich and grand one—in the great abbey or collegial church dedicated to Mary Magdalen, which stands high on the hill of Vézelay. One of the most beautiful of the monuments of France, the church of Ste-Madeleine has evoked universal praise and admiration—from the religious, art-lovers, antiquarians, architects and (not the least) engineers. To write of the beauties of Vézelay would require a book to itself—and it has had many. About the year 860 Girard de Roussillon, who was related on his mother's side to the Counts of Autun, was himself Duke of Lyons, regent of Provence, and celebrated in the *chansons de geste*, established a convent at St-Père on the banks of the Cure and at the foot of the hill of Vézelay. The Normans destroyed this in 887, and some years later, the nuns having been replaced by monks, a monastery was founded on the hill, on the site of an early *oppidum*. Reformed by the ancient house of St-Martin d'Autun, the abbey was first dedicated to the Virgin. Then, in the early years of the eleventh century, the monk Badilon gained possession in Jerusalem of the supposed remains of Mary Magdalen, and brought them home in triumph for his monastery. The abbey of Vézelay, rededicated to Ste-Madeleine, quickly became a celebrated place of pilgrimage and, later still, one of the four rallying points in France for the most popular pilgrimage to the shrine of St James of Compostella in Galicia. Between the years 1027 and 1037 the abbey fell under the ascendency of Cluny, despite vigorous protests from the bishops of Autun—and, indeed, from some of its own monks. Although the Provençals claimed already to possess the relics of the Magdalen at St-Maximin and were vociferous in pursuing their rights, in 1058 the Pope recognized the validity of the pretensions of Vézelay, and this was confirmed by Pope Paschal II in 1103.

The building of an enlarged abbey church to replace the Carolingian edifice was begun by Abbot Artaud, and it appears that of this the apse and transepts were consecrated in 1104. Two years later, so great were the financial burdens placed by the Abbot on the towns-people that they rose in revolt and murdered him. He was succeeded by the nephew of St Hugh of Cluny, Renaud of Semur, of the feudal family who were lords of the Brionnais. When in 1120 a disastrous fire destroyed much of the existing fabric, Abbot Renaud began afresh, basing his

plans for the nave and aisle not on all-powerful Cluny, but on
the little pilgrim church so famous in his part of the country—
Anzy-le-Duc. By 1132 this building was completed, and work
was begun on the narthex, which too was finished by 1138.
Finally, for reasons which are unknown to us, a gothic choir
and apse was substituted for the original romanesque east end
under Abbot Girard d'Arcy, between 1185 and 1190. The great
abbey church of Ste-Madeleine de Vézelay stood complete,
gleaming in the brilliant whiteness of its stonework, the amaze-
ment of the crowds of pilgrims, who were captivated as much
by the allegories of its superlative sculpture as by the beauty of
the building itself.

Here in the abbey church St Bernard preached the Second
Crusade in 1146; in 1190 on the hill of Vézelay gathered the
chivalry of France to embark on the Third Crusade. Meanwhile,
the Provençals continued to press their claims against the
Burgundians; finally in 1279 they produced their trump
card—the bones of the Magdalen herself. It was asserted that
the relics, many years before, had been secretly buried at the
approach of the Saracens, and forgotten until now. . . . Bowing
before this irrefragable evidence, Pope Boniface VIII decided
in favour of St-Maximin. Almost at a stroke, the stream of
pilgrims to Vézelay dried up. In 1537 the Benedictines were
replaced by canons regular; in 1568 and again in the following
year the abbey was sacked by the Protestants. On the night of
21st–22nd October 1819 the building was struck by lightning,
set on fire and seriously damaged. Then, in 1840 the enlightened
custodian of ancient monuments, Prosper Mérimée, appointed
Viollet-le-Duc in charge of restoring what remained of the
mouldering fabric. It has been too easy to criticize the restoration carried out by Viollet-le-Duc; but before we become over-
censorious we should recall that but for his work we should
have no Ste-Madeleine extant today.

From the entrance to the nave, the visitor will recognize how
the design of the building follows, allowing for the vast
difference in scale, its model, Anzy-le-Duc. There are the same
elevation in two storeys, the same windows set high in the nave
wall, the same rounded arches, the same composition of the
nave piers with their engaged columns, the same groined

vaulting. But at Vézelay the structural elements are all picked out by moulding, exquisitely carved in rosettes and garlands; and the voussoirs of the ribs of the nave vaulting alternate in light and dark stonework. Some see in the last feature the close connection of Burgundy with Moslem Spain; but this might indeed have been inherited from Carolingian building—we may recall St-Philibert of Tournus. However, perhaps the first impression of the visitor to Vézelay is one of its lightness and grace—and of light, everywhere, splendid in the full rays of the sun, and no less effective on dull days, when at times the choir seems bathed in mother-of-pearl. A miracle of grace and light.

And then there is the sculpture. The façade of the narthex is a pastiche of Viollet-le-Duc, and does little to prepare us for the great western entrance within. Two lateral doorways complete the design of the magnificent central portal: that on the right represents scenes from the Childhood of Christ; on the left are depicted events succeeding the Crucifixion. In this marvellous ensemble we have perhaps one of the high points in the romanesque sculpture of Burgundy, a culmination of the influence, and visible proof of the excellence, of the *ateliers* of Cluny. The whole may be taken to represent to the pilgrims the Mission of the Church. On the central *trumeau* is the figure of the Precursor, John the Baptist, standing directly below the Christ in Glory, whose swirling spirals of drapery may suggest strongly also the scene of Pentecost. The Word is listened to by the Apostles, who are grouped on either side of the *mandorla*, as well as by the peoples of the earth, who are depicted on the lintel and innermost band of the lunette. On the archivolt are shown the signs of the zodiac, alternating with the labours of the months. This extraordinarily suggestive and beautiful work was executed about the year 1120.

It would appear that the creator of this marvellous group of sculpture over the three doorways, who from it is known as the Master of the Tympanum of Vézelay, thought that he had represented here sufficient of the Christology for the edification of the pilgrims, since within the church the carving on the capitals hardly refers to Christ; and there is no reference at all to Mary Magdalen to whom the church is dedicated. The subjects treated on these astonishing capitals seem to defy logic, but most of them would be familiar to the iconographical understanding of mediaeval pilgrims; yet the *Education of Achilles* and the *Rape of Ganymede* must have caused some searching for their relevance. Here are depicted in a wealth of decorative imagery and sculptural skill the *Fall*, the *Sacrifices of Abel and Cain*, the *Death of Cain*, the *Lives of Jacob* and of *David*, the story of *Judith and Holophernes*, and the *Lives* again of *Saints Peter, Anthony, Martin, Benedict* and even *Ste Eugénie*. Perhaps a word of warning should be given: Viollet-le-Duc found much of the sculpture in a poor state; some capitals he copied, and the originals can be seen in the Musée Lapidaire; others he had executed himself on what he thought likely themes. The official guides will distinguish these—not that they are in themselves negligible.

The strictures of St Bernard of Clairvaux against the magnitude and magnificence of these great churches, and in particular their sculptural decoration, brought a powerful reaction with the Cistercian Order. The beautiful abbey church of Fontenay (see illustrations) may be considered as embodying St Bernard's thoughts on the architecture and simple decorative style most suitable to his more austere kind of Catholicism. It has been said that with 'Fontenay we have the extreme end of the romanesque period in Burgundy'. The way is already prepared for the triumphant gothic of the Ile-de-France. But the influence of Burgundian Cluny had spread far. So far that Bruce Allsopp in his book, *Romanesque Architecture*, makes bold to declare that 'The great pilgrimage church of Santiago de Compostella is perhaps the supreme achievement of Burgundian Romanesque architecture.'

CHAPTER VI

Gislebertus of Autun

GISLEBERTUS HOC FECIT—'Gislebertus has done this'. Standing before the tympanum above the west door of St-Lazare at Autun, the visitor reads these words carved directly beneath the feet of the majestic Christ in Glory, the centrepiece to this magnificent representation of the *Last Judgement*. Although there are other examples of romanesque sculptors signing their work—there is in Burgundy the '*Renco me fecit*' of the crypt of St-Philibert de Tournus and the '*Unbertus me fecit*' of St-Benôit-sur-Loire in nearby Loiret—these are discreetly, unobtrusively placed; there is nothing so bold as the way Gislebertus proudly proclaims his authorship at Autun. St-Lazare was built by that great patron of church reconstruction, Etienne de Bagé, Abbot of Saulieu, and Bishop of Autun from 1112 until 1136, who in emulation of Hugh of Semur's famous church of Cluny III rebuilt also his abbey of Saulieu as well as the collegial church of Notre-Dame in Beaune. Since Gislebertus' tympanum was completed in the Bishop's lifetime, he and his chapter would have of necessity given their permission for the sculptor's signature to appear in the prominent place it occupies. We must, therefore, conclude that Gislebertus was already a name to conjure with, an artist sufficiently celebrated to shed some of his fame over this new church for whose decoration he was almost entirely responsible. At Cluny and at Vézelay, although there were sculptors-in-chief engaged on the carving (for example in the narthex of Vézelay the so-called Master of the Tympanum), the immensity of the work at these places required the existence of a regular *atelier*. Yet at Autun, not only the west doorway and the now destroyed north doorway (which included the famous *Eve* as part of its lintel) but all of the some sixty historiated capitals (with the exception of a possible two) were the work of

Gislebertus. The sculpture of Autun was virtually the work of one man, and therefore fully justifies the assertiveness of *Gislebertus hoc fecit*.

Lazarus, the 'friend of Christ', who raised him from the dead, together with his sisters Mary Magdalen and Martha, was said to have come by sea to Provence, where he became the first bishop of Marseilles. As early as the tenth century, long before the monks of Vézelay could claim to possess the relics of the Magdalen or the cult of St-Lazare was added to that of the Virgin at Avallon, St Lazarus, who was confused in the popular mind with the poor Lazarus of the parable, whose sores were licked by dogs, was venerated at Autun, and his supposed tomb there in the cathedral church of St-Nazaire had long been a place of pilgrimage for lepers. To avoid the inconvenience of the too close proximity of those unfortunates, Bishop Etienne de Bagé and the chapter of St-Nazaire began the building about 1120 of a new church dedicated to St-Lazare, which was to contain the saint's tomb; this was on land lying to the south of their cathedral and given to them by Duke Hugh II of Burgundy. It was only later, in 1195, that St-Lazare was raised to the dignity of a cathedral and the older edifice allowed to fall into ruins, until it was eventually demolished in the eighteenth century. The still unfinished church of St-Lazare was consecrated by Pope Innocent II in 1130.

The researches of a number of scholars—archaeologists, architects and art-historians—have allowed us to piece together, with some degree of likelihood, the earlier career of this out-standing artist among romanesque sculptors, Gislebertus of Autun, concerning whose life contemporary documents are silent. When in 1125 Bishop Etienne appointed Gislebertus in charge of the sculptural decoration of his church, he was already a mature artist, acknowledged as a master in his profession, otherwise he would never have been employed as the sole sculptor for the work that he had in mind by anyone so experienced in church-building as Bishop Etienne. At Cluny the local stone-carvers of the Brionnais and elsewhere had been swept up in the creative *élan* and carried thence to new heights of achievement by the great Abbot Hugh of Semur. In 1088 work on the abbey church had been begun, and by 1115 the great west doorway was completed. There is strong evidence that Gislebertus was employed in this, and even if he did not begin his career at Cluny, it is clear that it was there he gained his *maîtrise*. Yet of all those trained in the Cluniac *ateliers*, he is, if imbued with their ideals, among the few sculptors who managed to free themselves from any academicism which may be associated with a school and to develop an imagination and a technique of their own—in a word, an individual style. The Master of the Tympanum of Vézelay was another. Two heads which were excavated by Professor K. F. Conant from among the ruins that are all that remains of the Cluny west doorway——one of a bearded man and the other of a woman, with hair swept back straight from the brow—bear a strong resemblance to the *Head of an apostle* at Autun and to that of the famous *Eve* of the Musée Rolin.

From Cluny, it appears, Gislebertus went in about 1120 to Vézelay, which inherited not only its tradition but also its craftsmen. There M. Salet's identification of the work of some nine different sculptors would allow us to see among them pieces of sculpture which are without a doubt by the hand of Gislebertus. In the lapidary museum at Vézelay are several fragments of which the style, different from any other work there, leaves no doubt that they were carved by him. Of particular interest is one fragment which shows the feet and dresses of two figures; the folds, the decoration on the hems, the arcaded stool on which one figure stands—all these and other features point to the presence of Gislebertus at Vézelay. From there, his reputation already established, Bishop Etienne would have called him in about 1125 to Autun. Further, there is some reason to think that Gislebertus returned to Vézelay after 1135, on completing his work in Autun. And that is about all that archaeology can tell us of his life. There remains his work.

Until 1939 the choir at St-Lazare was encased in marble of the baroque period. When this facing was then removed, a most important discovery was made, which has allowed us to see and to date the first work of Gislebertus at Autun. The lower-level capitals of the apse are seen to be done by a sculptor, or sculptors, working in the tradition of the Brionnais and of Cluny. Two damaged capitals on the upper level, however, are unmistakably the work of Gislebertus. One, the third capital from the north, shows a headless figure seated on a throne, resting its feet on an arcade consisting of three beaded bands. The delicacy of the carving of the decorative folds, the modelling of the limbs, and in particular the position of the knees reveal the hand of the sculptor of the *Last Judgement* of the west tympanum. Other evidence points to the date of the part of the building as about 1125. This is the first scuplture carved by Gislebertus on his arrival at Autun, and it shows that his characteristic style was already evolved, not differing essentially from his last work, that of the west front.

It is usually considered that Gislebertus spent some ten years on his carving in St-Lazare. After the capitals of the choir, he appears to have worked on the doorway in the north transept, which, facing the cathedral of St-Nazaire, was for long the principal entrance to the church. In 1766, on orders from the chapter, the sculpture of the tympanum (the *Raising of Lazarus*), the trumeau (*St Lazarus*, as bishop of Marseilles) and the lintel were removed, and the door baroqued over in stucco. Fragments of these carvings may be seen today in the Musée Rolin. The reason for this act of vandalism is perhaps not far to seek. On the lintel was represented the *Fall of Adam and Eve*, and the *Eve* (the only part of the lintel remaining), besides being possibly the best known of all romanesque sculptures, is perhaps also the most sensuous. In Burgundy it is rivalled, indeed, by the figure of *Luxury* on the door-jamb of St-Fortunat of Charlieu, where the swirl of the drapery only serves to heighten the naked form, and points forward in time to Agostino di Duccio. *Eve*, resting on her elbow and plucking the apple unseen behind her, seems to be swimming in the waters of the sea or flying effortlessly through the air, so lightly and gracefully is she poised, as she whispers to Adam from behind her cupped hand. Gislebertus' conception in representing the Fall in this way is quite unique in romanesque art. Not perhaps since antiquity had the female nude been so straightforwardly displayed. The composition and technique are equally brilliant; the surface planes are exquisitely controlled, the modelling being so deeply cut as to be almost in the round. To the right, where the stone is broken away, Satan's claws can be made out, grasping the rifled Tree of Knowledge. If this fragment were all we possessed of the work of Gislebertus he would have still been known—as the Master of the *Eve* of Autun.

As building on the nave and aisles progressed Gislebertus was required to carve the historiated capitals. Only some of the foliage capitals and those placed too high for close inspection were left to his assistants—with the exception of the two capitals on the fourth pillar on the south side of the nave. This pair, *Samson and the Lion* and *Christ Washing the Apostles' Feet*, has been ascribed, with good reason, to the author of the capitals from the destroyed abbey of Moûtiers-St-Jean, now in the Fogg Museum, Cambridge, U.S.A. During the restoration work carried out by Viollet-le-Duc, which was begun in 1860, certain of the capitals were restored in part and others were replaced by copies, the originals being housed today in the cathedral museum, upstairs in the former sacristy. Among these is the well-known *Flight into Egypt*, a very beautiful and touching piece of sculpture, which may be compared with the similar representation at Saulieu. (Although the matter is still subject to learned debate, it is considered now by competent authorities that the capitals at Saulieu were either contemporaneous with or later than those of Gislebertus, and not earlier, as some have claimed. However, they, with some of those at Vézelay, must rank very high among examples of romanesque sculpture, comparable indeed with that of Gislebertus in Autun.)

In the decoration of romanesque churches the abbot or bishop intimated to the sculptor the subjects he wished to be depicted, but left to the artist considerable freedom of choice in the design. Although as a rule the sculptures, which were usually highly coloured, were chosen to instruct or edify the people, there was often a curious medley of religious and secular themes: scenes were represented from both the Old and New Testaments, from popular hagiology or even pagan myths, with real and fabulous animals jostling against saints, sirens, acrobats, personified virtues and vices, and hybrid monsters. In St-Lazare religious and moral subjects preponderate; Gislebertus, for all his fascinated interest in the world about him, appears eminently serious, of a mind which turned naturally to eschatological ideas. As in so much else, Cluny was the iconographical source; but if the themes and symbols were largely traditional, the sculptor's imagination had wide scope to innovate, especially in matters of detail and style. Here Gislebertus excelled; his imaginative powers were as fertile as his technique was sure. His sense of composition; his control over his figures, whether they were foreshortened or elongated; his treatment of materials—of linen, wool, leather or metal; his surface texture; his rhythmical movement—in all the elements of his art he was a master. His subjects were chiefly illustrations of scenes from the Bible; *Genesis* and the *Gospels of St Matthew* and *St Luke* were his most frequent sources. Often Old Testament subjects formed allegories for those from the New Testament; *Daniel in the Lion's Den, Samson and the Lion,* the *Three Jews in the Fiery Furnace* or *Jacob Wrestling with the Angel,* all had their allegorical interpretations readily appreciated by the mediaeval mind. The *Death of Cain* prefigured the *Suicide of Judas.* (Here again, this last should be compared with the similar representation at Saulieu. No doubt Cluny was the common source, as it was for the *Fourth Tone of Music,* the *Four Rivers of Paradise* and the *Faun and the Siren* of Gislebertus.)

But brilliant as these historiated capitals are, so satisfying alike to simple and sophisticated tastes, they are quite overwhelmed by the grandeur of conception and execution of the great *Last Judgement* of the tympanum of the west end of St-Lazare. The only existing sculpture of the period that can be safely placed by the side of this masterpiece of Gislebertus is the tympanum in the narthex of Vézelay, carved about 1125, some five years or so earlier. Of Gislebertus' work here Denis Grivot and George Zarnecki wrote: 'No narrative composition of the *Last Judgement* on that vast scale had been attempted before. Here he displayed his full powers of originality and imagination. It is above all on the strength of his *Last Judgement* that he must rank as one of the greatest inventors of the mediaeval period.' M. André Malraux goes further: 'Gislebertus is not a primitive but a Romanesque Cézanne . . . The tympanum of Autun is an achievement without precedent—an epic of Western Christendom.'

It is fortunate for us that the vandalism carried out by the cathedral chapter in 1766 prevented an even more serious act of

destruction being committed by the Revolutionaries of less than
a generation later. In that year the canons, not relishing this
reminder of an 'age of superstition', destroyed the heads of the
Elders of the Apocalypse which then decorated the innermost
band of the archivolt, removed the figures from the trumeau and
covered the whole tympanum with bricks and plaster. The
existence of Gislebertus' work was rediscovered by the Abbé
Devoucoux on 23rd May 1837, and the covering was removed
later in that year. The work was restored by Viollet-le-Duc
after 1860, but the head of Christ, which was broken off in 1766
and was missing, found its way later purely by chance to the
Musée Rolin, where it was recognized for what it was, and it was
replaced on the tympanum only in 1948.

The centre of the composition is occupied by the formalized
representation of Christ, with his arms outstretched; this
majestic figure is enclosed in a mandorla, the decoration of
which is identical with that which once stood above the great
west door at Cluny. On the mandorla is inscribed OMNIA
DISPONO SOLUS MERITOS CORONO QUOS SCELUS EXERCET ME
JUDICE POENA COERCET (I alone dispose of all things and
crown the just. Those who practise crime I judge and punish).
Four angels support the mandorla, but the upper pair, which are
flying head downwards, have been much damaged. Above them
are represented by symbols the sun and the moon. And above
these again, in the outer band of the archivolt, the squatting
figure of *Annus* (the Year) occupies the centre of a series of
alternating medallions, which depict the *Months of the Year*
and *Signs of the Zodiac*. The areas to the left and right of Christ
are divided by a band of arcading into an upper and a lower
register. At the extremities of the upper register, which
represents heaven with the Virgin sitting on Christ's right, two
angels sound the Last Trump that calls all to Judgement.
Beneath the lower register, to the right of Christ, is the
inscription: QUISQUE RESURGET ITA QUEM NON TRAHIT IMPIA VITA
ET LUCEBIT EI SINE FINE LUCERNA DIEI (Thus each shall rise again
who does not live an impious life, and endless light of day shall
shine for him). On this side of the tympanum, on both upper
and lower registers and below on the lintel, are represented the
Elect, with *St Peter*, who carries an enormous key and holds the

hand of a child, in the centre. An angel pushes another child up through the arch into heaven, while another still buries its face shyly in the angel's dress. Noticeable is the charm and elegance of these elongated figures, particularly the beautifully modelled limbs of the children. Everywhere is manifested joy—surprise and joy. Even excited expectation.

To the left of Christ all is different; wild dismay and terror seize the minds of the damned. *St Michael* weighs the souls, and the *Devil*, a fearsome figure, exults in a horrible grimace as he makes ready to receive his own. *Leviathan* has already one of the lost souls in his maw. The devils are not caricatures so much as terrifying embodiments of evil. The effects of this choice which lay thus represented before him, when the stonework was heightened by brilliant colour, must have left an uneffaceable impression on the minds of even the most hardened mediaeval sinner. And the words above the lintel reinforce the moral to be drawn: TERREAT HIC TERROR QUOS TERREUS ALLIGAT ERROR NAM FORE SIC VERUM NOTAT HIC HORROR SPECIERUM (Here let terror terrify those whom earthly error binds, for their fate is shown here by the horror of these figures).

On this side of the tympanum, as opposed to the expressions of heavenly felicity on the other, everything suggests tension— vividly and eloquently, by means of gestures and distortion— —craven, hysterical, uncontrollable fear. In his *Last Judgement* Gislebertus has achieved a composition of dramatic extremes, with a force and an originality which are unique. It has been said of him that 'he was a visionary who created an image as full as any in the *Book of Revelations*'. When one considers the range of his art, taking the western tympanum in conjunction with the capitals within the church and the *Eve* and the *Assumption of the Virgin* of the Musée Rolin, the visitor to Autun may feel disposed to agree with the judgement of M. Paul Deschamps, who was 'left in no doubt that Gislebertus was one of the greatest sculptors of Western civilization'.

CHAPTER VII

St Bernard and the Cistercians

It HAS BEEN well said—by Archdale A. King in his informative *Cîteaux and Her Elder Daughters*—that 'for wellnigh fifty years the life of St Bernard of Clairvaux was the history of Europe'. Not only is this true, but there is an immediacy, a freshness and clarity, in the authentic voice which comes through to us, particularly from his *Letters*, that makes him in so many ways our contemporary, rather than a Burgundian monk who lived more than eight centuries ago. If some would stress his saintly side, that his words and deeds were the inspiration of his love for God, others would look to the human, claiming that his interest and importance for us come from his essential humanity. Nor are these differences of view incompatible; one does not have to be a Catholic, even a Christian, to admire Bernard the man. Born in all probability in 1090, a postulant at the abbey of Cîteaux in 1112, when he was twenty-two, three years later he was sent to found the abbey of Clairvaux, in a remote spot known as the 'Valley of Absinthe', near Bar-sur-Aube, on the borders of Burgundy and Champagne, on lands presented to the Order most likely by his relation, Josbert de la Ferté. Although for nearly fifteen years he seldom left his monastery except on visitations to its daughter foundations, his marvellous gifts of preaching, soundness of doctrine and extraordinary success as a recruiter to the monastic ranks, brought it about that, as one of the leading churchmen of France, he played a conspicuous part in the Council of Troyes in 1128.

His powers of persuasion were formidable; it is said that mothers hid their sons (and husbands) at his approach, lest they heeded his injunction to leave all and follow him. Of noble birth himself—although he was by nature genuinely humble, and sought above all humility in others—his appeal was addressed to men of all classes, if especially to those of birth and some culture, and it was among the young of the nobility that he chiefly found his adherents. In 1131, when he was on a visit to northern France, thirty youths of the best families in the regions of St Quentin and Cambrai answered his call to the monastic life. Yet he had little to offer them in the things of the world; he is reported to have uttered this harsh warning to these young men, who wished to make their oblation at Clairvaux: 'Leave your body at the door; here is the kingdom of souls; the flesh has nothing more to do with it.' Nevertheless, we hear of very few cases of backsliding.

Within fifteen years of his becoming abbot of Clairvaux, St Bernard's fame had spread from Burgundy to all France, and from thence it went on to embrace Western Christendom. His importance in the history of Europe may be said to have begun at the disputed election that followed the death of Pope Honorius in 1130. He was indefatigable in support of Pope Innocent II against the antipope Anacletus II, visiting in the Pope's company or alone the Emperor Lothair and King Roger of Sicily; intervening in the quarrel between Genoa and Pisa; taking a prominent part in the Council of Pisa; settling the affairs of the monastery of Monte Cassino; and persuading the Milanese to submit to the Emperor. Writing, preaching, incessantly travelling, his immense gifts were put at the disposal of the Papacy, and it was his personal influence that healed the schism in the Church with the abdication of the antipope. When the Cistercian Bernard of Aquae Silviae, who had made his oblation at Clairvaux, became Pope Eugenius III in 1145, St Bernard was no more than expressing the truth when he wrote to the Supreme Pontiff: 'They are saying that it is not you but I who am the Pope, and from all sides they are flocking to me with their suits.' While in his heart he sought the life of the simple monk among his loved community at Clairvaux, his exalted position demanded that he protect his widespread Cistercian Order and lend his counsel to popes, kings and bishops, and to all those of any station who sought his guidance. His correspondence was immense. 'I have become,' he wrote, 'a sort of modern chimaera, neither cleric or layman. I have maintained the tonsure of a monk, but I have long ago abandoned the life.'

Professor Joan Evans, in her study, *Life in Mediaeval France*, has this to say of St Bernard: 'In spite of his mystic and ascetic piety, he kept the saving common sense of the Frenchman, and defended a wise man as "one to whom all things taste even as they really are" . . . For a quarter of a century he dominated the religious life of France, giving new life to monasticism; reforming the secular clergy, warning against heresy, dogmatical, intellectual and superstitious, ending the papal schism, and preaching the Crusade . . . Bernard was the greatest monk of the Middle Ages.' With this assessment one would agree, perhaps substituting 'Burgundian' for 'Frenchman' and 'Europe' for 'France'. All the time he kept an astonishing sense of balance, a down-to-earthness, suiting his words to the need of the moment, with an irony which at times could be gentle, mocking, but at others caustic. To the mystic Ste Hildegarde, the 'Sibyl of the Rhine', who wrote to him of a vision she had had in which he appeared as a 'man in the sun', he replied in a guarded letter: 'That other people should believe me to be better than I know myself to be, is an indication more of human stupidity than of any virtues in myself.' He had a gentle rebuke for somnolent monks in one of the many sermons he preached to them: 'The long Vigils last night excuse your yawns, but what am I to say to those who slept at the Vigils and are sleeping now?'

Bernard was fearless in reminding popes, kings and others in high places of their duties. At times he was inclined to call a spade a bloody shovel, as in the famous dispute over the canonicity of the election of William Fitzherbert, the King's nephew, to the see of York in 1141. This contentious issue dragged on for years, Bernard taking up the cause of the Cistercians of Yorkshire with all the vigour of his powerful pen, not mincing his words in letters to King Stephen and a succession of four Popes. To Pope Lucius II he wrote, protesting at the support given by Henry de Blois, Bishop of Winchester and Papal Legate, to William Fitzherbert: 'Winchester has arrogated to herself the venerable name of Rome, and not only the name but the prerogatives as well . . . let Rome in the sole interest of justice crush the contumacy of this stubborn man, and with the hammer of severity throw down the idol [William Fitzherbert] he has set up and break his throne to pieces. If any of them should come to Rome for the pallium, it behoves your Holiness manfully to resist them, despising Ananias and Sapphira with their money bags. For we fear and dread lest that old whore of Winchester should be asked in some way by the new prophet he has set up [Fitzherbert] to share in the government, yea in the full power of his diocese. . . .' This is a letter from an abbot in a remote Burgundian monastery to the Pope. Needless to relate, in spite of the bitterest opposition, Bernard had his way. But something must have gone amiss, since William Fitzherbert did eventually obtain his archbishopric—this man of whom Bernard once wrote that his case was 'weak and feeble, and I have it on the authority of truthful men that he is rotten from the soles of his feet to the crown of his head'—and, what is more, since the archbishop, dying in the odour of sanctity, was later canonized as St William of York. But this, too, was St Bernard of Clairvaux.

St Bernard was born of military stock, his father, Tescelin le Sorrh, coming from the lesser nobility, Lord of Fontaines-lès-Dijon and one of a body of knights, the *milites Castellionenses*, dedicated to the defence of Châtillon-sur-Seine. On the side of his mother, Aleth, he was related to some of the first nobility of Burgundy, she being the daughter of Bernard of Montbard, who was connected with the Counts of Bar-sur-Seine, the Lords of Couches and of Mont-St-Jean, and the Viscounts of Beaune. Gaudry, Aleth's brother, who was to follow his nephew Bernard into Cîteaux, became by marriage Lord of Touillon. Bernard was the third of the seven children, six boys and a girl, born to Tescelin and Aleth, at Fontaines-lès-Dijon. From an early age his ardent temperament and somewhat frail constitution seem to have marked him out in his parents' eyes for the Church. He was sent to school in Châtillon, to that conducted by the canons of St-Vorles. The little eleventh-century church of this foundation still exists, above an even more primitive crypt, its blind arcades suggesting that it was the work of Lombard masons. It stands on the hill overlooking the town and the subterranean source of the River Douix, and is at the moment in the process of restoration. If we accept the date of Bernard's birth as 1090, which seems most likely, he would have been fourteen in 1104, when his mother, Aleth, died, leaving a deep and lasting effect on the impressionable, imaginative boy. His education must have been thorough; he was well read in the Latin authors that were the intellectual fare of the time, but in particular his knowledge of the fathers of the Church and of the Bible, both the Old and New Testaments, was profound. Furthermore, he had early given evidence of possessing remarkable gifts of expression, equally in the spoken and the written word, a style of great range and variety, at once subtle and pungent, diplomatic and outspoken, homely and visionary, appealing to the head but more especially to the heart, impelling in its power to move men.

In fact, it might be claimed that St Bernard's first miracle was one of persuasion. How otherwise, it might be asked, could a young man of twenty-two have gathered around him a group of nobles trained to arms, which included his own two uncles, Gaudry and another, all his brothers (save the youngest who was still a child), and the sons of the leading families in the neighbourhood, to the number of thirty or more; and, after preparing them by a six-month retreat near Châtillon, have led them at Easter 1112 to present themselves as postulants at the gates of the abbey of Cîteaux? Only someone possessing the rarest of gifts could achieve as much. His contemporaries were puzzled why he had chosen impoverished Cîteaux, which was notoriously unhealthy and on the point of failing, and not powerful Benedictine Cluny, where the cultivated way of life was such as might have been expected to suit the taste and talents of one like Bernard himself. He answered the question: 'I chose Cîteaux in preference to Cluny not because I was unaware that the life there was excellent and lawful but because I was conscious that my weak character needed a strong medicine.' The strength of the dose of the medicine, administered to a constitution not overstrong and weakened by self-mortification, was wellnigh lethal; but, he might have claimed, it did something for his alleged 'weakness of character'.

The abbey of Cîteaux stands fourteen miles south of Dijon and some seven miles due east of Nuits-St-Georges on the flat,

featureless plain through which flows the Saône, a wet countryside of woods and fields, with everywhere the presence of water
in scattered ponds, small streams and draining ditches. To this
desolate place of stagnant pools and reedy marshes, as it then
was, there arrived on Palm Sunday 1098 a party of some twenty
monks, under the leadership of their abbot, St Robert, who had
journeyed south from the Benedictine abbey of Molesmes, whose
ruins may be seen today near the village of that name in the
wooded country to the west of Châtillon-sur-Seine. At first
Cîteaux was known simply as the 'New Monastery'; the name
Cistercium, which came to be given to the house, and from that
to the Order, has been variously derived—from *cistelli*, the
reeds cut from the neighbouring swamps, or from *cisterna*, the
cisterns built by the White Monks to drain their waterlogged
fields. The purpose of this migration from Molesmes was the
earnest desire of a group of monks to maintain the Rule in its
primitive purity by observing to the letter the ordinances laid
down by St Benedict of Nursia. In the Benedictine houses,
which followed the pattern of observances of Cluny, with the
many accretions to the canonical offices had come a relaxation
in other matters and a complete cessation of the choir monks
from manual labour. The adoption of the *Carta Caritatis*, the
Charter of Charity, to which the finishing touches were put by
the second successor of Abbot Robert, the Englishman St
Stephen Harding (1108–33), and which was confirmed by
Pope Calixtus II at Saulieu on 23rd December 1119, marks the
beginning of the Cistercian Order of reformed Benedictines,
the White as distinct from the older Black Monks. It would
appear that the regulations as to such matters as clothing,
sleep, food and manual labour were established by the second
abbot St Alberic, and supplemented by Abbot Stephen
Harding chiefly with respect to the religious usages in church,
which were reduced to bare necessities of ritual and a greater
simplicity. In this newest reform the liturgical richness of Cluny
was sacrificed in the interest of daily work in the fields.

If the habit to be worn was to be of natural wool, undyed,
there was nothing at first symbolic in this; the diet prescribed
was of the greatest frugality, barely sufficient to support life,
the use of meat and wine being severely restricted. The monks

were permitted some seven hours sleep, retiring, without removing their habits, on wooden planks covered with straw in a common dormitory. The sole addition to the observance of the regular canonical offices allowed by the Cistercian Rule was the daily recitation of the Office of the Dead. (In their cemetery they dug and kept open the graves that one day were to receive their dead bodies.) The monks rose between one and two in the morning, descending by the stairway which led directly from the dorter to the church. In the course of the day the choir monks would follow the canonical hours—matins, lauds, prime, terce (mass), sext, none, vespers and compline, necessitating in all more than seven hours in church. The greatest reform, however, from the Benedictine Rule as practised by Cluny and those monasteries that followed it, was the return to manual labour, consisting primarily in field-work, which was obligatory on all monks. A further innovation was introduced here, with far reaching consequences to the development and improvement of European farming methods. The time spent by the choir monks in their religious duties limited the amount of labour they could perform, so there was introduced the practice of employing laymen (*conversi*), who though not ordained lived under their own rule, to assist the monks in their work in the fields. By means of these lay brethren outlying properties (granges) could be worked even at a considerable distance from the abbey, since the choir monks by their Rule could not, except on specifically laid down occasions, be absent overnight from their monastery. It was in this way that the monks of Cîteaux cultivated the famous vineyards at Meursault and Clos de Vougeot. European agriculture owes much to the labour and acquired skill of these 'consecrated peasants', for the clearing and draining of vast tracts of hitherto virgin and unoccupied lands and for improvements in viticulture, the raising of cereal crops and fruits, and the breeding of sheep, cattle, pigs and horses. The horses raised by the abbey of Morimond, the last of the 'four eldest daughters' of Cîteaux, were already famous at the time of the Second Crusade. By the thirteenth century the monasteries had almost a monopoly in Europe of the production of wool.

All this, however, came later. The first years after the

foundation of Cîteaux were a period of great hardship, despite the support of Raymond, Viscount of Beaune (a relation of St Bernard), who had given the land to the new monastery, and Odo I, Duke of Burgundy. In recognition of their indebtedness to the ducal house, Cîteaux, which like all Cistercian foundations was dedicated to the Virgin Mary, adopted the arms of Burgundy. And there many of the ducal family were buried.

The locality was at the outset most unhealthy from the presence of stagnant water, and a number of monks sickened and died. Added to this mortality, the austerity of the rule was such that it attracted only the bravest spirits; yet, rather than relax its rigours, the Abbot Stephen Harding persisted in living according to the way he had helped to lay down. The numbers had become reduced to a bare eighteen monks and *conversi*, when at Easter 1112 Bernard and his thirty companions arrived. From that moment the future of the Cistercian movement was assured. Recruits and donations of land—the Charter of Charity forbade the acceptance of tithes, rents and benefices—began to pour in. In the following year, on 16th May 1113, overcrowding had necessitated the founding of La Ferté, the first of the 'four oldest daughters of Cîteaux'; almost exactly a year later the influx of aspirants brought about the foundation of a further offshoot at Pontigny. By the time of St Stephen Harding's death in the spring of 1134, more than seventy-five abbeys had sprung from the filiation of Cîteaux and her own daughter houses. *Ora et labora*, by prayer and work the Cistercians were to cause these inaccessible, wild and desert places, which they invariably selected for a fresh creation, to blossom like the rose. A severe critic of the Order, the Welsh historian, Giraldus Cambrensis, felt himself obliged to acknowledge: 'Give the Cistercian a wilderness or a forest, and in a matter of few years you will find a dignified abbey in the midst of smiling plenty.'

Today the abbey of Cîteaux is once again inhabited by the White Monks, some hundred religious, both choir monks and lay brethren, carrying on their communal life, based as it was from the beginning on agriculture. But regrettably little remains

of the early monastic buildings beyond the thirteenth-century
library, which was largely rebuilt in the fifteenth, and a couple
of the bays for copyists in the innermost of its former three
cloisters. Fortunately, a plan of the building and grounds has
survived, showing the arrangement of the abbey about 1720,
before the vandalistic destruction that followed the French
Revolution. On 13th February 1790 the National Assembly
abolished by decree all the ancient religious houses of France,
and on 4th May of the succeeding year the abbey, with 9,800
acres of land, was sold for the sum of 862,000 pounds. The
library was dispersed, and of the mass of early manuscripts
only some 312 are preserved today in the municipal library in
Dijon. The buildings passed to a succession of owners, for five
years after 1841 being put to use in an unsuccessful attempt by
two Englishmen to found a phalanstery according to the
socialist ideas of the Frenchman Fourier. Thereupon Cîteaux
was bought by the Abbé Joseph Rey of Lyons as a home and
agricultural school for abandoned children. Then, in 1889,
some eight hundred years after the foundation of the abbey, at a
meeting in Rome of the general chapter of Cistercians of the
Reformed, or Strict, Observance (that founded in the seventeenth century by the Abbé de Rancé at La Trappe in
Normandy), it was decided to unite forces and to restore the
Order. In 1892, the abbey having been bought by the Baroness
de Rochetaillée and presented to the Order, the monks of the
'second spring' entered into possession, under the supreme
direction of Dom Sebastian Wyart, as the 63rd Abbot of Cîteaux
in the succession of St Robert of Molesmes.

To understand something of the appearance of a Cistercian
monastery in the middle ages, and to recapture some vestige of
its former life, one should go today not to the abbey of Cîteaux
but to that of Pontigny, or better, Fontenay. Dispossessed, as
were other French religious foundations at the Revolution,
Pontigny passed through several hands before coming back in
the last century into the ownership of the Church, to house
again a religious community; and with them it remained
until these fathers too were expelled by the anti-clerical

legislation at the beginning of this century. The abbey was then bought by the philosopher Paul Desjardins, and up until the outbreak of the Second World War Pontigny achieved some celebrity from the meetings that were held there, the so-called '*Decades*', informal discussions which took place at intervals and were attended by such intellectual figures as Thomas Mann, André Gide, T. S. Eliot and François Mauriac. Desjardins having died in 1940, the monastic buildings have been used since the last war by an educational institution, and are not open to visitors. However, the magnificent abbey church is.

In the middle ages the Abbey of Pontigny had close connections with England and particularly with the see of Canterbury, no fewer than three of whose archbishops sought the shelter of its hospitable walls. In November 1164 Thomas Becket found sanctuary there in his quarrel with King Henry II, who ultimately threatened to confiscate the Cistercian houses in England and Normandy if Pontigny continued to harbour the rebel. At the request of the abbot of Cîteaux, St Thomas left after a residence of two years and moved, as the guest of Louis VII, to the royal abbey of Ste-Colombe near Sens, where he stayed until his return to England in December 1170, to be followed so soon after by his murder in Canterbury Cathedral. In 1207 there appeared at Pontigny another exile from England: Archbishop Stephen Langton, whose appointment to Canterbury had not been recognized by King John in his dissension with the Church of Rome, a dispute which had as a consequence that all England was placed under an interdict. Langton remained at the abbey until the King's submission in 1213, when he returned to his country, to take part with the barons in the struggle against King John that resulted in Magna Carta. The third Archbishop of Canterbury to seek refuge in the abbey was Edmund Rich, whose opposition to King Henry III drove him to France, where for a short time he lived the life of the religious of Pontigny, before his death at Soissy on 16th November 1240. Edmund was buried at Pontigny, and from the first his tomb was the object of pious pilgrimage, his cult becoming one of the most popular in Burgundy after his canonization in 1247. In 1254 the shrine of 'Blessed Edmund the Confessor' was visited by King Henry himself, as an act of expiation, and he gave twenty-five marks from the revenues of Canterbury to provide for four lamps to burn there in perpetuity. To the tomb of 'St Edme' in Pontigny church pilgrims still come, particularly on the saint's day, 16th November, and again on Whit Monday.

The abbey church of Pontigny is the best preserved of all such Cistercian buildings as remain in Burgundy. Built in the second half of the twelfth century, largely through the munificence of Count Thibault of Champagne, the style is of the transition from romanesque to gothic, but remaining completely within the austere manner adopted by Cistercian architects. How beautiful this style can be is seen in the view of the abbey across the fields, from which it appears like some great skeleton of a ship upturned and stranded on the banks of the River Serein, its ribs the bare, unornamented buttresses, its keel the great horizontal length of roofline. Or again, as the visitor approaches the western entrance along the shaded lime avenue and sees the perfection of the proportions of the narthex and high gabled façade, with their elegant blind and open arcading, which reveal the interplay of surface light and recessed shadow. But the simplicity and austerity of the interior, this reliance the Cistercians placed on harmonious proportion and the effect of clear, uncoloured light, without the addition of extraneous ornament, surprises and delights the visitor from the purity of its conception and the sober brilliance of the stone from Tonnerre. Not far from the abbey, in the village, is a fine thirteenth-century bridge, the successor to that which gave its name to Pontigny. It was said that on this bridge three bishops (of Sens, Auxerre, Langres), three counts (of Auxerre, Tonnerre, Champagne) and an abbot (of Pontigny), could dine together, while each remained on his own land.

But unquestionably the place where the visitor can best evoke today the sense of the life of those early Cistercian monasteries in Burgundy is the abbey of Fontenay, to the southeast of Pontigny, standing remote in a delightfully verdant valley not far from the hillside town of Montbard. More so even than Cîteaux and Clairvaux—the buildings of the latter, after the depredations and destruction of the post-Revolutionary period, being used today, alas, as a place of detention—the abbey of Fontenay brings visitors close, perhaps closest, to St Bernard. Four years after the establishment on 25th June 1115 of Clairvaux, with Bernard as its first abbot, he in person led a party of twelve monks, the number thirteen symbolizing Christ and the Apostles, to found a hermitage near Châtillon; then, when aspirants came flocking in, to create a new monastery at Fontenay (October 1119). Not only was the land for the new abbey the gift of an uncle of St Bernard, but the first abbot of Fontenay was his own cousin, Godefroy de la Rochetaille. Further, the abbey church and the conventual buildings reveal perfectly the monastic ideals of the founder in their sober architecture and the internal domestic arrangements. In his famous letter to his friend, William of St Thierry, Bernard says that it is not for him, 'the most miserable of men . . . to judge the world . . . what would be more intolerable than to criticize the most glorious Order of Cluny and impudently slander the holy men who live in it such praise-worthy lives?' He then, notwithstanding, goes on to lay about him with vivid strokes of his pen, inveighing against the luxurious, over-delicate, often slothful and even grossly sensual lives, of some Benedictines. Finally, he comes to their churches, and all the faults of the older Order are summed up, for St Bernard, in these buildings. 'But these are small matters,' he writes, referring to his earlier strictures; 'I come to greater abuses. I do not speak of the excessive height of their churches, their inordinate length, their superfluous breadth, these sumptuous ornaments, these curious paintings which divert the attention of those praying and impede devotion . . . we monks who have quitted the world of men, who have renounced anything precious or attractive for the love of Christ . . . whose devotion, I ask, do we expect to arouse by these means? . . . but let it be. I assume it is all for the honour and glory of God.' For St Bernard the Cistercian reform offered a sure, if not the sole, way of righteous living; and in Burgundian Fontenay the visitor can see what is the most perfect structural embodiment existing today in France of his monastic ideal.

At the dissolution of the monasteries and the disposal of Church property in the Revolution the abbey of Fontenay was spared demolition, becoming at length converted into a paper manufactory. In 1906 the property was acquired by MM. Edouard and René Aynard, who set out with the admirable intention of removing all trace of its secular use, of repairing the mouldering fabric and, apart from one wing of the buildings converted for their own use, of restoring and maintaining the abbey, with its woods, fountains, lawns and gardens, as a national heritage. The beauty of the natural setting of Fontenay is perhaps only rivalled by that of Fountains Abbey in York-shire—the names, by the way, of the two Cistercian founda-tions both deriving from their abundant supply of running water.

The abbey church, which carried out faithfully St Bernard's precepts and which has been since the model of most Cistercian ecclesiastical building, owes much to the liberality of Everard of Arundel, Bishop of Norwich, who had retired to and died at Fontenay. The work of construction was extraordinarily rapid, and the church was consecrated in 1147 in the presence of St Bernard by the former Cistercian monk who had ascended the throne of St Peter as Pope Eugenius III. The structure is remarkable for its—if the barbarous term may be forgiven—aesthetic logicality. The nave is blind in that it is not lit from on high; the walls (which open on to the aisles in eight bays, separated by piers of pilasters and engaged columns) support pointed barrel-vaulting (*berceau brisé*) and are themselves buttressed to a great extent internally by the height and lateral strength of the aisle vaulting. The lighting comes from the windows in the aisles and from those strikingly placed in the east and west ends. (The effect of light was always carefully considered by Cistercian architects.) The capitals of the nave-pillars are of extreme decorative simplicity, and everywhere is noticeable the absence of any superfluous decoration, the impression of lightness and grace deriving in great part from the sober purity of the mouldings, and from the harmonious rhythms of the openings—from the sense of controlled space. Of particular architectural boldness is the square *chevet* or apsidal end—a requirement of St Bernard—which from the nave is seen through a triumphal arch, above which five circular-headed windows ascend and descend again like steps; and below the light floods in from the tiers of windows, one horizontal, consisting of three with rounded arches, and above them a further triad with pointed arches, which follows the line of the vaulted ceiling. Fontenay is a miracle of restrained grandeur, of a nobility which is the result of a refinement that is still at the same time robust—not of austerity entirely, for this last quality does not enter here, forgotten in our admiration of this supreme achievement of grace (perhaps, it might be said, there is something here of both senses of the word). In the church is the late thirteenth-century statue of Our Lady of Fontenay, the earliest example to have been preserved of such church ornament among the Cistercians, who, although they held in special veneration the Virgin Mary and dedicated all their abbey churches to her, appear to have resisted for nearly two hundred years the introduction of her figure into their churches, bare of all such ornament. With the decline in spiritual fervour of the Order, this proscription of St Bernard too was later relaxed. It was in this abbey church of Fontenay that the abbot of Cîteaux and vicar-general of the Order, Dom Gabriel Sortais, in the presence of sixty Cistercian abbots, celebrated mass on 13th September 1953 to mark the eight-hundredth anniversary of the death of St Bernard of Clairvaux.

In the adjoining monastic buildings at Fontenay we may see the typical arrangement of a twelfth-century Cistercian abbey, the model that was to be followed in the more than seven hundred monasteries that spread with such rapidity throughout France, Switzerland and Germany, to Poland, Scandinavia and the British Isles in the north, to the Iberian peninsula, Italy, Sicily in the south, and as far east as Syria, until it was said that 'the whole world has become Cistercian'. From the church, stairs led to the dormitory of the choir monks; the lay brothers, the *conversi*, had their quarters apart, with their own dorter and refectory usually in connection with the *cellarium*, the storehouse for the monastery. This could be of a vast size— at Fountains Abbey it measured a full hundred yards in length. Abutting on the nave of the church, most frequently (when the terrain permitted) to the south, was the great cloister, arcaded to allow the monks shelter in inclement weather. To the east opened the chapter house, where the monks met under the presidency of the abbot or prior. On the southern side of the cloister was the entrance, first, to the calefactory, a room in which the monks could warm themselves in the coldest season and dry out their habits, if caught by rain showers while working in the fields. Next followed the large refectory, on one side of which steps led up to a reading loft, where a monk read to his companions during meals. Next door were the kitchens and pantries. In the cloister garth immediately in front of the entrance to the refectory, was the *lavatorium* (often circular or octagonal in shape, and of a beautiful design), where the community washed, face and head in the morning, hands before meals—baths were frowned on. In the siting of a monastery a plentiful supply of running water, usually from a stream, was essential, not only for drinking, cooking and washing but also for flushing the lavatories and disposing of soluble refuse. In this respect Fontenay was profusely provided. Set apart from, but connected with, the main building was the infirmary, most often with its own kitchens and chapels; and further there were the accommodation for the abbot, the dormitory and common-rooms for the novices, the library, cells for copyists, and the rest. In the grounds were the guest rooms and those offices serving the essential needs of the monks—the bakery, smithy, barns, granaries, stables, animals' byres and pens, wine-press, pigeon-lofts, fish-ponds and flour mill, the vegetable and herbal gardens and the orchards. Frequently, too, buildings were erected by the monastery walls, providing accommodation, a hospital and chapel for pilgrims and wayfarers. The monastic ideal envisaged a self-contained, self-sufficient community; and in achieving this, the Cistercians contributed greatly to the religious life no less than to the economic and social progress of Europe from the twelfth century onwards; until events at length overtook them and the decline set in. Not least as a contribution to this inevitable falling away from the spirit that animated the century of St Bernard was the very success of the monastic movement, which brought with it great riches, and in consequence the system of 'commendatory abbots', of outside appointees who battened on the accumulated wealth of the abbeys—that 'leprosy of the monastic state', as Montalembert described it. But it was the Revolution that dealt the death blow to the religious houses of France, when the National

Dijon—General View

The Abbey of Cluny

Sculpture at Autun (St-Lazare)

Sluter's *Well of Moses* from the Chartreuse de Champmol, Dijon

Autun (St-Lazare): detail from the West Front

Cloisters at
Fontenay

Charles the Rash (from a painting by Van Eyck)

Philip the Bold

The death of John the Fearless on the Bridge of Montereau,
10 September 1419

The château of
Bussy-Rabutin

The château of
Ancy-le-Franc

Vauban

Comte Roger de Bussy-Rabutin

Alphonse de
Lamartine

Lamartine's
childhood home at
Milly-Lamartine

Vendanges at Clos Vougeot

Tasting the new wine at Beaune

Colette

Assembly on behalf of the people reclaimed their 'usurped patrimony'.

It was said that at first Guy and Gerard, brothers of St Bernard, who served as early cellarers, were scandalized by seeing a lay brother named Christian planting vines on a nearby hillside. However, by 1134 they had changed their minds, since the abbey then possessed several vineyards and later owned at least thirteen, their first wine-press being set up in 1153, the year of St Bernard's death. The Queen of Sicily, on a visit to Clairvaux in 1517, was most impressed with the monastery's existing wine-press, vat room and cellar, particularly a huge square storage tun, which seems to have been the same as amazed Dom Meglinger a century later. If the measurement, which is given in hogsheads, is accurate, then the quantity of wine made and stored was vast, since a hogshead contains between 60–140 gallons. One record describes 'a great room . . . containing from four score to a hundred hogsheads . . . The wine flows into the tuns through leaden pipes into a cellar where there is a large tun which contains four hundred hogsheads of wine. It is thirty feet in circumference and eighteen feet high . . . in a normal year 1,700 to 2,000 hogsheads of wine are produced.' The historian Gibbon, who visited Clairvaux in the eighteenth century, had some caustic comments to make on the falling off from the earlier practices, the dearth of books and the plentiful supply of wine: 'St Bernard would blush at the pomp of the church and the monastery; he would ask for the library, and I know not whether he would be much edified by a tun of 800 muids (914 hogsheads), which almost rivals that of Heidelberg.' When one considers the revenue from sheep-rearing—the Queen of Sicily visited a building capable of holding 5,000 to 6,000 sheep, and was informed that the abbey's flocks numbered more than 18,000—as well as the return from other pursuits of the *conversi*, one may gauge the wealth of sixteenth-century Clairvaux.

When St Bernard died on 20th August 1153, after more than thirty-eight years as abbot of Clairvaux, sixty-eight daughter-houses had been established in France alone, and the whole of

E

its filiation amounted to no fewer than one hundred and sixty-four foundations. The number of religious at Clairvaux at the time of his death was 700, of whom about 100 were novices—a further 800 forms of profession were found in the saint's cell. During the lifetime of Bernard, Clairvaux of itself gave to the Church a pope (Eugenius III), five cardinals, nine bishops and more than seventy abbots, of whom one, Rainald de Bar, became abbot of Cîteaux. The amount of work St Bernard managed to get through was prodigious. Although the prior was his right-hand man and took charge during his many absences, he had his eye on everything, particularly the education and welfare of the novices; we have noticed the extent and importance of his correspondence; he, rather than the abbot of Cîteaux, was the active head of the Cistercian Order; visitations of affiliated houses and travelling on affairs of the Church took him away from Clairvaux for long periods, particularly at the time of the Schism and when he was preaching the Second Crusade. Nor did he overlook the relief of temporal suffering—in the famine which afflicted Burgundy in 1125 he is said to have fed 2,000 persons daily, 'so that the provisions of the house were often exhausted'. The aesthetic side of Bernard's many-sided nature came out, apart from in his writings, in his care for the quality of the singing, his insistence on the purity of the chant, he himself composing an antiphonal to purify abuses which had crept in. The professed and the novices chanted the Office on alternate days; any slip in the choral singing was met with punishment.

That punishment played a large part in the formative process of the monks is seen from a fourteenth-century custumal from the Benedictine (the more tolerant Order) St-Bénigne of Dijon, quoted by Joan Evans. Boys might be entered as oblates from the tender age of seven. The sense of original sin lay heavy on the minds of these mediaeval masters. '. . . at all the Hours, if the boys commit any fault in the Psalmody or other singing, either by sleeping or such-like transgression, let there be no sort of delay, but let them be stripped forthwith of frock and cowl, and be beaten in their shirt only. . . . Let the masters sleep between every two boys in the dormitory, and sit between every two at other times. . . . When they lie down in bed, let a master be always among them with his rod and (if it be night) with a candle, holding the rod in the one hand and the light in the other. If any chance to linger after the rest, he is forthwith to be smartly touched; for children everywhere need custody with discipline, and discipline with custody. . . . When they wash, let masters stand between each pair. . . . When they sit in cloister or chapter, let each have his own tree-trunk for a seat, and so far apart that none touch in any way the skirt of the other's robe. . . .'

It might be thought that there was not much sweetness and light here, yet most remarkable as evidence of the influence exercised by St Bernard was the spirit that animated Clairvaux, and spread throughout the Cistercian Order, the spirit that emanated and radiated from this one man. It seemed that the abbey of Clairvaux and the daily life carried on there were the physical embodiment of the spirit of St Bernard. From this arose the well-known *nostalgia claravallensis*, the longing of every monk who had passed through there to return, especially to end his days at Clairvaux and to find his last resting-place in the monastic cemetery. A feeling of deprivation, separation and loss was felt by St Bernard himself in his enforced absences from his abbey. This human intimacy and bond between all members of the community, and communities, must be close to the secret of the Cistercians' success. It is revealed in a letter written by St Bernard to his monks, when he was far from Burgundy: 'This twofold grief will never leave me until I am restored to you, for you are part of my life. I have no doubt of what you are feeling for me, but I am only one person. You have only one reason for your grief, but I have many because I grieve for each of you. It is not only that I am obliged, for the time being, to live away from you, when even to be a king would be but a sorry servitude without you.' It is a very human sentiment that inspired the *nostalgia claravallensis*, and it is a mark of the greatness of St Bernard that, with the harsh rigour of his asceticism and his mystic flights, he could have fostered a feeling so human.

CHAPTER VIII

The Grand-Dukes of the West

IN THE LIFETIME of Philip the Good, the third and greatest
of the Valois dukes of Burgundy, the ideals of mediaeval
chivalry, and the exclusive predominance of the nobility in
society, had already passed their apogee. This period marked in
no mistaken terms the waning of the middle ages; yet chivalry
was to expire in a blaze of vividly resplendent pageantry, to
the sound of music of hitherto unheard-of technical accomplish-
ment and formal beauty. The Burgundian court under Philip
the Good was unparalleled in contemporary Europe for its
material riches, for the brilliance and variety of its public
displays at those solemn or joyous entries, tournaments, recep-
tions of princes or foreign ambassadors, ducal family weddings,
or those fantastic state occasions, like the celebrated *Voeu du
Faisan*, when lavish and ostentatious expenditure on visual
magnificence became a conscious political act. For Philip the
Good employed the romantic concept of chivalry—and with it,
its outward trappings and panoply, and its martial reality—as
an instrument of state. In 1430 the Flanders King-at-Arms
proclaimed the Duke's foundation of the Order of the Golden
Fleece, 'from the great love we bear to the noble order of
chivalry'. The possessor of widely separated and disparate
states—we hear the triumphant ring of his titles: 'Duke of
Burgundy, of Lothier [Lower Lorraine], of Luxembourg, of
Limburg and Guelders, Count of Artois, of Flanders, of
Burgundy [Franche-Comté], Prince-palatine of Hainault, of
Holland, of Zeeland and Zutphen, Marquis of the Holy
Roman Empire, Lord of Friesland, of Salins, of Malines . . .'—
Philip the Good had of necessity to rely on the armed strength
derived from his feudal overlordship to counterbalance the
ever-active pretensions of the Third Estate, of a proud
municipal patriciate and restless proletariat, especially those

of the flourishing cities of the Low Countries. In the judicious use of these chivalric forces of late feudalism Duke Philip was successful in maintaining and extending the boundaries of his hereditary state. With his son, Charles the Rash, we already see chivalry outmoded in the renaissance prince. In pursuit of those ideals of a more modern age, Charles was to lose both his duchy and his life on 5th January 1477, his body being found two days later, stripped and partly eaten by wolves, buried beneath the heap of slain, in a frozen pool outside the walls of Nancy.

In 1031, Henry I, the grandson of Hugh Capet, the founder of the Capetian dynasty, succeeded his father, Robert the Pious, on the throne of France, and confirmed his brother, like their father named Robert, in possession of the duchy of Burgundy, 'to enjoy in full proprietary and to pass on to his heirs'. This fief, which was one of the largest and richest in the kingdom, remained for over three hundred years in unbroken succession with the descendants of Hugh Capet, until the line failed in 1361 on the death of Philippe de Rouvres. In strict feudal law the duchy did not revert to the crown; Burgundy devolved on King John the Good, of the house of Valois, by virtue of his personal rights of succession. This point was made amply clear at a meeting of the Estates of Burgundy in Dijon: the duchy was to remain an autonomous entity, retaining its ancient administration in its bailiwicks; it was not to be absorbed as a province in the kingdom of France. The Estates and the individuals of the higher nobility swore allegiance to John the Good as their feudal suzerain.

Some years previously, on 19th September 1356, King John had suffered a disastrous defeat at Poitiers, where, despite the valiant defence of his fourteen-year-old son Philip the Bold, he was captured by the English. The scene was graphically described by the Florentine chronicler Villani, who tells how Philip, throwing himself against the King's assailants, shouted: 'Look out, father, . . . There, to your right . . . to your left!' In reward, on 27th June 1363 King John appointed Philip, who was the youngest son, his lieutenant-general in Burgundy, and on the 6th September (secretly, at first) he invested him and his heirs with the duchy, creating him premier peer of France as well as the first Valois Duke of Burgundy. In 1369 Philip the Bold married the young widow of Philippe de Rouvres, Margaret, daughter of Louis de Maele, Count of Flanders, and heiress of the five counties of Flanders, Artois, Burgundy, Nevers and Rethel. On the death of Louis in 1384 these rich counties came into the possession of Philip the Bold, who had acquired by the time of his own death in 1404— through marriages, purchase or treaty—a substantial buffer state between the territories of the Empire and the kingdom of France, which was then in the nerveless hands of his mentally unbalanced nephew, Charles VI. After the death of his eldest brother, King Charles V, in 1380, and especially after madness had first struck his nephew in 1392, Philip the Bold, supported by his brother, the art-loving Duke of Berry, was virtually the ruler of France, challenged only in his latter years by his nephew, Louis of Orleans. But Philip did not allow his business at the French court to impede the consolidation of his own growing duchy of Burgundy. Philip the Bold always looked on himself as a Frenchman—indeed, was he not the first peer of the realm—but it must have been only too apparent to someone as clear-seeing as he that the interests of his Burgundian duchy, particularly those arising from the rich trade of the Low Countries, were not always compatible with those of France. It was this fundamental opposition of interests that was to drive his successors to attempt to create an independent sovereign state, to revive the post-Carolingian kingdom of Lotharingia, and to cast off their French links.

This division widened when John the Fearless succeeded his father in the duchy of Burgundy. In Paris, at the court of the demented King Charles VI, Philip the Bold's former authority in direction of affairs had been assumed by the brilliant Louis of Orleans. Friction between the cousins quickly grew into open enmity. On the night of 23rd November 1407 Orleans was set on by an armed gang and done to death in the streets of Paris. The instigator of this crime was John the Fearless, motivated partly by personal jealousy; but in public he gloried in having rid the country of a tyrant. The defence of the Duke of Burgundy was undertaken by a member of his council,

Jean Petit, who pleaded before the princes of the blood in justification of the murder, taking as the basis of his argument the axiom '*Dame convoitise est de tous maulx la racine*', which he developed in the manner of a mediaeval disputation, in accordance with the syllogism in *Barbara*. The presence in Paris of Burgundian troops and the open support of the Parisian mob prevented the Orleanist faction from pursuing the matter; although later, when John the Fearless had returned to Burgundy, the dead man's family, through the mouth of the Abbot of Cérisy, publicly refuted Petit's paradoxical defence of tyrannicide. Again, the Abbot based his counter-argument on the irrefutable assertion, '*Radix omnium malorum est cupiditas*—Covetousness is the root of all evil'! Sentence was passed against the absent Duke, but was never carried out. France thenceforth was rent for years with civil war between the Burgundians and the supporters of the Orleans, who took the name of Armagnacs from their leaders. John the Fearless was thus driven by these events, and by the needs of his Flemish subjects, into negotiations with the English; and although, when Henry V landed in France in 1415, John seems to have made some lukewarm efforts to support his King, neither he nor Burgundian troops were present at the battle of Agincourt.

On Sunday, 10th September 1419, with the connivance—indeed the complicity—of the Dauphin Charles whom he had gone to meet, John the Fearless expiated his crime against Louis of Orleans on the bridge at Montereau-Faut-Yonne. Advancing to the centre of the bridge, he was separated from his escort and cut down with an axe. His successor, Philip the Good, the third Valois duke of Burgundy, was thus thrown—both to revenge his father's death and to protect his state of Burgundy—into the arms of Henry V of England. The result was the Treaty of Troyes of May 1420 and the formation of the Anglo-Burgundian alliance against what remained of French resistance grouped around the Dauphin, become 'the King of Bourges' on the death of Charles VI in October 1422. In Paris Bedford, the brother of the late King Henry V, was regent for the young King Henry VI. Henceforth Philip the Good shaped his policy between the claims of his English ally and his rightful

king, Charles VII, as in all respects an equal sovereign. This
policy was centred on the vital independence, the protection
and advancement of his own duchy of Burgundy. He saw that
the struggle in France between the houses of Valois and
Lancaster could only help his own cause—the creation of his
Burgundian states into a resuscitated kingdom of Lotharingia.
Doubtless Philip the Good, like Bedford, looked on Joan of
Arc as something very different from the God-inspired saviour
of France. After the capture of the Maid in 1430, and before he
sold her to the English, the Duke had an interview with her,
at which the chronicler Monstrelet was present, although he
declared later that he had heard nothing. The inference is that
what the outspoken Maid said to his Duke was not to the credit
of his loyalty or of his honour. However, Joan's victories had
turned the tide; thenceforth it flowed in favour of the France of
Charles VII. Aware of the change and looking to the future,
Philip the Good dropped his English alliance; by the Treaty of
Arras in 1435, in which the Treaty of Troyes was abrogated,
the new *rapprochement* with France was sealed. King Charles
VII publicly and solemnly disavowed the murder of John the
Fearless, and made territorial reparation to his son by a cession
of Auxerre and the Auxerrois and the cities of the Somme.

Philip the Good, nevertheless, maintained his independence,
refusing angrily when cited to appear in Paris. If his constant
efforts to obtain from the Emperor the crown he so much
desired were unsatisfied, he gave his subjects the peace they
longed for, which enabled the duchy of Burgundy to become
the richest state in Europe and its court second to none in
princely magnificence. It is calculated that the income of the
Duke of Burgundy in 1455 was 900,000 ducats anually, a sum
equalled among European powers by the Republic of Venice
alone, while the revenues of Florence were only one-quarter of
this, those of Naples a third and of the Papacy and Milan
one-half. Philip the Good had thus at his disposal funds eight
times in excess of those which allowed his contemporary, the
great Federigo da Montefeltro, to build his celebrated palace
of Urbino.

The reign of the fourth Duke of Burgundy, Philip's only
legitimate son, Charles the Rash (we prefer this nineteenth-

century French sobriquet to the usual 'the Bold') is one of the 'great might-have-beens' of history. Disposing of such great forces in the unsettled political conditions of fifteenth-century Europe, Charles the Rash was driven by a restless ambition that knew no bounds. King, why not Emperor? There was no longer a question of seeing in Louis XI of France his suzerain: Charles rightly considered Louis the principal opponent of his ultimate success. If ever the character of the prince was decisive in history it was so in the struggle between Charles the Rash of Burgundy and Louis XI of France, 'the universal spider'. Philippe de Commines foresaw what was to be the outcome, and switched his allegiance from the insatiable, headstrong Charles to the patient, pliant and faithless Louis. And the end was as Commines had foretold. Determined to teach a lesson to the baseborn townsmen and peasants of the Swiss cantons, who had inflicted a defeat on some of his troops, Charles the Rash led his splendidly equipped army (the last flowering of the age of chivalry) to the field of Grandson in March 1476. Grandson, Morat—the names of these disasters sounded a knell to the hopes of Charles the Rash. In 1816 Byron picked up a skull, one of those of the 8,000 slain, on the field of Morat. In the museums of Switzerland today we may see the tapestries, carpets, jewels, highly-wrought armour and crystal cups that formed part of the booty of the Swiss mountaineers in their overwhelming victories over the foremost prince of his day. Louis XI moved to Lyons, to wait. The end was not long in coming. The last of the Valois dukes of Burgundy perished on 5th January 1477 in an unsuccessful attempt to relieve Nancy. Louis ordered his army to move in, and the duchy of Burgundy reverted once again, this time for good, to the crown of France.

The court of Burgundy under its four Valois dukes was itself a conscious work of art. If the motive for this outpouring of vast sums of money on the building of the palaces at Dijon and elsewhere and the Charterhouse of Champmol, on the precious works of sculptors, painters, gold and silversmiths, jewellers, armourers, tapestry makers, engravers, illuminators, weavers of silk, satin and brocades, furriers, makers of musical instruments and ingenious mechanical devices, and all the other purveyors of the requirements of a rich and luxury-loving court—if the purpose behind this costly magnificence was primarily diplomatic, to bring to the eyes of an impressionable world the wealth and the might, the power and the glory of the Grand Dukes of the West, this was not the sole reason for this immense expenditure and sumptuous display. Nor does it explain the quality of what was achieved. These Valois princes were great patrons, but also they were great connoisseurs: Charles V with his library in the Louvre, Louis of Anjou, John of Berry (the memorial to whose taste is the *Très Riches Heures de Chantilly*), and, not the least, Philip the Bold of Burgundy. At the end of the fourteenth century Paris had become the cultural centre of northern Europe, possessing links through the papal court in Avignon with the painters of Siena, and attracting crowds of artists from the rapidly developing schools of the Low Countries. Philip the Bold, who remained at heart a Frenchman, was not only the transmitter of French taste to his new capital, but it was he, after he had become ruler of the Low Countries, who gathered together those sculptors and painters who were to make Dijon the *foyer* of a truly Burgundian school. The Burgundian style in sculpture and (to a much lesser degree) painting, with its source at Dijon, and the Burgundian style in music, with its sources chiefly in the cities of the Netherlands, owe everything to the patronage of Philip the Bold and his three successors. Valois Burgundy in the fifteenth century became one of the principal centres of those tendencies in art which are now distinguished by the term International Gothic.

No sooner settled in his duchy, Philip the Bold began to rebuild the palace of the former dukes in Dijon, beginning in 1366 with the Tour de Bar, and employing as his architect-in-chief Drouet de Dammartin of Paris, who had previously worked for his brothers, Charles V and the Duke of Berry. From 1382 the Duchess Margaret of Flanders employed Drouet on her château at Germolles, near Chalon-sur-Saône (alas, now destroyed), with Jehan de Beaumetz in charge of the painting and Claus Sluter, a native of Haarlem, to carve the stonework. Philip the Bold brought from his northern states architects, sculptors and painters, often choosing them himself, to work in Dijon. Perhaps as early as 1372 Jehan de Marville, probably a Fleming, was employed as a sculptor by Philip, and in 1381 he was commissioned to design the Duke's splendid alabaster tomb, which is today in the Dijon Museum. Claus de Haine of Tournai was also engaged on this tomb. On Marville's death in 1389, he was succeeded by Claus Sluter, who was thought of so highly by Philip that he appointed him '*ymagier et varlet de chambre*'. Further, he sent him to Mehun-sur-Yèvre, to the court of the Duke of Berry, to study the work of the celebrated André Beauneveu of Valenciennes; also to Paris, to buy alabaster from the Genoese, as well as to Dinant and Malines for supplies of glass and marble. If Sluter brought from the Netherlands his native genius and his techincal knowledge, it was under the discriminating patronage of Philip the Bold that he came in touch with the French and Italian influences then current, and absorbed the native Burgundian traditions of romanesque and gothic sculptors. It is from these sources that Sluter may be seen as the founder of the 'Burgundian' school, having as his immediate followers his nephew, Claus van Werve, and later the Aragonese Jean de la Huerta and the sculptor from Avignon, Antoine le Moiturier, the last-named the nephew and pupil of Jacques Morel. The magnificent tomb of Philip the Bold was finished only in 1470, and set a fashion in funeral sculpture, as is seen in the monuments of John the Fearless and his wife Margaret of Bavaria in Dijon and of the Seneschal Philippe Pot by Antoine le Moiturier in the Louvre.

As early as 1377 Philip the Bold began the building of the Charterhouse of Champmol, at the gates of Dijon, to house a prior and twenty-four monks, whose task it was to pray incessantly, day and night, for the spiritual and material welfare of the Duke and his family. Their church was to constitute a ducal mausoleum of unparalleled splendour. Today little of this great monastic establishment, which became famous throughout Europe, remains, save the doorway to the church and the sculptured well. Jehan de Marville designed the sculptural group on the west portal, where kneel the figures of Philip the Bold and his duchess, Margaret of Flanders, accompanied by their patron saints, John the Baptist and St Catherine, who all turn towards the beautiful representation of the *Virgin and Child*, the type and model for so many similar statues by Burgundian sculptors. This is the work of Sluter; and nearby, in what was the centre of the cloister, stands his masterpiece, the *Well of Moses*, one of the outstanding sculptural works of all time. These six majestic figures of the prophets originally formed the plinth on which rose a representation of the Crucifixion, with the sorrowing figures of the two Marys and St John. Of this only the beautiful, resigned head of the Christ has survived and is today in the Musée Archéologique in Dijon. Very little remains, too, of the magnificent decoration of the interior of the church, with its paintings, altars and statues by Sluter and such painters as Jehan de Beaumetz, Jan Malouel and Henri Bellechose. Some idea of the magnificence of these furnishings may be gained from the retable by Jacques de Baërze, with its shutters or wings (*volets*), painted by Melchior Broederlam, now in the Dijon Museum.

John the Fearless and Philip the Good carried out and brought to completion much that was begun under Philip the Bold. In the palace of Dijon the third Duke commissioned the architect Jean Poncelet to add the upper storeys to the Tour de la Terrasse (or de Philippe le Bon), from which on an exceptionally clear day can be discerned the snow-capped peak of Mont Blanc, some two hundred kilometres away to the south-east. At this period were built the fine Salle des Gardes and the stupendous ducal kitchens. In Dijon the Duke's subjects reflected their prince's taste for luxury in the sumptuous hôtels de Rochefort, Rolin and de Chambellan and the Maison des Sauvegrain, known as the house of the English Ambassadors. Outside Dijon, Philippe Pot constructed his château of Châteauneuf-en-Auxois, and, under Philip the Good, his chancellor Nicolas Rolin built the remarkable Hôtel-Dieu in Beaune and his town house in Autun.

To Philip the Bold goes the credit for having discovered the so-called Limbourg brothers (Pol, Jehan and Herman, nephews of the painter, Jehan Malouel), the creators of the *Très Riches Heures* now at Chantilly. But the high point in painting was reached under Philip the Good, when the incomparable Jan van Eyck was his *varlet de chambre*, and produced such master-pieces as the *Madonna of the Chancellor Rolin*, today in the Louvre. Rogier van der Weyden painted the Duke and his son, Charles Count of Charollais, later Charles the Rash, and the *Last Judgement*, commissioned by the Chancellor Rolin for his Hôtel-Dieu in Beaune. Contemporary with these artists were such masters of painting in the Low Countries as Dirk Bouts, Hans Memling, Robert Campin, Jacques Daret and the gracious, melancholy Hugo van der Goes. Among native-born painters in Burgundy were the father and son, Guillaume and Pierre Spicre. Painters at the Burgundian court were expected to put their hand to what was required of them at the moment —the painting of banners, devices, escutcheons, mural decorations, backcloths for pageants and statues. Claus Sluter's sculpture on the *Well of Moses* was carved to be covered with brilliant colour by Jehan Malouel—gold, reds, browns, greens, shades of blue heightening the realism of the figures; that of Jeremiah actually being given a pair of spectacles in gilded copper, the work of Henniquin de Hacht.

Prominent were the illuminators of the precious books for the ducal library which, added to by all four dukes, rivalled the finest contemporary collections in Europe. Besides the Limbourg brothers, we hear of the work of Jehan de Beaumetz, Jacquemart de Hesdin, Jacques Coene, Henri Bellechose, as well as, under Philip the Good and Charles the Rash, Leyset Lyédet, Haincelin de Haguenau, Jehan le Tavernier and Guillaume Vrelant. Allied to the art of painting was that of the weavers of tapestries, which at the court of Burgundy achieved a rare excellence. The subjects were taken from mythology, history, battles or scenes from courtly life. Even on campaign the Dukes were accompanied by the tapestries; among the booty taken by the Swiss at Grandson was the splendid carpet now in the museum in Berne. On a deep blue background are scores of exquisitely worked plants in the most beautiful colours, surrounding the arms of Burgundy. So exact are the power of observation and fineness of execution that botanists have been able to identify some thirty-five species. In fact, it might seem that the scenes of Burgundian court life might themselves be best represented as pieces of gorgeous tapestry

A fitting accompaniment to all this visual splendour was the Burgundian court music. This was the great period of Netherlandish musicians and composers, themselves much influenced by the Englishman, John Dunstable. Of such outstanding names as Guillaume Dufay, Gilles Binchois, the Fleming Jan Okeghem and the Hainaulter Josquin des Prez, the first two served the Burgundian court, and though Okeghem worked in Paris and des Prez in Milan, their music was universally played. The music heard was both religious and secular. Philip the Good is said to have had his twelve trumpeters drawn up beneath his window to wake him each morning with a brazen fanfare. Charles the Rash, who had as master the Englishman Robert Morton, as well as Dufay, took with him on his travels 'his entire musical chapel and master-singers, who performed a beautiful musical service and office all day long in honour of the Mother of God'. When in camp at Neuss in 1475, Charles is said to have had 'every evening something new sung in his quarters and sometimes his lordship sings . . .' Although a skilled musician, his voice was not good. At banquets and pageants music played a most important part, as in the Feast of the Pheasant, when we are told of a huge pastry which contained within twenty-eight musicians, who regaled the company. Each of the many interludes which were part of the banquet was preceded by music: one by choristers who sang the chanson *La Saulvegarde de me Vie* and a motet; another by a boy mounted on a beautiful white stag with gilded antlers, the boy singing in a pure, clear voice the chanson *Je ne vis onques la pareille*, accompanied by the stag! On this occasion we are informed of the instruments employed: organ, harp, lute, viol, fiddle, flute, German horn, trumpet, oboe, bagpipe, and tambourine. No contemporary court could rival the musical resources at the disposal of the Grand-Dukes of the West. Every courtly activity had its appropriate music; what we would give to have heard in their colourful Burgundian setting such songs as these, or others—*De plus en plus, Le joli tetin, Hé, Robinet* or *Filles à marier*. Some of these Burgundian melodies appeared in the *Orchésographie*, a book on music and dancing, published in 1588 by the canon of Langres, who signed himself 'Thoinot Arbeau' (an anagram for Jehan Tabouret), on whose work Peter Warlock based his well-known *Capriol Suite*.

In an age when men were required to maintain a high state of physical fitness by a life spent largely on horseback in the open air, in hunting or hawking or in the practice of martial exercises, as preparation for the field of battle, it is small wonder that blood ran high. It is with this background in mind that we may understand the extraordinary proliferation of etiquette to cover every public action at the ducal court, the place of chivalry at that court, and the development of an esoteric symbolism in colours, devices, signs and mottoes. Like his brother the Duke of Berry, with his motto, *Le temps viendra*, Philip the Bold had his, *Il me tarde*; both indicating their personal attitude to political events. As devices Philip the Bold displayed a flint and steel or sparks and flames. At the time of the struggles between Burgundians and Armagnacs, it was said that priestly supporters of the former crossed themselves in the manner of the cross of St Andrew, the Burgundian emblem. When in response to the hop and the nettle, the devices of John the Fearless, Louis of Orleans adopted the cudgel, with the motto *Je l'ennuie*, John the Fearless replied with a replica of a carpenter's plane and of shavings, with the motto *Ic Houd*, I hold. In 1406, we are told, he presented 315 gold planes, many studded with diamonds and inscribed with his motto, to his courtiers, and he used the device on his armours and clothes. Philip the Good's favourite motto, *Aultre n' arai*, was hardly appropriate, since he was well-known for his marital infidelities.

At this period, when princes and the nobility still considered it their right to permit their passions free and uninhibited play, it was only natural that, as some compensation or protection, the greatest importance should be placed on the due acceptance of forms, on etiquette. As we learn from the courtier Olivier de la Marche, every detail of life at the court of Burgundy was strictly regulated; it took long study to acquire a thorough knowledge of courtly observances. The daily functions were conducted with a ceremonial that was almost liturgical in its decorum and dignity. Nothing was held dishonourable if performed in the service of the Duke, two points above all being kept in view: to protect him from injury and to show him those marks of deepest respect that were owed to his exalted rank. Otto Cartellieri in *The Court of Burgundy* has described the service at the table of the Duke: 'The napkin with which the prince dried his hands was kissed when the *sommelier* delivered it to the *panetier*; in the same way the *valet-servant* touched with his lips the handles of the two knives, which were laid at the Duke's place at table; the *fruitier* in like manner kissed the torch which was intended for the ruler. Bareheaded, the valets and pages of good family carried the dishes from the kitchen to the dining hall, the squires kneeling frequently before the prince. The manner in which the various articles were to be held was carefully prescribed, the salt-cellar between the base and the waist, the drinking vessel at the base. When the prince had finished drinking, the cup-bearer received the cup with great reverence.' Dishes and goblets were carried high above the head; all food and drink was tasted in the Duke's presence, and a unicorn's horn was placed on the table as a preventative against poison. But not all was done in accordance with a rigid etiquette and decorous gravity. We hear of orders given by Philip the Good to his *varlet de chambre*, the painter Colard Le Voleur, 'to make conduits and suitable contrivances low down and all along the wall of the gallery, to squirt water in so many places that nobody in the gallery could possibly save themselves from getting wet, and other conduits and devices everywhere under the pavement to wet the ladies from underneath'.

Visitors to the Burgundian court, like the Bohemian Leo of Rozmital, were sometimes surprised at the small regard paid to legitimacy—or rather, at the fair treatment given to the numerous 'bastards of Burgundy'. If Philip the Bold had a son who became an innkeeper, his legitimate son and grandson were both more sensuously inclined and more considerate of their offsprings' welfare. John, the Bastard of Burgundy, son of John the Fearless and Agnes de Croy, became bishop of Cambrai and archbishop of Trier, and was once said to have celebrated mass attended by thirty-six of his illegitimate sons and grandsons. Philip the Good, according to his panegyrist, Bishop Guillaume Fillastre, suffered from what the bishop described as 'the weakness of the flesh'. (The bishop himself was the bastard son of an abbot and a nun.) The Duke's mistresses were too numerous to be accurately counted but a recent genealogical work has attributed to this amorous prince twenty-six bastards, who were mostly brought up at court, and thirty-three mistresses, who were not (openly at least) received there. In this he was unlike his contemporary, Charles VII, who forced on his wife and court the regal mistress, Agnes Sorel. Although scandal was carefully avoided and decorum assiduously maintained, calculation has shown that some five per cent of the court of Philip the Good were illegitimate, and his courtiers, taking their cue from their prince, went about it with a will, if the number of legitimizations granted by the Duke is any indication. Philip the Good's favourite, Anthony, a celebrated jouster and connoisseur, was favoured with the honorific title 'the Grand Bastard of Burgundy'.

This openness in sexual matters was carried to some strange lengths. For example, a young couple, married at court, would be accompanied to the bridal chamber by a joyful band of companions of both sexes, who remained in an ante-room, with music and singing, until a cry from within told them that the marriage had been consummated. Women, then, held a high place in this pleasure-loving court, Philip the Good being with his brother co-founder of a famous Court of Love, formed to give the lie to those calumniators of women, the authors of the *Roman de la Rose*; and for this attention to the rights of her sex the Duke was thanked by that women's-liberal before her time, Christine de Pisan. There is something fresh and healthy about the bawdy tales collected for Philip the Good, the *Cent Nouvelles Nouvelles*, that compilation which echoes somewhat distantly Boccaccio's better-known *Decameron*. Among the ducal treasures was a curious Madonna, richly wrought in gold and ornamented with gems, which, when a door was opened, revealed the Holy Trinity in the womb of the Virgin. It will perhaps seem strange to our age, when we find the staid Chastellain, the official court historiographer, writing of the dress of a certain countess that it 'represented the womb of her late mother'—one can only wonder how she achieved it. In a court, then, where these tolerant views on the relations of the sexes were prevalent, it is

perhaps a matter of small surprise that the last of the Valois
Dukes of Burgundy, Charles the Rash, whose attitude towards
women was very different from that of his father—he let it be
known that he would rather spend an hour in the company of
his *chambre des comptes* than of the female sex—was given
little credit for his chastity by his courtiers. In fact, his illegitimate half-brother, Baudouin, seems to have hinted at his
homosexuality.

We have already remarked on the policy of Philip the Good of
employing chivalry as an instrument of state. Such was the
fame of the Court of Burgundy for its passages-at-arms, the
chivalric tournaments held in the presence of the court ladies,
that knights from all over Europe journeyed there to break a
lance with its most celebrated jousters, the Grand Bastard
Anthony, Duke Adolph of Cleves and Jacques de Lalaing.
Exercising his sovereign rights, Philip the Good had constituted
in 1430 his Order of the Golden Fleece, in emulation of the
English Order of the Garter and in advance of the Order of
St Michael of Louis XI of France. As a matter of deliberate
policy the Duke revived expiring chivalry to serve his political
ends. Himself an enthusiastic jouster, Philip the Good staged
tournaments that became more and more elaborate and
spectacular, passages-at-arms with such bizarre names as the
Pas de l'Arbre Charlemagne, *Pas de la Belle Pèlerine*, *Pas de l'Arbre
d'Or*, or *Pas de la Dame Sauvage*.
    In 1450, to take advantage of the jubilee year, when many
pilgrims would be passing through Burgundy on their way to
Rome, the famous Burgundian knight Jacques de Lalaing
instituted, with the Duke's approval, the *Pas de la Fontaine aux
Pleurs*, remaining a whole year in residence near Chalon-sur-
Saône for this purpose. Lalaing concocted a fantastic tale
about an imagined Lady of the Fountain of Tears to serve the
occasion, and assessed his challenge to the courts of Europe.
Splendid multicoloured pavilions and galleries were set up near
the lists for the Duke, the Golden Fleece King-at-Arms, the
Charollais Herald, the ladies of the court and the noble visitors.
Beneath the figure of the Madonna a picture was hung of a
mysterious weeping woman, whose tears fell into a ewer held by

a unicorn, which bore also three painted shields besprinkled with blue tears. Any knight who wished to succour the *Dame de la Fontaine aux Pleurs* had to touch one of the shields—the white if he wished to fight with the axe, the violet if he chose the sword, and the black shield if he wished to combat mounted and with a lance. Lalaing fought all comers, removing parts of his armour at times, risking wounds, to provide variety. This passage-at-arms was a resounding success, the visiting knights vying with each other in extravagance of fanciful display. The prizes distributed by Lalaing (or rather, by Philip the Good, since Lalaing was penniless) were axes, swords and lances, all of gold. Two magnificent banquets, with music and interludes, brought to a fitting close this *pas d'armes*, one for the ladies of Chalon, at which the *entremets* (representations of ships, towns, woodland scenes, fountains, symbolic *tableaux*, etc.) brought Lalaing universal approbation for their fantasy of imagination, intricate contrivance and the artistry displayed.

But far outstripping in costly magnificence these frequent chivalric exercises were the state occasions, of which a splendid tournament usually formed an essential part: the visit of a foreign prince, a ducal marriage, like that of Charles the Rash with Margaret of York in 1468, or gatherings with a diplomatic purpose, where oaths were sworn at banquets of unsurpassed brilliance and ostentatious extravagance. By far the most bizarre and spectacular of Burgundian court banquets was, by common consent, that held in Lille on 17th February 1454. The fall of Constantinople to the Turks in the preceding year had stunned Europe, and Philip the Good was determined, if events at home permitted, to take the lead among European princes in the recovery of Christian Constantinople from the infidel. It was the custom among the nobility to swear oaths to the specific performance of some hazardous undertaking, such as a military campaign or a crusade. To render the ceremony more solemn and binding a bird was selected as a symbol of the vow; we have many instances of this extraordinary ritual for oath-taking: the *Voeu du Héron*, the *Voeu du Paon* and others. On this occasion a living pheasant was chosen, with a collar of gold richly studded with pearls and precious stones. The Feast of the Pheasant was preceded by jousts, presided over by the Knight of

the Swan. Dr Richard Vaughan, in the volume on Philip the
Good of his learned series on the Dukes of Burgundy, quotes for
the first time a letter of a minor court official, written home to
Burgundy, and describing the scene, when the oath to take the
cross was sworn by the Duke and his court: 'Last Sunday my
lord the Duke gave a banquet in the hôtel de la Salle in this
town. . . . The dishes were such that they had to be served with
trolleys, and seemed infinite in number. There were so many
side-dishes, and they were so curious, that it is difficult to
describe them. There was even a chapel on the table, with a
choir in it, a pasty full of flute-players, and a turreted tower
from which came the sound of an organ and other music. The
figure of a girl, quite naked, stood against a pillar. Hippocras
sprayed from her right breast and she was guarded by a live
lion who sat near her on a round table in front of my lord the
Duke. The story of Jason was represented on a raised stage by
actors who did not speak. My lord the Duke was served at table
by a two-headed horse ridden by two men sitting back to back,
each holding a trumpet and sounding it as loud as he could,
and then by a monster, consisting of a man riding on an
elephant, with another man, whose feet were hidden, on his
shoulders. Next came a white stag ridden by a young boy who
sang marvellously, while the stag accompanied him with the
tenor part. Next came an elephant . . . carrying a castle in
which sat Holy Church, who made piteous complaint on behalf
of the Christians persecuted by the Turks, and begged for help.
Then two knights of the Order of the Golden Fleece brought in
two damsels, together with a pheasant, which had a gold
collar round its neck decorated with rubies and fine large pearls.
These ladies asked my lord the Duke to make his vow, which
he handed in writing to Golden Fleece King-at-Arms to read
out. . . .' At this elaborate and fantastic ceremony Philip the
Good pledged, on certain conditions (which, in fact, were
never fulfilled), to undertake the crusade for the recovery of
Constantinople, and his example was followed by other
members of the ducal family and nobles present.

The writer barely mentions the lavish splendour displayed at
the Feast of the Pheasant: the great hall decorated with
tapestries depicting the labours of Hercules, the canopies and

cloths of silk damask, the embroidered coats of arms, devices
and mottoes, the profusion of candelabra and the magnificence
of the colourful dresses in damask, satin and silk, and the jewels
worn by men and women alike. The symbolic *entremets* and
interludes ranged from the gorgeous, through the whimsical
and far-fetched, to the downright absurd. Beside the naked girl
who served as a fountain of spiced wine, a naked boy placed high
on a rock spurted rose-water. The amount of food and strong
wines of Burgundy consumed was immense; carriages and
litters covered with golden and blue material and displaying
the Burgundian arms were let down from the roof by pulleys;
these contained the food, the meat course consisting of forty
different dishes and each carriage containing eighty-two
joints. And all this was accompanied by performances of
dances, acrobats, freaks, dwarfs and strange animals, to the
sound of religious and secular music composed by Dufay and
Binchois. The brilliant pageantry of the Burgundian court on
this occasion, and fourteen years later at the marriage of
Charles the Rash to Margaret of York, this blending of material
riches, chivalry and the fine arts to serve the political purposes
of the Valois dukes, was unsurpassed in princely splendour by
any of the European courts of the waning middle ages.

CHAPTER IX

Gothic Burgundy

WHY GOTHIC BURGUNDY and not Burgundian gothic? The reason—which is not pure pedantry—is not far to seek. In the romanesque period of French art, in church architecture and sculpture particularly, Burgundy was in the vanguard of creative activity, so that one may properly speak of a Burgundian romanesque style; indeed, within that style valid distinctions can be made, between the 'Cluniac' and the 'Martinian', for example, both equally Burgundian. In the succeeding gothic period, however, it is perhaps more appropriate to speak, not of Burgundian gothic, but rather of the gothic style in Burgundy. Not that all art historians have denied the employment of this term; it has been used as recently as 1960 by R. Branner in his most interesting *Burgundian Gothic Architecture*. But since the principal centres of innovation and development were elsewhere—in the Ile-de-France and Champagne pre-eminently—the most beautiful gothic churches in Burgundy, and there exist some outstanding examples of the period, reveal native elements which are in the main but a continuation of its own romanesque tradition—especially that tradition of fine stonework, of clearly cut mouldings and vigorous sculptural forms—and not such a distinctive originality or recognizable homogeneity of style as to merit the term *Burgundian* gothic. The sources of the new styles lay outside the province.

This may be thought to carry the matter too far, and to fly in the face of opinion better founded than one's own. For instance, the French historian Joseph Calmette has written of 'the marvellous jewel of Notre-Dame de Dijon' as 'perhaps, with St Louis' Sainte-Chapelle, the most perfect, the most accomplished work of French architecture'. This, too, may appear an exaggeration; but Calmette was making the point

that in Notre-Dame gothic architecture in Burgundy equalled
the finest in France. Yet it may be plausibly argued that
Notre-Dame, supremely beautiful as it is, should not be looked
on as specifically Burgundian at all. And again, in the allied
art of sculpture, although Claus Sluter (*c.* 1350–1406) and his
numerous followers in Burgundy have rightly been regarded
as constituting a truly Burgundian school, and one of great
significance in French, and European, art, nevertheless they
must be held to be already belonging to the period of the
renaissance. By one of those curious anomalies in the history of
art, sculpture had already gone on ahead, when painting, with
a backward look at a past age, lingered over forms that were
already anachronistic, however exquisite at times—in that
somewhat capricious, if magnificent, expression of courtly
nostalgia which is the International Gothic Style. If this style
has been so closely associated with Burgundy, with the court
of the Grand-Dukes of the West, where the pursuit of the ideals
of an outmoded chivalry was a matter of internal and foreign
policy, yet the justification of the use of this inelegant, but
meaningful, term 'International Gothic' is primarily to point
just the essential difference between the highly artificial art of
the fifteenth century and the gothic art, properly so understood, of the two preceding centuries.

The distinctive features of gothic church architecture were
the use of the pointed or ogival arch, the employment of ribbed
vaulting, and the grouping of slender columns in clusters
which, soaring to heights hitherto unattempted, permitted
stained-glass windows to replace the walls of ashlar, and
frequently necessitated, in order to counter the formidable
stresses and lateral thrusts, the construction of often elaborate
systems of flying buttresses. It will be recalled that the word
'gothic' was used, first by Vasari and later by Christopher
Wren, as a term of disparagement, synonymous with
'barbarous'. Few would hold this view today; and in Burgundy
the amateur of church architecture is perhaps uniquely placed
to observe the transition from masterpieces of the romanesque
period to equally splendid examples of the succeeding gothic.

It is usually considerd that the pointed gothic arch first
appeared in Burgundy in the narthex of Ste-Madeleine of

Vézelay. Undoubtedly among the earliest examples of the use
on the grand scale of this imported gothic style from the
neighbouring Ile-de-France is that in the beautiful transept
and choir, with its deambulatory and apsidal chapels, of this
same church of Ste-Madeleine. This was at the end of the
twelfth century. Here the three storeys of arcades, triforium
and clerestory of the gothic choir, which was influenced by
St-Denis, have a lightness and grace that are in perfect harmony
with the romanesque nave, consisting as it does of the arcades
and high windows of a familiar type of two-storey structure—
the form of Burgundian romanesque which is known as
Martinian or Brionnais. In churches of this type, of which
Anzy-le-Duc was the progenitor and Vézelay the most splendid
example, the passage from the romanesque to the gothic was
achieved by the substitution of pointed-arched ribs in place of
the former arches or groins of the rounded vaulting. The
simple romanesque system of nave vaulting evolved step by
step into the fully developed style of flamboyant gothic by
means of the use of ribs and intervening panels, revealing at
first a new elegance and later an ever-increasing intricacy of
decorative pattern. It passed, that is, from the simplest quadri-
partite to sexpartite vaults; thence, as the fourteenth century
progressed, to a highly stylized, web-like composition, derived
from the employment of transverse, diagonal, ridge, intermediate (*tierceron*) and lierne ribs and their ornamental bosses;
and finally, in the late flamboyant period, to an over-
sophistication (at times), when structural demands seem to
have given way before decorative effect, and the proliferation
of ribs in fans and pendants appears, even with an element of
perversity, to defy the force of gravity.

In Burgundy the romanesque two-storey churches of the
Martinian type have their gothic analogues in the splendid
examples from the second half of the twelfth century—the
abbey church of Pontigny and the collegial church of Montréal.
The architectural ideals of St Bernard of Clairvaux, which
found their most perfect expression in the austere refinement of
romanesque Fontenay, were carried a further step about 1150
in the great abbey church at Pontigny, the second of the
'daughters' of Cîteaux, and one of the earliest of Burgundian

churches to adopt gothic ribbed vaulting for their naves. In the early thirteenth century the square apse at Pontigny —a common Burgundian feature—was replaced by the existing circular east end with deambulatory and radial chapels, and the beautiful closed porch added—another architectural element, deriving from the Carolingian narthex, commonly found in Burgundy. Pontigny, with its high windows above the nave arcading, its purity of proportion and line, simplicity of mouldings and absence of extraneous ornament became the model for that Cistercian church-architecture which, arising in Burgundy, spread through twelfth- and thirteenth-century Europe, and has remained as an exemplar for much church building ever since.

The small mediaeval town of Montréal, rising on its hilltop above the River Serein, was the 'Mont Royal' of Queen Brunhilda and a favourite residence of the Capetian dukes of Burgundy, who in 1255 had dispossessed of their ancient fief its earlier owners, the ancient noble family of Anséric de Montréal. From the Lower Gate (*Porte d'En-bas*), with its thirteenth-century arcades, the street ascends, flanked by houses of the fifteenth and sixteenth centuries, some with the characteristic *tourelles*, to the Upper Gate (*Porte d'En-haut*) on the further side of the town, at the summit of the hill. By the latter gate, which serves as its bell-tower, stands the collegial church, founded in 1168 by Anséric II. Viollet-le-Duc, who restored the church in the middle of the last century, was enthusiastic in its praise, considering the western gallery, which rests on consoles and a single slender column, as unique in France. Although the early gothic architect, who appears to have been trained in the traditional idiom of the Burgundian romanesque, has revealed some uncertainties in his use of the new style, nevertheless this little church is a splendid example of the nascent gothic, with its fine, sharply contoured mouldings, the surety of articulation in its main members, the clarity of design in the rose window of the west end and the beautifully carved doorway, and the decorative motif of marguerites of the façade. Moreover, in the quite magnificent carvings of its sixteenth-century oak pews Montréal has furnishings worthy of their gothic setting. These are the work of the brothers

Rigolley, and they must be ranked among the finest examples of sculpture in wood in all Burgundy. The end of one stall depicts the scene in the carpenter's shop in Nazareth. Above, the artists have represented themselves in an interval from their labour; seated at a table, one brother offers the other some wine from a generous *pot de bon bourgogne*. On the left of the choir is a beautiful retable in alabaster, excellent English work of the fifteenth century.

Likewise at St-Seine-l'Abbaye, the church, which may date from as early as 1209, has remained true to the romanesque Martinian tradition of two-storeyed building, but here we find an intrusion from outside the province, in the gallery running below the high windows of the nave, a feature which, originating in Normandy, was introduced from neighbouring Champagne. We shall find this gallery again in the cathedrals of Nevers (1213) and Auxerre (1215) and in the beautiful Notre-Dame of Dijon (1230). If, as seems probable, the date of the rebuilt church of this ancient abbey, which was founded in 534, was indeed 1209, then St-Seine-l'Abbaye was the first church in Burgundy to adopt this high internal gallery, which was to become an important element in the structure of the larger gothic churches of the province.

But the masterpiece of this type of church is undoubtedly the beautiful Notre-Dame of St-Père-sous-Vézelay, which, small though it is, remains, from the elegance of its architecture and the excellence of its sculpture, a jewel of the thirteenth-century gothic. The west front is preceded by a deep porch of two open lateral bays, an excellent example of its kind from the early fourteenth century, restored by Viollet-le-Duc. The voussoirs of the central opening, above the trefoiled arch, are carved with a representation of the *Last Judgement*. Behind the crocketed pinnacles of the porch rise the gable of the façade, above the deep-recessed arch enclosing the beautiful rose window, and to the left of the gable-end the lofty tower, where high up, beneath gargoyles, sculptured angels sound their trumpets of stone. The mastery of the architect is shown in this tower, built as it is over the first bay of the left aisle (one angle thus supported by the nave pier), by the perfection of its proportions, and the inventiveness of the design. The topmost storey, beneath the short, modern spire, passes most successfully from a square to an octagon, the vertical line being continued in pairs of slim columns. To the purist it may be found a fault in this beautiful building that the gable of the façade serves no structural purpose, the roof of the nave only rising to the height of the top of the recessed central arch.

The elegance and technical virtuosity of the architecture are equalled by the beauty of the sculpture, both without and within the church. In Notre-Dame of St-Père we may see how in Burgundy the romanesque tradition of carving was maintained at a high level in pre-Sluterian sculpture, that of St-Père being executed about 1250. The floral capitals and the corbels of the nave reveal the characteristic Burgundian robustness, the firmness of outline and the vigour, the sap of the vegetal forms. Much of the sculpture has suffered from the ravages of time and the iconoclasm of men; the central doorway, for example, has lost its tympanum, statues and carving on the voussoirs, the north portal alone retaining in its tympanum a good *Crucifixion*. But it is the statues on the western gable that excite our profoundest admiration. Eight figures of saints in echelon ascend to the seated figure of God the Father, crowned by two graceful kneeling angels; on the left are the Virgin Mary, St Peter, St Andrew and St James; to the right stand the Magdalen, St Paul, St John and, possibly, an Evangelist. Directly below the benign figure of God, his right hand raised in blessing, is a remarkable statue, seemingly in the round, of a youthful, almost boy-like, St Stephen. The Marys are supported by the two large heads of resignedly subservient grotesques. This magnificent group which, it is conjectured, served as a model for the distinctly inferior western façade of Ste-Madeleine of Vézelay, marks one of the high points, with the carving on the west front of the cathedral of Auxerre, in the gothic church sculpture of Burgundy.

In the interior of the church we find, instead of the familiar flat apse, a deambulatory and radial chapels; and again the two storeys, with gallery beneath the high windows, as in St-Seine. Two other notable churches show similar features: Notre-Dame in Cluny, built in the thirteenth century by the powerful abbots of the place, and that, contemporaneous with it, of Benedictine nuns at Rougemont, near Montbard, both of which contain some good sculpture.

A further type of romanesque church—that known as 'blind-nave' from having no high windows lighting the nave from above the aisles—is found to have its gothic counterparts throughout Burgundy. Many of these, restricted in size and sometimes rather squat in form, were built as parish churches in the country villages and small towns. However, from this type of church building has derived a form of gothic which, as at Vermenton in Yonne, is singularly successful by reason of—strange as it seems—the brilliant effect of its light. Here the first two bays, of the late twelfth century, are two-storeyed; from this point the aisles have been planned a century later to rise to the height of the nave, thus resulting in a 'church-hall', arresting in its grace and abundance of light. Vermenton is perhaps unique in Burgundy, and seems again to betray an influence from across the border in Champagne.

The best known of gothic churches in Burgundy is doubtless the admirable Notre-Dame de Dijon, so much has been written of it by art historians, travellers and by literary men, such as the neo-catholic J.-K. Huysmans, who described its highly original façade in the over-ripe prose of *L'Oblat*. Citizens of Dijon, perhaps understandably in their provincial pride, have seen in Notre-Dame 'all the purity and originality of the Burgundian ogival style of the thirteenth century'. This is a mistake. Certain gothic churches in Burgundy do reveal a remarkable family likeness and suggest by their build, their carriage and physiognomy a common ancestry. This filiation is borne out not only by the analysis of comparative architectural anatomy but also by well attested historical facts.

In 1212 the bishop of Nevers, Guillaume de Saint-Lazare, rebuilt the choir of his cathedral which had been destroyed by fire. Although this choir was reconstructed later after another calamity, it is generally believed that it resembled that which we see today in St-Etienne of Auxerre, which was begun a little after 1215 by Bishop Guillaume de Seignelay, and completed by 1234. A few years later was built the church of St-Martin in Clamecy. These three buildings, all to the west and north-west of the ancient duchy of Burgundy, showed close structural affinities: all were of three storeys, had a gallery above the triforium and below the high windows, possessed similar proportions, the same slender height, the same elegance. Their determining influences came from across the borders— to the north from Champagne, to the north-west from the Ile-de-France. Historically, from the eleventh century the counties of Nevers and Auxerre were linked, and the viscounts of Clamecy were of the family of the counts of Nevers. In 1225 was begun the beautiful church of Notre-Dame at Semur-en-Auxois, and here again the triple elevation in the choir, the upper gallery (but no triforium in the nave), and especially the slender aerial elegance, reproduced the structural characteristics of Auxerre. While these influences were felt to the west of the duchy, in its heart, in Dijon, they appeared also, with the construction of Notre-Dame and the Sainte-Chapelle.

In 1187 the Capetian duke of Burgundy Hugh III had granted the mayor and aldermen of Dijon municipal rights of 'the kind enjoyed by the commune of Soissons', and some decades later the municipality resolved to rebuild in more fitting style their official church of Notre-Dame-du-Marché. The son of Duke Hugh III, another Hugh, married in 1229 Yolande, daughter of Robert, Count of Dreux. The *chantiers* of the cathedral of Laon had become in the early thirteenth century a school of gothic architects and masons, from which had gone out the builders of Saint-Léger of Soissons and Saint-Yved of Braisne, the latter church the family burial place of the counts of Dreux. In 1230 the city council of Dijon appealed to an architect trained in this school to design and build their Notre-Dame, and thus set in train the construction of this masterpiece of the gothic style in Burgundy and a model to the whole of western Europe. All these churches have structural elements in common: a triple elevation, a lanter-tower at the crossing, the gallery above the triforium, an external gallery around the chevet at the level of the high windows, thus passing through the buttresses, and a small hood capping the head of those same buttresses. The parental likeness is striking: Notre-Dame de Dijon is clearly related by birth to these churches of Champagne and the Ile-de-France.

The architect of Notre-Dame was presented with the problems arising from the restriction of the space at his disposal. From the Place E.-Renan and the Rue de la Chouette we can see the solutions that he arrived at—in the remarkable façade and in the refined logic of the chevet, where the choir and apse are clearly differentiated from the transept, with throughout an admirable disposition of the stonework and the intervals of space. The west front is unique, the flat surface being relieved by the deep recesses of the porch, seen through the triple opening of perfectly proportioned arches, by two storeys of arcades unsurpassed for the elegance of their slender supporting columns, as well as by three wide bands of sculptured frieze. The excellence of the carving here is proof of the continuance of the high tradition of Burgundian sculpture. Between decorative panels of powerful, deep-cut leafage and formalized floral design figures project in the manner of gargoyles. These depict animals, both from the everyday world and that of the mediaeval bestiary, and human beings, some of whom hold masks, each human face possessing its own individual character, some realistic to the point of caricature, others given a natural expression or even idealized, grave and gay, elderly and smilingly youthful. For the most part these are modern, and they have deceived many, including the erudite Huysmans. This 'copying'—for it surely must not be called counterfeiting—raises questions not adequately answered either by Prosper Mérimée or by Viollet-le-Duc. (In restoration the former thought that the aim should be to revive the spirit; the latter was content with nothing less than the letter.) Within the porch, on the jambs and *jumeau* and in the archivolts, the sculpture was brutally disfigured during the excesses of the Revolution.

At Notre-Dame the familiar Burgundian porch itself will be seen to form an integral part of the building. This is contrary to a prevalent practice in Burgundy, where the narthex-porch was frequently an addition, as we see at Semur-en-Auxois, St-Père-sous-Vézelay, Pontigny and Notre-Dame of Beaune, or in some beautiful examples in smaller churches, such as those at Escolives, Civry, Vignes, Savigny-en-Terre-Plaine or Ste-Sabine (Côte-d'Or). However, it seems that those of

Rougemont and the curious structure of St-Albain, near Tournus, were contemporary with their churches.

From the entrance of Notre-Dame, especially on a sunny morning when the central door is open, the interior of the church presents, by reason of the height and narrowness of the nave and choir, with its polygonal apse, a singular lightness and elegance. The nave arcades are formed of round pillars, which are surmounted by capitals of boldly-cut crockets (a form commonly found in Burgundian gothic churches), and the soaring arches at the crossing spring from graceful piers, composed of a central core and a cluster of slim columns, each distinctly articulated, which rise up unimpeded to where capital and shallow abaci mark the springing of the vaults, and then flow on in crisply defined mouldings and delicately rounded shafts. It is this uninterrupted, untrammelled flowing of vertical lines, bending gracefully to meet in keystone of arch or vault, that draws our eye continuously upward and contributes to the illusion that the sexpartite vaulting is suspended in light and air, rather than materially supported. The effect is admirable; our intellectual awareness of the architect's mastery of structural composition is momentarily withheld in our immediate response of recognition and pleasure to the majesty of his conception, the perfection of his achievement in this aerial, etherial grace.

The illumination, from which much of our first impression derives, comes from the high windows of the nave (beneath which, and above the triforium, runs the Champenois upper gallery), the lantern at the crossing, the windows of the transept, and those of the choir, where the triforium wall was pierced in the seventeenth century with eye-windows. In the five lancet windows of the left transept is some stained glass contemporaneous with the building. The tendency of these gothic builders to construct churches where the stonework was reduced to a structural minimum—to a mere framework of masonry—aimed at an ever greater diffusion of light, filtering through stained-glass windows, the art of the glazier reaching a high perfection at this period. This development culminated in St Louis' Sainte-Chapelle in Paris, which resembles a *châsse*, a reliquary of coloured enamels, or an ornate Victorian conservatory, where the light penetrated its walls of glass in an extraordinary chromatic richness of yellows, reds, browns, greens, blues and purples. About 1240 Hugh IV and Yolande of Burgundy began their Sainte-Chapelle in the ducal palace of Dijon. This building, which was wantonly destroyed by the Revolutionaries, became later under Philip the Good the meeting place for his celebrated Order of the Golden Fleece. A painting, once hanging in the Charterhouse of Champmol and today in the Louvre, depicting the *Presentation in the Temple*, shows that the chapel reproduced the Champenois features of Notre-Dame and that it surpassed the latter in its illumination. But undoubtedly the Burgundian church which carried furthest these later gothic developments in structure and window-lighting, while retaining the influence of Champagne, was the beautiful church of St-Thibault-en-Auxois.

The liberality of Duke Robert II of Burgundy and his wife Agnes, the daughter of St Louis, ensured the magnificence of this priory church, rebuilt in part at the end of the thirteenth and beginning of the next century to contain the relics of St Thibault of Provins. In 1686 the nave and transept collapsed, and all that remains today of this remarkable edifice—itself evidence of the inherent dangers from the attenuating tendencies of some gothic builders—are the sculptured porch, once the entrance to the transept, and the lofty apsidal chapel of the choir. The height of the four-storeyed apse is arresting; and the elevation is accentuated by the extreme slimness of the columnar mouldings, a pronounced vertical line being given by the single columns, as slender as a conductor's baton, which carry the eye irresistibly upwards from the blind arcading at ground level, beyond lower windows, triforium and high windows, right to the key of the vault, some ninety feet above the floor. Here again the presence of two galleries reveals the influence of architects of Champagne, the gallery of the second storey running between a highly decorative double trellis of stonework, and that above passing behind the parapet of the elegant triforium. The admirable openwork of the second storey is clearly modelled on the choir of Troyes cathedral. The effect of this sheer verticality, this perpendicular armature of stone, however impressive it is as an architectural *tour de force*, and however beautiful the choir must once have looked, when it glowed with all the richness of colour of its mediaeval glass, nevertheless may give rise to a sense of inappropriateness in the minds of some visitors. And if this feeling stems from an awareness of the structural fragility of the building, it also comes from a recognition of an aesthetic inadequacy. Unlike the architect of St Louis' Sainte-Chapelle, the builder of St-Thibault might be thought to have failed in attempting too much.

It appears that the sculpture on the door of St-Thibault, which is almost unique in Burgundy in being practically intact, comes from two periods. The tympanum and archivolts were carved about 1260 and represent scenes from the life of the Virgin Mary (the *Dormition, Assumption* and *Coronation*) and the figures of the *Wise and Foolish Virgins*. Towards 1310 were added the five statues, four of which, unusual at so early a period in church sculpture, seem to be protraits from life of the church's benefactor, Duke Robert II, his son Hugh V, the Duchess Agnes, and the Bishop of Autun, Hugh d'Arcy, the tutor of the young Hugh. On the *trumeau* is the figure of St Thibault. In addition, within the church are some most interesting examples of gothic carving: a late fourteenth-century statue of the young St Thibault in painted wood, two retables (also in wood) illustrating the life of the saint, and in the apse a Crucifix of the same period. On the right of the choir is the fine tomb of the founder of the priory, Hugh of Thil, from a century earlier. That of his wife has unfortunately suffered considerable damage.

If, then, this Champenois style of gothic church with three storeys and an upper gallery is found widely diffused in Burgundy, it is largely from the success and celebrity of the builders of Notre-Dame of Dijon, which undoubtedly has been the model for other churches. Among them is the cathedral of St-Vincent at Chalon-sur-Saône, which has romanesque arcades in the nave, but is gothic in its apse and upper storeys, being rebuilt from about 1260 onwards and incorporating the characteristic gallery. Similarly, the rebuilding of Notre-Dame of Auxonne led to the gallery finding its place in the nave, but not—and this applies equally to the reconstructed St-Bénigne

F

of Dijon—in the choir and apse. At St-Bénigne, the romanesque tower having collapsed in 1272, the abbot Hugues d'Arc set about the rebuilding of his church. The choir and apse, of harmonious proportions, were finished by 1280, but the raising of the nave continued well into the fourteenth century and, although it too is well proportioned, it is lacking in distinctive decoration.

It was the attraction to the church of St-Gènes at Flavigny-sur-Ozerain of pilgrims, who came in large numbers to the town, drawn by the sanctuary of Ste-Reine in the Carolingian crypt of the nearby abbey of St-Pierre, that brought about its deviation from the type of Notre-Dame de Dijon. The relics of the virgin Reine, a young Gallic Christian who was held to have suffered martyrdom at Alesia for having refused to marry the Roman governor Olibrius, had been brought to Flavigny as early as 864. It was in order to accommodate these crowds that in the fifteenth and early sixteenth centuries the ecclesiastical authorities found it necessary to modify considerably the beautiful thirteenth-century church, by constructing wide galleries, with a wooden balustrade, over the aisles and west end of the building, and by the erection of a rood-loft. St-Gènes remains unique of its kind in Burgundy. Of considerable interest are the late fifteenth-century stalls, several with amusing carved figures on the arm-rests. And in the last chapel on the right is the exquisite *Angel of the Annunciation*, discovered in a mutilated state in 1938, and now recognized as a masterpiece of late Burgundian gothic statuary (fifteenth century?).

Although Bishop Guillaume de Seignelay, who was an admirer of the new, the 'French style' of architecture, began the rebuilding of his cathedral church of St-Etienne of Auxerre in 1215, progress was slow; by the year 1234 the choir, indeed, had been completed, but it was not until about 1400 that the nave and aisles, the southern transept and the chapels were finished. Work finally seems to have come to an end about 1560 with the raising of the north tower of the western façade, leaving the south tower unachieved. In the decoration of the façade of St-Etienne we find one of the earliest uses of a form of arch that became peculiarly associated with later French gothic—

the ogee (reversed arch, *accolade*). Paradoxically, however, if we follow the theory of M. Camille Enlart, we shall have to attribute this style of arch not to French but to English architects. What is clear is that from 1358 to 1370, when the work on St-Etienne was progressing, the English were in possession of the city of Auxerre during the fighting of the Hundred Years War. The cathedral suffered much damage during the Wars of Religion, but was mercifully spared the worst excesses of the Revolution. Within, seen on a sunny day, St-Etienne is a miracle of light, of lightness and soaring grace, a splendid example of the structural elegance of French thirteenth-century gothic at its best. And the church, too, is fortunate in the remains of its stained glass, contemporary with its early building and, like it, revealing the influence of Champagne, in this case the workshop of the glaziers of Troyes. Of the windows at St-Etienne M. C. Oursel writes: 'This church is alone in Burgundy in offering, despite grave damage, the most beautiful collection of stained glass and one of the finest decorative schemes of this art in France.'

The sculpture of the western doorways of St-Etienne d'Auxerre is outstanding in quality. In the tympanum of the central doorway Christ is shown with the kneeling figures of the Virgin Mary and St John; on the lintel is represented the *Last Judgement* and on the jambs appear the *Wise and the Foolish Virgins*. To the sides, under canopies, are pairs of seated figures, now decapitated, and thought to depict either *Kings and Queens of Judah* or, more likely, *Prophets and Sibyls*. Particularly beautiful is the carving in low relief of the panels beneath; in these medallions it seems that the arts of the miniaturist and the glass painter have joined to inform the sculptor's chisel. Furthermore, a close study of this carving in St-Etienne reveals—as has been frequently remarked—how close were the links at this period between gothic sculptors in France and Italy; we think of the contemporary carving in Northern Italy or of that of Orvieto. Of particular interest is the treatment of the nude in the figures of the medallions representing the *Creation and Fall of Adam and Eve* on the north doorway. Noteworthy, too, in these scenes is the sculptor's attention to the disposition of the hands—those, for example, of God, when he touches Adam, or where at the birth of Eve, with an almost feminine delicacy, he gathers up his dress; also the hands, curiously poised, of the angels above. Remarkable likewise are the representations in low relief of the *Story of Joseph*, the *Loves of David and Bathsheba*, the *Prodigal Son*, and in high relief the figures of the *Liberal Arts* and, unfortunately mutilated, the *Judgement of Solomon*. The doorway to the south transept shows no falling off in the portrayal, powerfully executed in the second half of the fourteenth century, of *Scenes from the Life of St Stephen*. It would appear that a veritable school of sculptors was working in Auxerre on the sculpture and decorative carving of the façade for something more than a hundred years from the middle of the thirteenth century.

The visitor to Auxerre will not fail to see the early examples of fresco in St-Etienne and in the crypt of the neighbouring abbey of St-Germain, founded in the ninth century, and once famous for its mediaeval school of philosophy. The earlier of the two frescoes of St-Etienne, which dates from the last quarter of the eleventh century, depicts Christ, the rod of iron of the Apocalypse in His hand, mounted on a white charger; four angels, also on horseback, accompany Him in rectangles formed by the arms of the cross. This painting is unique of its type in France. Another fresco in the crypt, of the thirteenth century, shows Christ with the four evangelists. The Carolingian frescoes in St-Germain d'Auxerre are numbered among the oldest surviving in France. A series in faded red and yellow ochres represent *Scenes from the Life of St Stephen*, and were painted about 850. The crypt here is itself full of architectural and antiquarian interest.

Another distinguished example of the thirteenth-century gothic churches of Burgundy is Notre-Dame of Semur-en-Auxois, which was much admired by Viollet-le-Duc, who worked on its restoration from the 'forties to the 'sixties of last century. From the Place Notre-Dame the two square towers of the west façade present a somewhat severe aspect above the cavernous fifteenth-century porch. To appreciate fully the skill of these builders of the thirteenth century—work was begun on Notre-Dame about 1225—the church is best seen from the Place de l'Ancienne Comédie, which is gained by the Rue

Notre-Dame, which takes the visitor past the *Porte des Bleds*, where the sculpture, unlike that on the western doorways, has miraculously escaped the destructive attention of the revolutionaries. In three registers, the tympanum relates the *Legend of St Thomas*, the apostle of the Indies, and, although the figures are perhaps overcrowded, the carving has a certain fresh vigour; that on the voussoirs possesses charm and even elegance. From the *place* the mastery, the surety of touch, of these gothic architects is evident in the logical arrangement of the structural elements: the high choir and buttresses rising above the roofs of the clearly marked chevet, and the pronounced transept, with, at the crossing, the octagonal tower and spire.

Notre-Dame of Semur has been called 'a cathedral in miniature', and the interior of the church bears out the description in the beauty of the proportions of the nave, the remarkable choir flanked by a double nave, and the deambulatory and three radial chapels. The carving of the floral capitals and the human-headed corbels is of a remarkable quality; particularly beautiful is the large painted boss, forming the key of the choir vault, which represents the *Crowning of the Virgin*. In the apsidal chapel is some thirteenth-century glass, restored by Viollet-le-Duc, and in the chapels off the left-hand aisle are colourful fifteenth-century windows, presented by the guilds of butchers and drapers and illustrating their trades. From late in the same century is the *Mise au tombeau* in an adjoining chapel, by a follower of Claus Sluter.

These *Entombments*, which became such a feature of Burgundian church statuary, are all of the post-Sluterian period. Perhaps their origin goes back to the romanesque epoch, to such figures as adorned the tomb of St-Lazare, now in the Musée Rolin at Autun. Some of the best known *Mises au tombeau* are in Nevers, Tonnerre, Châtillon-sur-Seine and Dijon (Hôpital de Saint-Esprit and St-Michel). These were usually painted, as indeed were the tombs carved by Sluter and his school, and the figure of Nicodemus habitually was portrayed as a gorgeously dressed negro. These homely, stocky figures, most often of painted wood, are found everywhere in the churches of Burgundy, as, for example, at Brancion. Early in the gothic period statues of saints became detached from church walls and appeared free-standing in churches. The Cistercians, austere to the point of puritanism in church decoration, made the exception of permitting the presence of the figure of the Madonna, customarily with her Child—such is the charming *Madonna of Fontenay*. As the thirteenth century progressed, the smiling Virgins gave way to the more melancholy type of the fourteenth; after the time of Sluter the folds of the drapery became more voluminous and heavier, in a style almost baroque. Examples of these Virgins may be seen at the Musée Rolin, at the Hôpital de Moutiers-St-Jean, the churches of Joigny, Châteauneuf, Meilly-sur-Rouvres, Auxonne and elsewhere. At Rouvres-en-Plaine, near Dijon, as befitting a fief of the Capetian dukes of Burgundy, the beautiful twelfth-thirteenth-century church is almost a museum of statuary. It is interesting to compare there the strange, but excellent, earlier statue of *St John the Baptist* with the later examples from the school of Sluter.

Wall painting, as one would expect from its nature, has suffered from the passing of time, as may be seen in St-Bénigne of Dijon, Notre-Dame of Beaune and the cathedral of Autun. In the little church of Brancion, however, where the dukes of Burgundy possessed the nearby castle, the ruins of which we may still visit, have been preserved some most interesting mural paintings by an anonymous artist of the fourteenth century. With the celebrated *Danse macabre* of the little country church at La Ferté-Loupière we are already well into the period of the International Gothic Style, which will always be associated with the era of the Grand-Dukes of the West.

CHAPTER X

The Rabutinades of Bussy-Rabutin

UNLIKE MOST FRENCH châteaux, which are built on sites as
if chosen expressly to set off to the best advantage the perfection
of their individual beauties, the château of Bussy-Rabutin lies
withdrawn and hidden, encompassed by its woods. It stands at
the mouth of a narrow valley, pressed in upon on three sides,
almost submerged, by the magnificent growth of trees; the
remaining side forms an open terrace, a balustraded balcony,
which overlooks the brown-tiled roofs of the village of Bussy-le-
Grand below and away to the undulating hills beyond. The
countryside is some of the most delightful in Burgundy; a landscape of compact hills and secluded valleys, of woods and
streams and fertile meadows, of hill-top towns and villages—
Alise-Ste-Reine, with its great statue of the Gaulish chief
Vercingetorix; Flavigny-sur-Ozerain, with the remains of the
Carolingian abbey; and Semur-en-Auxois of the pepper-pot
towers, perhaps the most romantically situated town in all
Burgundy. To the north-west, some seven miles away as the
crow flies, is the abbey of Fontenay. This is the heart of the
country of the ancient Gauls, here where they made their last
stand against the Roman armies under Julius Caesar, and where
their survivors lived on, maintaining their Gallic qualities
intact, and finding their lineal descendant in Roger de Rabutin,
Comte de Bussy.

The entrance by which the visitor approaches the château
today is not that of former times. Leaving the road that runs
alongside a small stream, the Rabutin, we take the village
street of Rue du Château (curiously the name of the village, not
the street), which leads up between cottages and farmyard
entrances to an unimposing covered gateway. Since 1929
Bussy-Rabutin has been the property of the State, and visitors
are obliged to wait until a party is formed, to be conducted

round the château by an official. From where we stand by the
estate office the château is hidden from view by lofty lime trees
of great age, whose spreading branches sweep the ground, and
by an ivy-covered wall. Following our guide through a door
in this wall, we descend some steps to find ourselves facing the
cylindrical tower at the northern angle of the château; to the
right is a wide terrace which occupies the space between the
rear, the north-western façade, of the château and the stone
balustrade that terminates abruptly the platform on which it
stands. The terrace is laid out in ornamental garden beds and
gravel paths, with shrubs and box hedges in the French style.
The stone of the balustrade is caught up and repeated in the
stone of statues and follies, and in that of an open conduit of
water which supplies the central pool and is fed from a little
cascade in the enclosing wall through which we entered. One
is first struck, rather than by the architecture of the house, by
the size, the luxuriance, of the trees of the encroaching woods, a
backcloth of great beauty, whose variegated greens are picked
up and reflected in the still waters of the moat, and which acts
as a chromatic contrast, a foil of verdure and freshness to the
warm rose-apricot of the stonework.

As our party is conducted round the south-western flank of
the building, where the woods almost overhang the moat, we
feel as if we are intruders, interlopers, trespassers on the privacy
of the former owner, whose spirit remains so strongly attached
to the place. It is only when we pass the southern round tower
(the towers mark the cardinal points of the compass) and come
out into the open that we can conceive what was in the mind of
Le Nôtre, who planned the landscape setting of Bussy-Rabutin.
There is nothing grand about it, nothing ostentatious; rather
it is a sylvan setting of midsummer charm and grace. An
amphitheatre formed by the woods is carpeted with lawn; two
groups of statuary, the Rape of Proserpine and the figure of
Jupiter the Thunderer, are set beneath the foliage; flights of
stone steps lead down the gentle slope to the Louis XIII bridge
which, crossing the moat, gives access to the court of honour.
A certain romantic elegance, not feudal grandeur, is the key-
note. It was from this side, with this view of the château, that
the rightful proprietor, Roger de Rabutin, entered Bussy-

Rabutin, his principal country seat in Burgundy. And it is from this vantage point that the visitor today can best appreciate the architecture of the building.

The original fortified castle dates from probably as early as the twelfth century, and of mediaeval work there remain today the four cardinal round towers with their conical caps, the two nearer ones (over the chapel on the left and the 'donjon' on the right) being surmounted later with lanterns. The curtain wall on the side facing us was removed, possibly at the time of Henry II, when the two arcaded wings which join the towers to the *corps de logis* were built. These are of that charming amalgam by which French taste modified the style of the Italian renaissance, with its classical proportion and delicate low-relief carving, which was introduced into France by François Ier. Above doors in these arcades are two bas-reliefs in marble. One represents Ste Jeanne de Chantal, the intimate and disciple of St Francis de Sales and the grandmother of Mme de Sévigné and of Comte Roger de Rabutin's first wife, Gabrielle de Toulongeon. The other medallion is of the great Colbert, carved in 1706 by the sculptor Coysevox. The main body of the building was begun by Léonor de Rabutin, Lord of Epiry, and completed by his son Roger de Bussy-Rabutin, and dates from between 1610 and 1665. It is remarkable for the beauty of its apricot-coloured stone, the harmony of its proportions—the elegance, which combines both strength and a lightness that allows it to support with ease its high roof, being achieved by the harmonious distribution of its openings, the perfect placing and relationship of the main doorway and the fenestration with the intervening niches. It is the embodiment of good taste, of nothing too much, of clarity both of thought and feeling, of a joyous recognition and acceptance of what this life has to offer —it is peculiarly French.

The family of Rabutin, one of the most ancient and noble in Burgundy, distinguished for their deeds of prowess, their literary bent and a certain ebullience of spirit, left their mark on the French language, by lending their name to the coining of three words, which figure in Littré's nineteenth-century *Dictionary*—'*Rabutinade:* a witticism in the manner of Bussy-Rabutin. *Etym:* Rabutin, a relative of Mme de Sévigné.

Rabutinage: something concerning the family of Rabutin. *Rabutinement:* in the manner of Rabutin, truly Rabutin.' In this Littré is possibly not quite correct; the words may well be older than Roger de Bussy-Rabutin. Who was this singular man, whose reputation (or, to speak more accurately, whose notoriety) has been eclipsed by the fame of his cousin Mme de Sévigné?

He himself writes of the birthplace of his family: 'In the county of Charollais stands a great wood called the forest of Rabutin, in the middle of which there is a kind of marsh where one sees the remains of an old castle which one names still the château of Rabutin.' It could be the beginning of a fairy tale. The first of the race of which there is written record is Mayeul, who held the fiefs of Rabutin, Epiry and Chaseu, whose name appears in a document of 1118. Later the family, with its numerous bastards (*donnés*, 'given facts', as the Burgundians indulgently called them), all of whom proudly retained their patronymic, possessed estates throughout Burgundy, notably Bourbilly and Bussy-le-Grand. The château of Bourbilly, later the property of Mme de Sévigné, came into the family in 1467 by the marriage of Hugues de Rabutin, councillor and chamberlain to Charles VIII, to Jeanne, the legitimated daughter of Claude de Montagu, last prince of the royal house of Burgundy. A window in the church of Sully, near Autun, commemorates this alliance. It is likely that Hugues' father, Amé de Rabutin, who was killed in 1472 on the bridge of Beauvais, fighting for the Burgundians against the troops of Louis XI, was the first of the family to *rabutine*. His raillery and persiflage were said to have affected even his adversaries. This was the Amé de Rabutin whom Philippe de Commines praised as a 'very gentle knight for his fine and polished language (*ses beaux et aornés mots*), the wisest, most courteous and pleasant that one has known in Burgundy or knew anywhere else'. The use of *beaux et aornés mots* and this spirit of raillery were of the essence of the *rabutinades* of his descendant, Bussy-Rabutin. Hugues de Rabutin's legitimate son Claude, inheriting his grandfather's gifts, endeared himself to Louis XII, whom the chroniclers of the time say he 'governed'. A bastard of Hugues, Sébastien, was a favourite of

Henry II, a Knight of Malta (the family had a permanent stake in the Order) and a great hunter, who is reported to have cleared the wolves from the forest of Milly—Lamartine, three hundred years later, might have had good reason to bless him. King Henry regarded Sébastien so highly as to hang his portrait in the Salle des Suisses at Fontainebleau.

Another of Hugues' bastards, François, showed, besides his war-like exploits, a literary turn of mind. He read the Latin historians in translation, holding particularly in reverence Caesar, and agreeing wholeheartedly with the 'divine praises' accorded that martial author for the reason 'that the same hand that had fought his enemies wrote the *Commentaries*'. With François de Rabutin the literary side of the family found its first practical exponent. He knew no Latin, this 'poor gentleman and simple soldier' (as he described himself), and he felt his French to be shaky; but with the advice and assistance of some Parisian *littérateurs*, whom he assiduously frequented when not fighting, he produced in 1555 his *Commentaires* on the wars of Charles V and Henry II in which he himself had participated. When a kindly helping hand translated these into Latin, with the title *Commentarii de novissimo bello Gallico*, he felt his tribute to his hero Caesar was complete. In François de Rabutin an important side of the Burgundian character is revealed, a characteristic that has persisted throughout the centuries—an unequivocal down-to-earth realism. His expressed desire was to write his commentaries 'baldly, as things had happened'— that is, as he himself had witnessed them. He may have recalled Commines; but perhaps he was unaware of St Bernard of Clairvaux' description of a wise man as 'one to whom all things taste even as they really are'. François' descendant, Bussy-Rabutin, was to discover to his detriment that some things are better not written 'baldly, as they have happened'. They are better not written at all; not even spoken; and certainly not sung.

As we approach the generation of Roger de Bussy-Rabutin and Marie de Rabutin-Chantal (later Mme de Sévigné), other characteristics of the family, further *rabutinages*, disclose themselves. Gui de Rabutin, although already married, carried off by force his mistress, although she too was married. His son,

Christophe II de Rabutin-Chantal, in contradistinction to his father was known for his gentleness, his *douceur*. A soldier like all his forebears, he was noted for his gallantries, was something of a poet, and following the fortunes of Henry IV, was appointed governor of Semur-en-Auxois and gentleman of the bedchamber to the King. This charm of manner and mildness, we are told by Bussy-Rabutin, 'brought down on his head some quarrels with the brutal, who did not believe one could be brave without being a braggart. But he disabused them with great thrusts of his sword.' This gentle knight fought eighteen duels and his body was a latticework of scars. In 1592 he married the twenty-year-old Jeanne Frémyot (the future Ste Jeanne Chantal), the daughter of the second President of the Parlement of Burgundy. Christophe henceforth forewent gallantry, 'even during his absences on military service'. He was killed while hunting near his château of Bourbilly in 1600 at the age of thirty-seven, leaving four children, two of whom are of particular interest to us, the only son, Celse-Bénigne, and his sister Françoise, whom her saintly mother married to the Comte Antoine de Toulongeon, 'who was able to offer her a decent lodging'.

When the young Celse-Bénigne de Rabutin-Chantal appeared at court in 1617 he is said to have caused a sensation. He was imposing in stature and charming in manner; his skill at arms was out of the ordinary, he was ready with the '*beaux et aornés mots*', he was prodigal with the money he had (or did not have), and 'he danced with unparalleled grace'. He was a Rabutin, and he *rabutined*. Everyone fell under his charm. His mother looked on, between works of charity, with admiration and fear, and called in the assistance of Francis de Sales. Remonstration being of no avail, Jeanne Chantal, activated with a worldly prudence worthy of a Saint Teresa, found him a bride, Marie Coulanges, the daughter of an immensely rich farmer of the gabelles, Philippe de Coulanges. No Rabutin attended the wedding; for them it was a *mésalliance*, despite the fact that the girl was the 'Saint's' choice. Celse-Bénigne shared the family pride, but he had already gone through a sizeable share of his wife's money, before, fleeing from the rigour of Richelieu's decrees against duelling, he was killed on the Ile de Ré, fighting against the English of Buckingham. This was on 20th July 1627. He had combated for six hours, had three horses killed under him, and received twenty-seven wounds before he succumbed. He left one surviving child, a daughter aged seventeen months, Marie, afterwards Mme de Sévigné. '*Il etait joli, mon père*', she said later.

Of a cadet branch of the family was another François, Comte de Bussy and Baron d'Epiry, who was said not to have lacked good sense and even wisdom, although these sterling virtues were threatened by his being 'somewhat hotheaded', and nothing if not obstinate. His motto reveals the man: *Et si omnes, ego non*, which, in his case, may be roughly rendered, 'If all are for it, count me out'. His eldest son, Léonor, was gentleman-in-ordinary to the King, representative of the nobility of Autun at the Estates-General, captain of the royal cavalry and Lieutenant of the King in the Nivernais. In 1608 he married Diane du Cugnac, daughter of the Marquis of Dampierre. The eldest of their surviving children was Roger, our hero, who was born at Epiry in April 1618; his godfather was the Duke of Bellegarde, Marshal of France and Governor of Burgundy. At his birth his 'aunt' Jeanne Chantal, looking into the future, declared that he would be the saint of the family, which utterance suggests that either all historical reports of his career are untrue or that the gift of prophecy is not necessarily among the graces vouchsafed saints. Writing of his father, Bussy-Rabutin says, 'He was well educated, and he knew more than was necessary to know for a man of war.' For the rest, a person of some address, a friend of poets and men of letters, a lover of pleasure, choleric at times, yet of a temperament that was essentially sanguine—in short, a typical Rabutin. His advice to his son was simple and terse: fear God, hold honour higher than life, serve the King.

Bussy-Rabutin was an exemplary pupil, first with the Jesuits of Autun, subsequently at the Collège de Clermont, today Louis-le-Grand, which he attended shortly before Molière. By the time he was twelve he had an excellent grasp of Latin, and at thirteen he was so advanced as to be entered for philosophy without having to take the preliminary rhetoric. At sixteen his father sent him to Lorraine in nominal command of his regiment. After a brief return to the Académie de Benjamin, his military life began in earnest. It was to continue for twenty-five years. He now entered, too, into his intimate relations with women, which were to last all his life.

On the death of Celse-Bénigne Rabutin-Chantal in 1627, Count Léonor, as the senior representative of the Rabutin family, had claimed wardship of the infant Marie, but this was disputed by her maternal relations, the Coulanges, and the courts decided in their favour. In 1636, when Marie was ten and Bussy-Rabutin eighteen, her Coulanges guardian died, and a family council was convened in Paris to appoint a successor. Here, in his father's stead, attended the young Captain de Bussy-Rabutin, and he saw his cousin for the first time. His advice, to put her in charge of her aunt Mme de Toulongeon, daughter of 'Ste' Jeanne Chantal, was disregarded. In truth, he cared little at this time for this precocious cousin, who was already responding so brilliantly to the tuition of her illustrious preceptors, MM. Ménage and Chapélain, and the chief motive for his intervention was to thwart his father who saw in Marie Rabutin-Chantal, and her large fortune, a most suitable matrimonial match for himself. It was not until eight years later that he was to reverse this opinion entirely. But by that time he was the husband of Gabrielle de Toulongeon and Marie had married at eighteen the Breton Marquis de Sévigné. Then he declared Mme la Marquise to be 'the prettiest girl in the world to be the wife . . . of another'. Moreover, by the time the cousins had met again and discovered with infinite pleasure their common *rabutinage* and their mutual affection (it was indeed a stronger, much deeper feeling), Bussy-Rabutin was well advanced on a career which showed all too plainly that the family strengths and failings were developed in him to an extraordinary degree.

He had served his first campaigns under Prince Henry de Condé (the father of the 'Great Condé') in Burgundy and Picardy, and had made there his first essays in the course of gallantry. In 1638 he was at court, where Cardinal Richelieu appointed him, on his father's retirement, to his colonelcy of infantry. Provoked into a duel, he had fought and killed his opponent. Two years later, while on duty with his regiment at

Moulins, he had accompanied the attractive young Comtesse de Busset, in her husband's absence, back to her château deep in the country and in the depth of winter. While he was thus delightfully engaged in the warming arms of the Countess, his troops got out of hand and committed serious excesses. This coming to the ears of Richelieu, their colonel was summoned to Paris and found himself confined in the Bastille. While thus quartered at the expense of His Majesty for five months, he made the acquaintance of another resident—a long-term one— the celebrated Marshal Bassompierre, who has left us his entertaining *Memoirs*, and from whom Bussy-Rabutin learned much. Bassompierre had been an intimate of the now ageing Queen-Mother Marie de Médicis, and a story is told of their relationship, which illustrates perfectly the freedom of the period. Marie de Médicis had expressed her delight in both Paris and St-Cloud, and being unable to choose between the two places, she had declared that she would like to have one foot in each. 'In that case, Madame,' replied Bassompierre, 'I should not budge from Nanterre.' In 1643, Bussy having married Gabrielle de Toulongeon in the previous year, her dowry permitted him to buy for 12,000 écus a lieutenancy of light cavalry under the Prince of Condé. During the same year his favourite uncle Hugues de Rabutin became Grand Prior of the Knights of Malta, giving Bussy a splendid pied-à-terre in the Temple in Paris; and the death of his father, whom he regretted, brought him the appointment of Lieutenant of the King in the Nivernais. Furthermore, he was now made Councillor of State. Meanwhile, his military exploits had earned him the highest praises of his general, the Great Condé. During 1647 his Countess died, leaving him the father of three daughters. He had loved his wife, in spite of his infidelities.

On the annual cessation of hostilities during the winter months, Bussy-Rabutin had seen much of Mme de Sévigné in Paris. Their discovery of each other was a revelation, and thenceforth they delighted in spending their time together, or, when separated, in an exchange of letters. Their friend in common, the cultivated and charming Corbinelli, declared that they were 'made for each other. You were made,' he said, 'to live side by side.' They were Rabutins to the top of their bent—intelligent, high-spirited, articulate, filled with the *'beaux et aornés mots'*, looking facts straight in the face—and bursting into laughter.

From Les Roches, the Breton estate of the de Sévignés in March 1648, Mme de Sévigné wrote to Bussy-Rabutin, who was with the army under Valence:

> I find you a pleasant *mignon* for not having written to me for two months. Have you forgotten who I am and the rank I hold in the family. Ah, truly, little younger branch, I shall give you cause to remember. . . . You know that I have just completed my confinement, and I find in you no more dis-quiet over the state of my health than if I were still a girl. Well, I inform you, since it will make you furious, that I have been brought to bed of a boy, whom I am going to make hate you with the very milk he sucks, and that I shall have many more, solely for the reason of making them your enemies. You haven't the wit to do as much, you fine producer of girls!
>
> But this is enough to hide my tenderness for you, my dear cousin; naturalness carries the day over what is politic . . ., and I must revert to it to tell you that M. de Sévigné and I love you very much, and that we often speak of the pleasure of being with you. Adieu.

Bussy's reply speaks worlds for the state of their intimacy:

> Valence, 12 Avril 1648
> I will tell you, Madame, that I notice that you adopt a certain way of reproving me that has more of the suggestion of the mistress than the cousin. Take care of what you are embarking on; for, when once I have decided to suffer, I shall want to have the rewards of lovers as well as the asperities. . . . It is true that you are as quick to soften as you are to get cross, and that if your letters begin with 'I find you a pleasant mignon', they finish with, 'we love you, M. de Sévigné and I'.
>
> For the rest, my fair cousin, I don't regale you with the fecundity that you threaten me. Remain content then, if

you will trust in me, with this boy whom you have just produced! It is a very laudable action, and I avow to you that I have not had the wit to do as much: also I envy the happiness of M. de Sévigné more than all the world.

In the summer of 1648 the events which were about to break out in the first Fronde were forgotten for a brief moment while society was diverted by the *affaire Miramion*. Bussy-Rabutin, grand seigneur that he was and avid for military glory, and valuable as had been his services to the state, had seen no recompense for these, save the praises of the Queen-Mother, fair words from Mazarin and the favour of Condé. He was thirty, a widower with three children, and deep in debt. He must look about him for a rich wife. Listening to the suggestions and false reports of a venal monk, he allowed himself to be persuaded that he was looked on with favour by a young widow aged eighteen, the possessor of 400,000 écus, Mme de Miramion, whose confessor the monk was. In the precipitate actions Bussy now took he was supported by Condé, who had already in the single year 1645 abetted three successful elopements. Bussy would emulate the exploit of his ancestor, Gui de Rabutin. Aided by his younger brother, another Guy, and an armed band of gentlemen, he waylaid the coach of Mme de Miramion at the bridge of Saint-Cloud and carried her off, screaming her protests, to the Commanderie de Launay, a stronghold of the Knights of Malta. It was a rape rather than an elopement. 'I understood that she wished me to carry her off,' Bussy afterwards explained, lamely enough. He very soon discovered that indeed she did not. Immediately he knew the true situation, he courteously released her. Her relations, gentlemen of the robe and strong in the Parlement of Paris, were loud in their demands for justice. Bussy-Rabutin put himself under the protection of Condé; some money was paid over, but it was the outbreak of the Fronde that put an end to the matter. Mme de Miramion devoted herself and her riches to charity, and Bussy returned to the army and Condé.

He served with Condé in the first stages of the Fronde from motives of feudal loyalty; but after the princes' imprisonment and release, he refused to follow Condé into his alliance with

Spain, and went over to the royal service, fighting gallantly
and successfully against Condé's troops in his lieutenancy of
the Nivernais. At the conclusion of the disastrous second
Fronde, he was held in high honour at the court, winning the
praises and thanks of the Queen and Mazarin, but he received
nothing more, not even the back pay owed him and his troops,
yet he had spent more than he possessed and run into debt in
the royal cause. Then in 1653, having married Louise de
Rouville, he managed to purchase with her money and a loan
from Fouquet the honourable lieutenant-colonelcy of Light
Cavalry of France for the huge sum of 90,000 livres. In that
year he met and fell deeply in love with Mme de Montglas,
the love of his life. The next years he looked on in retrospect as
the happiest he had known. He was appointed lieutenant-
general under the Great Condé's brother, the Prince de Conti,
for the campaign in Catalonia. On excellent terms with his
commander, a man of his own spirit—they exchanged orders
and despatches in verse—he amused their leisure by writing a
parody of the then fashionable *Cartes du Tendre*, the *Carte du
Pays de Braquerie*, in which he satirized under the flimsiest of
disguises—a topographical description of an imaginary country
—the affairs of some of the highest ladies at court. His good
fortune seemed at its peak; he even won 10,000 écus at play.
On his return from Spain, ambitious to win the highest military
glory, he demanded to serve under Turenne in Flanders against
Condé and the Spanish. In the intervals between campaigns, he
was in Paris, enjoying endless *rabutinages* with Mme de Sévigné
and more in love than ever with the fascinating Mme de
Montglas.

It was during one of the intervals from fighting at the time
of the Fronde that Bussy offered his services to Mme de Sévigné
in the manner which he relates with such disarming frankness
in the *Histoire Amoureuse des Gaules*. His relations with both his
cousin and the Marquis her husband were of the most open
and cordial kind. Bussy remonstrated with Sévigné for his too
widely known gallantries, particularly with the amiable and
intelligent Mlle Ninon l'Enclos, remarking that his wife, who
was worth a dozen such women, would know how to revenge
herself for his infidelities. The Marquis merely laughed at this

and continued as before, so Bussy wrote to Mme de Sévigné offering himself as her lover, and sent the letter by a page. The Marquise being asleep and Sévigné entering the house at that moment, he intercepted and read the letter. Bussy was forbidden the house, but Mme de Sévigné let him know that all would soon blow over. Six months later the Marquis was killed in a duel with the Chevalier d'Albret.

The relations between the army commander, Turenne, and Bussy-Rabutin, lieutenant-colonel of the Light Cavalry, were difficult from the start. In temperament the two men were incompatible; and the fault for their disagreements lay on both sides. Turenne withheld from his subordinate the opportunities to gain that fame for which he thirsted. Bussy-Rabutin took his revenge by comparing Turenne disparagingly with his rival Condé, and ridiculing him in conversation, stories, epigrams and songs. These went the rounds of the camp, and were repeated in Paris. The laugh was first against Turenne, but ultimately it went against Bussy. Mazarin and the court learnt of Bussy-Rabutin's military skill and bravery not so much from his general but from the captured despatches of his opponent Condé. In secret reports Turenne had his revenge. He wrote of Bussy: 'The best officer in the army . . . for songs'. Bussy-Rabutin had made more enemies by his biting tongue and his brilliant pen than he had counted on, both at court and with the army. Then in the summer of 1658 he quarrelled with Mme de Sévigné.

In May of that year Turenne had left Paris for the army. Bussy, who was in honour bound to follow his commander was immobilized in Paris, without the means of equipping himself for the campaign. In his distress he turned to his cousin Mme de Sévigné. The Bishop of Chalon, their uncle, had recently died, leaving his nephew and niece a share in his estate. Bussy-Rabutin proposed that Mme de Sévigné advance him the money he so urgently required against the security of his share of their inheritance. She declared herself most happy to do this to assist her dear cousin. Then her uncle, the Abbé de Coulanges, made difficulties and delays. It was necessary to send to Burgundy to make enquiries. Bussy was at his wits' end; a battle was imminent and the commander of the Light

Cavalry was kicking his heels in Paris. Mme de Sévigné could not, or would not, help. Finally, Bussy's mistress, Mme de Montglas, raised the money by selling her diamonds. He left for the army, arriving at Dunkirk on the eve of the Battle of the Dunes, 5th June 1658. In the great victory that followed, Bussy-Rabutin was signalled out for his bravery—it was the common report that he shared the honours with Turenne. He returned to a triumphant Paris, to Mme de Montglas, but not to his Rabutin relation, Mme de Sévigné, from whom the rupture was complete.

For Holy Week 1659 M. le Duc de Vivonne, brother of Mme de la Montespan, issued an invitation to a small party of friends to gather at the château of Roissy, south of Paris, where they might 'devote themselves with less distraction to thoughts of eternity'. Among those present were the notorious libertines Vardes, Guiche, and Manicamp, the last two practising homosexuals; and the Abbé Le Camus, the future Cardinal and Bishop of Geneva. Seeing that the party lacked a guiding spirit, Vivonne invited Bussy-Rabutin at the last minute; he arrived on Good Friday in company with the violinists. The 'debauch at Roissy' created a scandal; the accounts of what went on there—the blasphemies, sacrilege, murder even—lost nothing in the telling. The part played by Bussy-Rabutin in all this may have been limited to the composition of some songs and to the telling of some scandalous and wounding tales; and for this he was to pay dearly. In the scabrous stanzas of the celebrated '*Allelulia*' song he ridiculed the young King's passion for Mazarin's niece, Mlle Mancini. Louis was twenty-one, and sensitive still. And he was the King, if not yet master in his Kingdom.

> *Que Deodatus est heureux*
> *De baiser ce bec amoureux*
> *Qui d'une oreille à l'autre va!*
> *Allelulia!*

Furthermore, he related the adventures of some highly placed court ladies (these were anyway common knowledge), that were later to appear in the *Histoire amoureuse des Gaules*. And he took his revenge on Mme de Sévigné's disloyalty in a brilliant character sketch. Shortly afterwards he received a letter from the King, banishing him to his estate in Burgundy.

In 1660 Mme de Montglas was ill with smallpox at Lyons, and Bussy ran to her bedside. During her convalescence he regaled her and her friend Mme de la Baume with the tales he had recounted at Roissy. They were charmed; and flattered by their praises for the truth, verve and literary style of the stories, he allowed himself to be persuaded, once back at Bussy-Rabutin, to commit them to paper. It was the making of his literary reputation, and of his personal disgrace.

Although his first banishment lasted only some months, on his return to court he found little favour with the King. After Mazarin's death in 1661, his 'portraits of the court', a sort of secret police dossier, gave Louis fresh reasons to be on his guard against this too intelligent and too presumptuous subject. The coming of peace with Spain had removed the need for Bussy's military services, and the King, treating him with an icy reserve, allowed his well-earned requests to go unheeded. With the removal by death of Mazarin, Louis XIV decided to be his own prime minister, and one of the first manifestations of his intention to be master in his own house was the arrest of the too-powerful Fouquet. It was rumoured that among papers seized were some which implicated both Bussy and the Marquise de Sévigné, but this report proved unfounded.

In 1662, yielding to the cajolery of Mme de Montglas, Bussy, much against his will and better judgement, let her friend Mme de la Baume, who had heard him relate his Roissy stories, read the *Histoire amoureuse des Gaules*, which no one but his mistress had seen. He lent her the manuscript for forty-eight hours. Some little time later he heard that a copy of the *Histoire* was going the rounds of the drawing-rooms of Paris. Furiously he confronted Mme de la Baume, who denied indignantly her culpability. Further, he was assured by a friend whom he trusted that the copy had been destroyed. Bussy had recently composed for Mme de Montglas some *Maximes d'amour* in verse, based largely on Ovid. The King, who had heard them praised for their elegance, wit and worldly wisdom, asked for the verses to read with his new mistress, Mlle de La Vallière.

Fortune seemed to be turning a more benign face towards Bussy-Rabutin. The King spoke to him at Court; but he let it be known that there were to be no more tales, no more portraits and no more songs. Bussy joyfully promised His Majesty. However, unknown to him the manuscript of the *Histoire* was still in existence. In the spring of 1665, Bussy-Rabutin, on the solicitation of his friend the Duke of Saint-Aignan, was elected to the Academie Française to fill the vacancy caused by the death of Perrot d'Ablancourt. The King gave his assent to his candidature.

But the clouds were gathering. Copies had been taken of Mme de la Baume's copy of the *Histoire* and everyone was reading and laughing at the stories of Mme d'Olonne and Mme de Châtillon and the cruel but perceptive portrait of Mme de Sévigné. Warned by the Duke of Saint-Aignan that the noise had reached the ears of the King, Bussy decided to put on a bold front and sent a version (the original one, he claimed) to the King. To his infinite relief, Louis read these scandalous tales and smiled. He also already knew what everyone knew, and he, the admirer of Corneille and Molière, appreciated a fine literary style. The complaints, however, of the injured followed; and to these were added the complaints of those who felt themselves injured in *not* figuring in the *Histoire*. It was the enmity of Condé that decided Bussy's fate; stung by the latter's observations on him, he threatened to assassinate Bussy in the street. On 17th April 1665 the Comte de Bussy-Rabutin, on orders of the King, was committed to the Bastille.

The *Histoire amoureuse des Gaules* is a minor masterpiece. The prose is clear, subtle, precise; the events related are scandalous, but they are a true picture of the period; the portraits are not caricatures but engravings of characters from life, presented with uncanny accuracy and a marvellous economy. The pseudonyms disguised no one. The truth of the representation was alone sufficient to procure the condemnation of its author; no such society could condone so candid and revealing a portrayal of itself. Who, for example, could fail to recognize under the masks of 'Crispin' and 'Ardélise' the living features of M. Paget and Mme d'Olonne?

"In the meanwhile, Crispin, a man of a certain age, of low birth, fell in love with Ardélise, and, having discovered that she was passionately fond of gaming, he believed that his money would be a substitute for merit, and founded his most cherished hopes on the sum that he resolved to offer her. He had the means of access to her house to speak to her himself, if he had dared; but he had not the courage to deliver a speech that might produce in its train unpleasant consequences, if it were not well received. He decided then to write to her, and he wrote her this letter:

LETTER

"*I have loved on occasions in my life, Madame, but I have never loved anything so much as I love you. What makes me believe this, is that I have never given to any of my mistresses more than a hundred pistoles to have their good graces; and, for yours, I will go as far as two thousand. Reflect on the above, I pray you, and consider that money is rarer than it has ever been.*

"Quinette, Ardélise's maid and confidante, brought her this letter of Crispin. Without a moment's pause, this beauty made reply as follows:

LETTER

"*I was well aware that you had intelligence from the conversations that I have had with you, but I was quite unaware that you wrote as well as you do. I have never seen anything so pretty as your letter, and I shall be more than delighted to receive often others of the same quality. Meanwhile, I would be very happy to have a chat with you this evening at six o'clock.*
Ardélise.
"Paget did not fail to turn up at the rendezvous, and to turn up suitably attired, that is to say, with his wallet. . . ."

Bussy-Rabutin's character-portrait of Mme de Sévigné cut her to the quick. It was malicious and cruel; but it was a true picture. Corbinelli, who was a good friend of them both, and loved them equally, confessed later to Bussy that he had read the portraits with a slight feeling of guilt for the hurt that he knew it must give Mme de Sévigné, but he finished reading in laughter. He read it again and again and laughed each time afresh, so brilliant and lifelike was Bussy's sketch of his cousin. Even beneath his carefully casual manner of writing, below the surface of these judicious praises and this gentle chiding are hidden barbs. And then there came some telling home truths.

> With so much fire, it is not strange that her discernment is only mediocre . . . a lively fool will always carry the day with her over a serious man of good common sense. The gaiety of people preoccupies her; she will not consider if one understands what she is saying. The greatest mark of intelligence that one can show her is to have admiration for her; she loves incense; she loves to be loved, and, for that, she sows in order to reap; she bestows praise in order to receive it . . . [Mme de Sévigné is indiscriminate in the objects of her affection, Bussy goes on:] Among men, she prefers a lover to a friend; and among lovers, the gay to the sad. The melancholy flatter her vanity, the lively her imagination; she amuses herself with the latter, and flatters herself with the opinion that she has the merit of having been able to cause the melancholy of the former.

He then becomes extremely personal, and all the more wounding for being veracious.

> She is of a cold temperament, at least if one may believe her late husband . . . her warmth is all of the intelligence. To tell the truth, she compensates for the coldness of her nature. If one judges by her actions, I believe that conjugal faith has not been violated: if one looks to intention, it is another matter. To speak frankly, I believe that her husband is untouched before men, but I hold him a fool before God. . . .

He then taxes Mme de Sévigné with social hypocrisy and snobbery.

Finally Bussy-Rabutin comes to the action of his cousin that has caused this devastating attack:

There are people who put only things holy as the limits of their friendship, and would do everything for their friends short of offending God. These people are called friends right up to the altar. The friendship of Mme de Sévigné has other limits: this beauty is a friend only as far as her purse. . . .

It was a terrible accusation. Unfortunately for the reputation of Mme de Sévigné her cousin's words were true.

When he was arrested and was searched Bussy-Rabutin had nothing more incriminating on his person than an aide-mémoire against Mme de la Baume and a copy of an *Epistle* of Boileau. No charge was preferred against him, but his surveillance was of the strictest. The scandal of his imprisonment was widespread, echoing to the capitals of Europe; the *chansonniers* of Paris were busy, and much in his favour. He fell ill, and his faithful wife was allowed to tend him. Meanwhile, his friends, who left messages but were not permitted to see him, interceded for him with the King. It was then that Bussy learned that his mistress for thirteen years, Mme de Montglas, had deserted him for the President Mesnard. He did not know that Mme de Sévigné had called to enquire news of his health —was this suppression of her visit through negligence or on instructions? Ultimately, his wife prevailed on the King to allow him on 16th May 1666 to be moved to a doctor's house, where he was operated on for a fistula. There all the Court flocked to greet him. Finally, on 10th August, after seventeen months detention, he was permitted to retire to his Burgundian estates. This banishment, despite pleas from influential friends at court, and apologetic and even abject personal letters from Bussy to Louis XIV, was to last virtually until his death.

It was in his château of Bussy-Rabutin that he spent for the most part the long years of his exile, and it is here today that

we can see the marks of his presence, in the rebuilding of the
house, but most of all in the extraordinarily revealing decoration of the interior. Even in the hopeless bitterness of failure,
Bussy-Rabutin wished to leave in these rooms a memorial to
the martial glory, whose ultimate triumphs had escaped him,
and to his loves—well, what had he to say of these? A portion
of each day he spent personally supervising his masons,
carpenters and artists, a portion in writing, and in the evenings
he would close himself in, like the disgraced Machiavelli, with
his memories and those representations that revived for him
his days of glory. He sent to Paris for paintings, copies for the
most part, of those women who had played a role in his life,
and he summoned indifferent local artists to work under his
direction to complete the decorating. It is as well to acknowledge that with the exception of a few Mignards the paintings
are not in general of high quality. Of his own portraits there
are two, one depicting him as a young man, dressed as a
Roman soldier, and the other by Claude le Febvre, the pupil
of the better known Lebrun. This shows Bussy in his maturity;
the face, under the clustering curls of the full wig of the period,
extremely handsome, with the undeniable presence of the
grand seigneur, the soldier and courtier. Yet it is the eyes and
mouth that claim our attention. The beautiful eyes, set far
apart, are large and smiling; but it is the mouth above all,
with the lips at once sensitive and sensual, lips on which plays
some unspoken shaft of amused malice, that reveals the family
characteristics, the Rabutin of the inexhaustible *rabutinades*. In
those private rooms—the Salle des Devises, the Salon des
Grands Hommes de Guerre, his bedroom (sometimes called
that of Mme de Sévigné, but she never visited Bussy-Rabutin),
the Tour Dorée and the Gallery—Bussy has gathered around
him all that his life held precious for him. The portraits of the
royal house of France, the Valois Dukes of Burgundy, the
military heroes of France, beginning with Du Guesclin and
ending with Condé, Turenne and himself; the royal palaces,
and the members of his own family—and the women who had
meant most to him for good or ill, for he was nothing if not
comprehensive in his choice. One of the principal motifs of
his decoration of these rooms is the interlaced monogram of his

own initial with that of his loved but faithless mistress, Mme de Montglas.

To those who criticized his bringing together here the *'terribles'* Comtesses d'Olonne and de Fiesque, Mmes de Châtillon, de la Ferté and de la Baume with the irreproachable Marquise de Sévigné, her daughter the Comtesse de Grignan, Mme de Scudéry and the Comtesse de Bussy-Rabutin, he might have replied that he left such moral delicacy to the Tartuffes of the age. All Paris learned that he had composed verses and mottoes—'posters', he called them—to be painted beneath the portraits, and all were agog to learn what he had written there. When one considers what some of those ladies were, how he had described them in the *Histoire amoureuse,* and how some had treated him, his comments must be regarded as approaching magnanimity. Even in his many references to Mme de Montglas the bitterness was tinged with regret, and a suspicion of lingering love. Yet once when he heard that Mmes d'Olonne, de Montglas and de Montmorency were seeing a great deal of each other, he wrote: 'You know indeed that they call the association of Augustus, Lepidus and Mark Antony the *triumvirat.* I call this the *triumputat.'* Beneath the painting of Mme d'Olonne he remarked that 'she was less celebrated by her beauty than by the use she made of it'. Under Mme de la Baume, whose treachery brought about his ruin, he limited himself to 'The most amiable and the prettiest, if she had not been the most unfaithful.'

The deep hurt that Mme de Montglas's desertion caused him is seen in the many devices in Latin and French in which he dwelt on it. Her portrait appears time and again. Represented as the moon, she 'has more than one face'; as a siren, with the warning, 'He who listens is lost'; as a rainbow, 'Less Iris, less ephemeral, less changing than mine'; as Zephyr, 'lighter than air'; as a swallow, *'Fugit hiems*—she flees the bad weather.' Writing one day to Mme de Scudéry, who mentioned her in a letter, Bussy pleaded, 'Ah, let me laugh on her chapter; she has caused me to weep enough!'

> *Cela soit dit en passant,*
> *Pour celle que j'aimais tant.*

But the woman for whom he had the deepest and most constant feelings was his cousin Mme de Sévigné. In the autumn of the beginning of his exile, Bussy paid a visit to the château of Bourbilly, near Semur; it was something in the nature of a pilgrimage to this home of his ancestors, and surely not unconnected with his affection for Mme de Sévigné, whose property it now was. He wrote to her on 21st November 1666:

I was yesterday at Bourbilly. Never have I been so surprised, my fair cousin. I found this house beautiful; and when I searched for the reason, after the little regard that I have had for it two years ago, it seemed to me that it came from your absence. For the truth is that the beauty of you and Mlle de Sévigné has the effect of making that which surrounds you seem ugly, and you had this effect two years ago on your house. . . .

And he went on in a lighthearted way to tell her how her tenant did him the honours of the place, and how the sun, which had not appeared for two days, suddenly gilded the rooms decorated with their armorial bearings.

I had gone there among the family, who seemed also as satisfied with this house as I was. The living Rabutins, seeing so many coats of arms, prided themselves even more, perceiving what the dead Rabutins made of their house. But we all burst out laughing when we saw on his knees the good Cristophe, who, after having put his arms in a thousand places and in a thousand different ways, had had himself a suit made of them. Surely that is to push the love of his name as far as it can go. . . .

Mme de Sévigné kept Bussy waiting until the following May before replying in a somewhat heartless letter. Bussy was hurt, and said so, but quickly resumed his lightness of tone. Not so Mme de Sévigné, who began a long series of reproaches against Bussy for his *Histoire amoureuse* sketch of her. Bussy tried to defend himself, to ask her forgiveness, but she was unsatisfied, and implacably returned to her attacks. He might, had he been a different man, have thought that with all the right on her side, as she claimed, she was protesting too much. On 26th July 1668 she was still reproaching him:

> We are close and of the same blood; we like each other, we love each other, we take an interest in each other's fortunes. You speak to me of advancing you money on the ten thousand écus that were coming to you from M. de Chalon: you say that I have refused you, and I say that I have lent it to you; for you know very well, and our friend Corbinelli is a witness, that my heart wished it from the first, and that when we sought certain formalities . . . impatience seized you. And having found myself by misfortune sufficiently imperfect in body and mind to give you subject to make a very pretty portrait of me, you did so, and you preferred to our long friendship, to our name and to justice even, the pleasure of being praised for your work. . . .

And so it dragged on, Bussy patiently explaining, yet for peace's sake yielding on every point; but Mme de Sévigné remaining unsatisfied, relentless. Finally, on 28th August she wrote: 'One further word, and then no more. . . . How the devil would you have me find twelve or fifteen thousand francs? Did I have them in my cashbox, does one find them in one's friends' purse?'

And the answer to this question, which was intended to, and did, floor poor Bussy-Rabutin, was Yes, she did have the money, and more, much more; that she had miserably failed her cousin in his need. It is fortunate that Bussy did not have the evidence which has subsequently come to light, which shows that Mme de Sévigné in May 1658, the month when he asked for the loan, had been repaid by a certain Sieur Lubin Petit, a bourgeois of Paris, a loan of over 50,000 livres, 22,272 livres of which had been handed over on 6th April, the receipt for which she had herself signed. Mme de Sévigné is a marvellous writer, the truth of her observations and of her sentiments standing out on every page that she wrote, but she lied to the cousin whom she loved, and then, when he took his literary revenge, she heaped her reproaches on his head. Bussy always gave as good as he received, but the female of the Rabutin species could be more vindictive than the male. However, this storm at last blew itself out, and they continued to write as old friends, who appreciated so justly each others' merits, until the end.

Bussy-Rabutin lived out his years of banishment in Burgundy, permitted on short occasions to journey to Paris to conduct his numerous law suits. When, late in his life, he was allowed to re-appear at Court, he saw that the King had forgiven him nothing, and that he was a figure from the past that was best forgotten. His enemies and calumniators were too many and too close to the King's ear; every vice was fathered on him, and his name was put to every piece of scurrilous prose that was circulated, every caustically critical or obscene verse, and every ribald song.

Like his literary model Petronius he became the *arbiter elegantiae* of his age. He was not idle; his correspondents were said to have numbered at least one hundred and fifty persons; his advice was sought on literary matters; he wrote verses (his *tonrelon-tontons*, he called them), composed his *Memoirs* and a genealogy of his family, and translated the letters of Heloïse and Abelard into beautiful French prose. He kept copies of his own letters and those he received from his numerous feminine admirers, who openly confessed their love for him; from statesmen, soldiers and the chief literary figures of the period. His prose style became a model; it was La Bruyère who said that the secret of good writing was 'to write like Bussy'. His literary taste was impeccable, and posterity has confirmed his judgement of his contemporaries. He supported with his pen Boileau, Racine, La Fontaine, and wrote an admirable criticism of the *Princesse de Clèves*, which, when it was first published, Mme de Sévigné sent him for his judgement. 'I have been very pleased to know your opinion,' she wrote, 'and still more that it accords perfectly with mine. . . . Your criticism and mine were just from the same mould.' He refused to be drawn into the controversies over the Jansenists and Port-Royal. 'Let us live well and let us rejoice. In matters of conscience too much delicacy makes

heresies. I only want to go to paradise, not higher.' He respected
Pascal for the quality of his prose, and when told that he might
regain the favour of the King if he wrote a rebuttal of the
Lettres provinciales, replied that Pascal could not be rebutted.

It was Bussy who 'discovered' Mme de Sévigné. When, three
years after his death in 1693, the volumes of his *Correspondance*
appeared, they contained a quantity of his cousin's, the Marquise's letters; but at first, and for some half century, his own
letters held the field as models of the best French epistolary
style. Only then did the Marquise de Sévigné outstrip him in
the esteem of the literary world, and relegate him to the
obscurity in which he has too long lain. Roger de Bussy-
Rabutin was the epitome of the Gallic spirit, seasoned with the
down-to-earth quality of his native Burgundy. But he had
rabutined too early and too well; Bussy-Rabutin was the victim
of his own *rabutinades*.

CHAPTER XI

The Châteaux

THE ATTITUDE OF the high ranks of the French nobility to their châteaux, whether their origin had been of the sword or the robe, became in the course of the *grand siècle* curiously anomalous. Following the lead given by Louis XIV, huge sums were spent in embellishing their country seats, whence their titles sprang, converting them into often ostentatious reflections of their family pride and position; yet banishment from the court at Versailles, to the seclusion of their country estates, from the presence of the *Roi Soleil* towards which all gravitated, appeared in their eyes a barren exile, a form of social extinction. Proud court ladies languished in the desert of the provinces; physically they pined away, while the King was endlessly petitioned for that letter of recall which, by restoring them to his presence, would save their lives. Bussy-Rabutin, dismissed from court to his native Burgundy for allowing his wit to run away with his discretion, wrote letter after letter, each more abject than the last, to Louis XIV and to influential ministers in fruitless efforts to be permitted to return from his beautiful château at Bussy-le-Grand to the futile unreality of Versailles. As the eighteenth century advanced, and there appeared those changes in society's thinking that heralded the end of the *ancien régime*, one such change was a newly discovered delight in the countryside and country pleasures, as exemplified by Jean-Jacques Rousseau at Ermenonville or by the lakeside retreat of the 'squire of Ferney'. Both Voltaire and Rousseau visited Burgundy as guests of Mme de Saint-Julien at the contemporarily built château of Fontaine-Française, north-east of Dijon. Furthermore, the heads of those great parliamentary families whose magnificent town-houses add so much to the architectural dignity of Dijon, following the fashion of the age, constructed for themselves country seats in the refined classicism of the eighteenth century. Dijon is encircled by these gracious châteaux, these charming *gentilhommières*: Vantoux, Talmay, Beaumont-sur-Vingeanne, Arcelot, Longecourt, Lantenay, Thenissey, Verry-sous-Salmaise, Grancey, Montculot among them.

Travellers who drive along the country roads in Burgundy, among the wooded or vine-clad hills, the verdant river valleys or the granite highlands of the Morvan, are frequently reminded of the evolution of the châteaux from the rude fortified keep, the donjon or castle, where defence was the primary concern, through the great seigneurial houses of the renaissance and the sixteenth and seventeenth centuries, to the refinement and restrained civility of the country seats of the last century of the *ancien régime*. These huge round or square towers of the middle ages are everywhere in evidence. Often to save the expense of demolition they have been left standing beside the later construction, as at Talmay, Ruffey and Chastellux, or by many a remote manor house; but perhaps almost as often they have been incorporated entire in the rebuilding, as at Bussy-Rabutin, Sully or Tanlay. At Chastellux-sur-Cure the eleventh- or early twelfth-century donjon stands isolated to the west of a château which has been constantly reconstituted from the fifteenth century onwards, remaining since the middle ages the property of one family, the Beauvoir de Chastellux. In Burgundy, as elsewhere in France, these cylindrical towers with their conical caps—the distinctive 'extinguisher' or 'pepper-pot' towers—are the visual symbols of the middle ages, in the same way as the appearance of a *corps de logis*, its façade enlivened by a central pediment, flanked by pavilion wings, suggests just as unmistakably the eighteenth century. When one considers what waves of savage warfare have devastated this opulent countryside from the fourteenth and fifteenth centuries—the Hundred Years' War, the Wars of Religion, the Fronde, the Revolution—it appears as a matter of some surprise that so much of this domestic architecture has survived.

South of Auxerre, in the lovely valley of the Yonne, through which also runs the Canal de Nivernais, stands a fascinating relic of the mediaeval past, the manor of Faulin. Here today the moat and encircling walls, the high entrance gate and

G

round towers, constitute the *enceinte* of this fortified farm of the fourteenth century. Set against the backcloth of trees, the manor itself, a beautiful small renaissance house of the sixteenth century, has great distinction and quiet charm. A survivor of the vicissitudes of time, the manor of Faulin is an eloquent witness to the quality of rural life in Burgundy in the age of Rabelais and Montaigne. In the valley of the Brenne in the Côte-d'Or, the château of Posanges could be taken as a perfect model of the fortified small castle of the early fifteenth century, with its three massive corner towers and their conical caps (the fourth was demolished by Henri Quatre) and its fine entrance gateway, which was once approached by a drawbridge and defended by a portcullis. Posanges was built by Guillaume Dubois, the maître d'hotel of Philip the Bold, and was restored some ten years ago.

Older still in its origin, and showing the marks of its tumultuous past, is the château of Pierreclos, a few miles west of Mâcon, once lived in by Lamartine's Mlle de Milly. Situated in an arresting position on a hill overlooking a wide valley, in the 'mountains of the Mâconnais', Pierreclos was a natural strongpoint, the remains of its keep and towers showing it to have been capable of an effective defence in the middle ages. Early in the seventeenth century domestic buildings were raised among the fortifications, and standing back from the wide terrace; and these include some spacious rooms, with the characteristic great beams of the period and good marble chimney-pieces. Later, additions were begun to face the semi-circular court, but these were never completed. It is a romantic spot still; and Lamartine, who knew it well and loved it, often visited the château and its owners, riding over from nearby Saint-Pont. He tells how the fierce old Count, returned after the relaxation of Thermidor, would point out the charred woodwork and the masonry damaged by crowbars, referring contemptuously to the evidence of the 'passage of the brigands', the revolutionaries of 1790. This Comte de Pierreclos possessed in Lamartine's day the nearby castle of Berzé at Berzé-le-Châtel, then a picturesque ruin, which added, as the poet said, 'the solemnity of the past ages and a touch of melancholy to the cheerful and varied aspect of the rest of the landscape'.

Since that time the château has been carefully restored—the sixteenth-century garden as well as the buildings—and today it is a most pleasant place, with its box-edged beds and its statues, its topiary yews and clipped hedges of hornbeam.

Berzé protected the southern approaches to Cluny; not far distant to the north of the abbey, standing in the valley of the Grosne, is another château once owned by relations of the Count and closely connected with Lamartine—Cormatin. Lamartine was a frequent and welcome visitor; indeed, he had a son by Nina, the wife of the owner, his friend Antoine de Pierreclos. The renaissance-style château, built in the warm local ironstone, which was begun about 1600 by Antoine du Blé and completed by his grandson, the Maréchal d'Huxelles, originally consisted of two wings and a *corps de logis*, these forming a court of honour; but the left-hand wing was demolished in 1830. The Maréchal was said to have been not particularly distinguished as a soldier, being rather 'a man of the table and of pleasure', and the lavishness of the interior decoration, if much of it is to be attributed to him, suggests that he gave free rein to his taste for splendour. The painted and gilded ceilings of the *salles dorées*, particularly that of the *Salle de Sainte-Cécile* (said to be by Pierre Puget), are remarkable for their richness, which is in keeping with the magnificence and the quality of the furniture, tapestries and paintings—even if the attributions of some of these last have been questioned. The painted panels of the *Salle des Gardes* are considered to be the work of Claude Lorraine. Visitors to Cormatin should without fail visit its church, where hangs a most interesting painting on wood of the fifteenth-century Burgundian school, the *Virgin of Pity*, in which the figures of Herod and Caiaphas are held to be portraits of Louis XI and Cardinal La Balue, hereditary enemies of the Valois Dukes of Burgundy.

A well-preserved example of a thirteenth-century castle is Ratilly, hidden away among the dense woods of the Puisaye, not far from Treigny (with its flamboyant 'cathedral'). Some miles to the north-west of Ratilly, in the same watery district of La Puisaye, is the château of Saint-Fargeau, on the edge of the small town of that name, and standing in its park, its walls reflected in the waters of the lake.

The original fortified stronghold here goes back at least to the tenth century. The present building owes its immense, squat, round towers to its fifteenth-century owner, Jacques Coeur, the financier of Charles VII. After Coeur's disgrace, his successor, Antoine de Chabannes, made some important additions to the structure. (The high bell-turrets on the towers are later still.) But it was from Mlle de Montpensier that Saint-Fargeau acquired the architectural elegance of its inner courtyard, and the decoration of its interior and chapel. When the Grande Mademoiselle arrived in 1652, banished by her cousin Louis XIV for her spirited part in the Fronde, she found the draw-bridge broken, the courtyard a tangle of long grass and weeds 'up to the knees', the windows and doors all shattered. She is said to have burst into tears on the spot. But she was not the daughter of Gaston d'Orléans for nothing; she sent off to Paris for the King's architect, François Le Vau, who converted the mediaeval edifice into a dwelling worthy of its châtelaine. Most effective is the junction effected by Le Vau of two sides of the court, where the obtuse angle is masked by wide fan-shaped steps, leading to a round-fronted portico, which is surmounted by a flattened cupola and a *clocheton*. Saint-Fargeau came into the possession of the Le Pelletier family, one of whom, Michel Robert Le Pelletier des Forts, turned against his King, and was assassinated in the Palais Royal on the very eve of Louis XVI's mounting the scaffold. His daughter was 'adopted' by the nation.

The western slopes of the granite outcrop of the Morvan—with its fir-forests and its woods of oaks and beech—are drained by the River Cure, which flows north, passing under the hill of Vézelay, to join the Yonne, winding through a broken, well-wooded countryside, with rich meadows, separated by trees and hedges—reminiscent, for all the freshness of the shades of green, of some familiar English landscape. Here in the autumn, on the great trees of edible chestnuts, their leaves turning molten gold, the pericarps of the nuts split open, letting the ripe fruit fall, and leaving on the branches the residue of covering turned back, like miniature stars of cream magnolia flowers. From the sixteenth century until recent times this was the district of the '*flottage à bûches perdues*', the cut logs from the Morvan being cast into the Cure, to be swept down by the force of the waters to the Yonne and thence to the Seine, to feed the household fires of Paris. At Arcy-sur-Cure, north of Vézelay, is the mediaeval Manoir de Chastenay. The date of the present building has been disputed, some authorities placing it as late as 1540. However, in the early middle ages Chastenay was a stage on the northern pilgrim route to the shrine of St James of Compostella, and parts of the manor may well be from the fourteenth century.

South of Vézelay, standing among the tall trees to the left of the N.458, is the very beautiful château of Bazoches, once the property of the great Vauban. Indeed, this might be considered his own country, for he was born in 1633 some miles to the east of here at the village of St-Léger-de-Foucheret, now known as St-Léger-Vauban; and in 1673 he acquired the vast domain of Bazoches, with another château three kilometres to the south, which now goes by his name. He lies buried in a chapel that he added to the twelfth-century church at Bazoches—all save his heart, which in 1808 was on Napoleon's orders removed to be re-interred in the Invalides. Vauban carried out extensive rebuilding, but he incorporated the machicolated round and square towers of the thirteenth-century defences in his beautiful house, whose very irregularity, with the red and brown tiles of its roofs and the buff colouring of its walls, contributes greatly to its charm. Unfortunately visits are not permitted. Likewise, the château of Chastellux-sur-Cure, which lies a few miles away to the east of Bazoches, is only visible from the outside. The former was at one time open to visitors, but their behaviour leaving something to be desired, the proprietor, M. Olivier de Chastellux, Duc de Duras, had one morning a placard placed on his gateway, which read: 'From today the château has ceased to be historic.' And that was that. . . . The remarks of Lemaitre in the introduction to his *French Châteaux* apply with a particular aptness to Chastellux and Bazoches: 'The châteaux of Burgundy always retain something of the rural and bucolic, setting less store by magnificence and dignity than by a kind of architectural realism which binds them more closely to their soil.'

To the east of the Morvan, in the rolling countryside of the

Auxois, is a château of great historical and architectural
interest, set high on the west side of a village whose houses
vividly recall the feudal age—Châteauneuf-en-Auxois. It stands
a little way south of the château of Commarin (which rises from
the still waters of its moat) and just north of the A6 motorway
from Paris. The original castle on this spot, which commands
an extensive ruin and lends itself to defence, was constructed
in the twelfth century by the Sires de Chaudenay. In the
fifteenth century it came into the possession of the famous
Seneschal of Burgundy, Philippe Pot, who rebuilt and added
to it from 1460 to 1493 in the style of the late gothic. Châteauneuf was rescued from falling completely to ruin—'the finest
military ruin in Burgundy'—by Count de Vogüé (whose family
built the beautiful hôtel de Vogüé in Dijon), who has restored
two wings, and who, in 1936, presented this beautiful example
of mediaeval domestic, as much as military, architecture to the
State. The decoration is somewhat plain for the period, but a
little decorative flourish has been given by the dormer windows.
In the eighteenth century a well-proportioned doorway was
opened from the court into the Salle des Gardes, a handsome
room, which retains its heavy beams and great stone fireplace.
Off it, in one of the round towers, is a charming little room,
whose walls are painted in soft greys and greens, and from its
long window and balcony there is a splendid view towards the
hills of the Morvan. In the chapel are remains of fifteenth-
century frescoes, in which figures of saints appear between
alternating bands of black and red. The château has a rare
power of evoking its own past and the distant age of the Valois
dukes of Burgundy.

The family of Rabutin was one of the oldest and most distinguished in the province, its members possessing among their
many fiefs those of Epiry, Chaseu (or Chazeu), Chantal, Bourbilly and Bussy-le-Grand. The château and grounds of Bussy-
Rabutin, near Montbard, the place of exile of the too audacious
Count Roger de Bussy-Rabutin, have a beauty, an Arcadian
charm and romantic elegance that match the historical interest
of its eccentric owner and the decorations that he carried out
there (see Chapter X). The ruins of the château of Chazeu may

still be seen in the valley of the Arroux, south of Autun; and to the north-west of that town, beside the stream of the Selle, stands the small country house of Chantal. The châteaux of Epiry and Bourbilly also still exist. Of Epiry there remains a high square tower on a hill overlooking the Yonne, south of Corbigny (Nièvre). It was here that Roger de Bussy-Rabutin was born in 1618, and where in 1660 Vauban married Jeanne d'Aunay. Bourbilly stands on the banks of the Serein in the Auxois, about six miles south-west of Semur-en-Auxois. The property came into the possession of the Rabutin-Chantal in the fifteenth century, and it was here that in the seventeenth century 'Sainte Chantal' spent her married life. On her and her husband's deaths the estate passed to her grand-daughter, Mme de Sévigné. Bussy-Rabutin visited Bourbilly in Mme de Sévigné's absence and wrote of its beauty in a delightful letter to his cousin. The château suffered greatly at the hands of the revolutionaries; and its Second-Empire restoration by the Comte de Frangueville, while it has retained its general shape, its pepper-pot corner towers and its dormer windows of the time of the renaissance, has left it somewhat cold and unfeeling, a shadow of its warm seventeenth-century self. Another château, a neighbour of Bourbilly, and also associated with Mme de Sévigné, is Epoisses, a most beautiful building in a remarkable setting. The oldest parts of the château go back to the thirteenth century, if not much earlier, but the two wings spared by the revolutionaries are of the sixteenth and seventeenth centuries. Mme de Sévigné visited here her friend, the Comte de Guitaut, on one such visit getting drunk in his company at a memorable supper party in Saulieu. Epoisses has some most beautiful furniture and fascinating historical momentoes.

But undoubtedly, after Bussy-Rabutin, the most outstanding of the châteaux of Burgundy are those of Sully, Tanlay and Ancy-le-Franc. The last two named are in the north of the province, near-neighbours in the valley of the Armançon, south-east of Tonnerre; the first, Sully, stands in a strangely uninteresting countryside to the south, in the Autunois.

Ancy-le-Franc, apart from the intrinsic excellence of its design and the splendour of its furnishings, is of outstanding importance in the history of French architecture, as being the only surviving building known for certain to have been designed by the Bolognese architect, Sebastiano Serlio, who was called to France in 1540 by François Ier to work on his palace of Fontainebleau. He appears, however, to have contributed but little to this; instead he devoted himself to bringing out his influential books on architecture, five of the eight volumes appearing before his death in 1554. Moreover, from Serlio's designs and from the decorations of Primaticcio (like Serlio a native of Bologna), Niccolò dell'Abate and their pupils, Ancy-le-Franc must be considered as a splendid monument to the School of Fontainebleau. This Italianate château was begun in 1546 for Antoine III de Clermont-Tonnerre, Grand-Master of the *Eaux-et-Forêts du Roi* and husband of Agathe de Poitiers, the celebrated Diane's sister. In 1684 the estate was sold to the Marquis de Louvois, Louis XIV's war minister, with whose descendants it remained until the middle of last century, when it reverted to the Clermont-Tonnerre. On the death of the last Duke, Ancy-le-Franc passed to the family of his nephew, the Princes de Mérode.

The austerity of the exterior of the building—of which the Duchesse de Dino, Talleyrand's niece, wrote in 1834: '*Le mot anglais "gloomy" semble fair pour Ancy-le-Franc*'—is belied by the architectural perfection of the classical form of the inner court. Here the design is modelled on that of the Belvedere of Bramante in the Vatican, having the walls of the two storeys broken by windows (or arcades), separated by pairs of fluted Corinthian pilasters that flank the niches. This decorative arrangement is used, with variations, in the panelling of several rooms, many of which have been plastered and frescoed in the Italianate manner of the period. An over-restoration in this last century has led one critic to say that these paintings 'now derive more from the reign of Louis-Philippe than of Charles IX'. Nevertheless, these rooms—there are some nineteen open to the visitor—present a sumptuous richness of decoration and furnishing that has few equals in Burgundy. In one room on the ground floor, which the restorers seem to have overlooked, the delicate faded arabesques may suggest the spirit of the original frescoing of these 'Fontainebleau' artists.

Neighbouring Tanlay has been described as 'one of the most attractive châteaux in Burgundy, or indeed in all France'. It owes much to its site—the abundance of water and the beauty of its park; in these it has a great initial advantage over Ancy-le-Franc. Tanlay was begun only a few years after the latter, about 1559, but already the Italian influence had been absorbed thoroughly and integrated with French taste. Tanlay was once the property of the ancient family of Courtenay, who constructed there the mediaeval fortress whose great round towers have been incorporated in the present building. In the mid-sixteenth century it was sold to Louise de Montmorency, mother of the Huguenot Admiral Coligny, who met his death in the massacre of St Bartholomew; in 1559 she ceded Tanlay to another of her sons, François d'Andelot, who began the château we now see. The Wars of Religion interrupted the building, and work was only completed in the following century under the celebrated architect Pierre Le Muet. The construction of Tanlay really falls under three stages. Firstly, the demolition by François d'Andelot of much of the mediaeval fortress and the rebuilding of a plain structure in a sober renaissance style. Of the château of this period an interesting part remains: a small room at the top of one of the towers, where the shallow domed ceiling has been frescoed by a follower of Primaticcio, with a scene representing the combatants in the contemporary religious wars. Between two groups of naked Catholics and Protestants appears a double-faced Janus. This is said to portray, beneath the beard, Catherine de Medici, who regards with a favourable eye the one side, while she looks daggers at the other. In 1574, on d'Andelot's death, Tanlay passed to his daughter Anne de Coligny, who married the Marquis de Mirebeau. It was this last who, instead of continuing the work of his father-in-law, began in 1610 the Petit Château in the highly ornamental style of Louis Treize. Here the visitor may be surprised to see in the rustication of the ground floor, not the usual imitation of roughly hewn stone, but perhaps an atavistic memory of the sculpture of Burgundian romanesque masons in the tangle of exotic vegetation through which roam curious reptiles and rodents.

The third, and final, stage came about after 1642, when

Tanlay was sold to the rich financier, Michel Particelli d'Hémery, who brought in Pierre Le Muet to complete the edifice. This he did by raising the three-storeyed *corps de logis*, building the two-storeyed wing on the right, to balance d'Andelot's wing of eighty years earlier, and by constructing the sturdy gatehouse, with its bridge and two obelisks. Within, on the garden side, is the notable Vestibule des Césars, with its marble busts in niches and the splendid ceiling in *trompe-l'œil*, depicting a scene of classical magnificence, all as if carved in stone, the work doubtless of Italian artists. Other rooms have been furnished with taste, much in the style of Louis Seize, and adorned with tapestries and paintings by such masters as Rigaud, Mignard and Philippe de Champaigne. It is the presence of water—the Grand Canal and the Château d'Eau —that adds so greatly to the beauty of Tanlay's setting in its admirable park. In 1704 the estate came into the possession of the family of Thévenin, for whom it was raised to a marquisate. Entirely escaping the attention of the revolutionaries, Tanlay has remained in the family to this day.

The construction of the château of Sully is roughly contemporaneous with that of both Ancy-le-Franc and Tanlay, being begun on the plans of Nicolas Ribbonier of Langres for the Maréchal de Saulx-Tavannes in 1567. Here, too, were incorporated the square towers from an earlier fortress, which are placed at an angle to the four façades. The moat, which widens out to a beautiful formal lake on the eastern side, is fed by the waters of the River Drée. A great flight of stone steps descends from the eighteenth-century façade to a large semi-circular terrace, surrounded by a fine balustrade, whence further steps lead down to the surface of the water. The entrance front, which is approached across a wide lawn separating well-set-back domestic offices, is of great simplicity and structural elegance, with its pediment in which two flying figures support a clock in a scroll, and above, at the level of the roof-line, a pair of stone lions hold up a bell and an heraldic device. It is unfortunate that visitors, although they may enter the grounds, are not permitted in the château, since the renaissance court-yard at Sully was described by Mme de Sévigné as 'the most beautiful in France'. This imposing building was the birthplace in 1808 of a descendant of an Irish supporter of the Stuarts who went into exile with James II, the Maréchal de Mac-Mahon, Duke of Magenta, President of the French Republic from 1873 to 1879.

While not so rich in châteaux as the Valley of the Loire or the Ile-de-France, Burgundy, like Normandy, possesses an architectural heritage of outstanding quality, and of all periods from tenth-century Brancion to the reconstituted La Rochepot of the nineteenth. In all parts of the province, often in the most unexpected places, the traveller comes on picturesque ruins of mediaeval donjons and towers, charmingly simple manor houses and farms, stately country houses and graceful eighteenth-century *gentilhommières*. Although no listing here could possibly be exhaustive, there are, in addition to those so briefly mentioned, such beautiful châteaux as those of Thoisy-la-Bergère, Fleurigny, Montjeu, Montcony, La Clayette, the celebrated Clos-Vougeot of the vineyard, and the remarkable villa-like stable-block at Chaumont.

CHAPTER XII

Alphonse de Lamartine

In *Les Confidences*, written when he had entered middle-age, Lamartine recalled a period of his youth when he, like so many of his contemporaries, suffered deeply from that *malaise du siècle*—'Before having lived, I was wearied of living.' He described his life at this time in a village in the Mâconnais:

> All my family were away. My father, staying with one of my uncles, shooting in the forest of Burgundy. My mother travelling. My sisters dispersed or at their convent. I spent the whole of one long summer entirely alone, shut up with an old woman servant, my horse and my dog in my father's house at Milly. This village built of grey stone, at the foot of a mountain carpeted with box, with its steeple in the shape of a pyramid, whose foundations seemed burned up by the sun, its steep tracks, rocky, winding, bordered by vignerons' cottages and middens, and its houses covered with slates blackened by the downpours, where grew mosses carbonized like soot, recalls for all the world a village of Calabria or of Spain.
>
> This aridity, this poverty, this burnt-up appearance, this lack of water, of shade, of living vegetation, pleased me. It seemed to me that thus this nature was the more closely linked with my soul. I was myself a vine of this hill . . . *un cep de cette colline.*

It pleased Lamartine always to stress his Burgundian origin, his childhood spent in the countryside of the Mâconnais. He was a '*cep de Bourgogne*', a *vigneron* like the others, if somewhat grander. As a '*bon propriétaire*' he 'manured his fields', the pastures and vineyards of 'this Burgundian desert', this '*pays sans physionomie grandiose*', scorched by the sun of the South; throughout his life he could not—nor did he wish to—dust from his boots '*le sol de sa patrie bourguignonne*'.

This side of Lamartine has been obscured, eclipsed by the celebrity of the poet, by the success (and failure) of the diplomat and statesman, by the magnificence, the grand style of this strikingly handsome aristocrat, who was yet (paradoxically) by temperament and by long meditation on his experiences a genuine democrat. To his contemporaries, and to posterity, Lamartine was, and remains, the elegiac poet of romantic, ill-fated love. The publication in 1820, when he was thirty, of the first volume of his *Méditations Poétiques* found a society whose 'sensibility' (the word, and still more the emotional condition, abhorred by Byron) was predisposed—too facilely attuned—to respond to this new and highly original poetry. In France the worldly cynicism of the *ancien régime* in matters of sexual love, its *libertinages*, had been followed by the bacchanalia, the unbuttoned excesses of the Directory and the Empire. The chastened society of the Restoration desired a chaste, an idealized, an etherial, incorporeal love. Society sighed through its tears with the poet of *Elvire*, and lost no time in preparing itself to perform these new and fashionable roles. Nature copied art, and then art nature: *Emma Bovary* was thus born. No one paused to ask if the '*Moi*' of the *Méditations* corresponded with the Lamartine of real life. When the second volume, the *Nouvelles Méditations* was published in the autumn of 1823, any change of tone was lost on the public, engrossed, obsessed with the *volupté* of the exquisite sentiments in which it had so quickly found its *soul*. No one, save the critic Sainte-Beuve, observed that the poems of the second volume were different and often superior to those of the first. In creating *Elvire* and the lover of *Elvire* the poet had in fact destroyed the *man*. In political life Lamartine could not shake off the approbrious role; to his political enemies, and they were many, he was always 'the Poet'. It was left to the mundane, philistine, essentially bourgeois mind of Louis-Philippe to see through this almost universal miscasting of Lamartine. The King, who disliked him intensely—and, indeed, he was to have good reason for his antipathy—always professed to regard him as the *vigneron* from the Mâconnais, referring to him in an execrable pun as '*le vain de Bourgogne*'.

The family of Lamartine was descended from a Pierre Alamartine, merchant-bourgeois of Cluny, who flourished about 1550. Ascending in social rank through the generations, it was in the person of his great-grandson Jean Baptiste de Lamartine that the family, now ennobled, came into possession of the estates of Milly (in 1705) and Monceau and of a town house in Mâcon. From these somewhat humble origins, the Lamartines passed from the counter by way of the *robe*, to become accepted as members of the *noblesse d'épée* with Louis-François de Lamartine, the grandfather of the poet, who in 1745 won the coveted Cross of St Louis for his bravery on the field of Fontenoy. It was he who acquired the estate of Montculot, near Dijon, and built in Mâcon the Hotel de Lamartine, which still stands today in the Rue Bauderon-de-Senecé (No. 3). Of the three sons of Louis-François de Lamartine, the eldest, François-Louis, a valetudinarian who never married, ultimately inherited Monceau; the second, who was obliged, by the custom then prevailing in noble families, to enter the Church, and was known as the Abbé de Lamartine, inherited Montculot; the youngest, Pierre, who was called, after an estate belonging to his mother, the Chevalier de Pratz, followed his father in the service of the King. On the outbreak of the Revolution, with the abolition of the law of primogeniture, the Chevalier de Pratz, in order to continue the family name, was eventually permitted by his father to marry, in January 1790, a Mlle Alix des Roys, daughter of noble parents in the household of the Duc d'Orléans, whose favour and friendship they enjoyed. It was from the first a love-match. The young couple were provided for by the gift of the small patrimonial estate of Milly, not far from Mâcon. On 21st October 1790 in Mâcon their first child was born, a son, who was christened the following day Alphonse-Marie-Louis de Lamartine. The house where the poet was born has also survived, No. 18 Rue des Ursulines, opposite the convent of the Ursulines, which today houses the Musée Municipale. It was in this convent that, after the birth of Alphonse, the Chevalier was imprisoned by the revolutionaries;

and it was here, as we learn from the *Confidences*, that he had those romantically clandestine meetings with his young wife.

Despite the wartime bombing of Mâcon, for the traveller curious to visit or see these houses so closely associated with Lamartine there remain today two others: the Hôtels d'Ozenay and Senecé. The Hôtel d'Ozenay, which is not far from the Ursulines, at No. 15 Rue Lamartine, was acquired by the Chevalier de Pratz in 1804; it is here that the poet lived when in Mâcon before his marriage, and it was in the study here that he composed much of the *Méditations*. His mother died in this house in 1829. The early, eighteenth-century Hôtel Senecé is today occupied by the Académie de Mâcon, the society founded in 1805 by the 'terrible uncle' François-Louis de Lamartine, where as early as 1811 the young Lamartine read a literary paper in order to placate his uncle and father, who were worried by his undesirable liaison with a Mlle Henriette Pommier. Later Lamartine was president of this learned body; and three rooms in the Hôtel Senecé now contain the Musée Lamartine, a collection which illustrates the poet's life, as well as his literary and political work.

Noblesse oblige. The pace of revolution quickening, duty called the Chevalier de Pratz to leave his wife in Burgundy and to return to Paris. There, on 10th August 1790, with loyal troops and the Swiss guard, he defended the Tuileries from the attack of the revolutionary mob. Wounded by a musket-ball, he escaped from the fury of the assailants by plunging into the Seine opposite the Invalides. Captured on the farther bank, he was imprisoned; happily he was recognized by a municipal officer of the commune, who formerly had been a gardener in the service of a relative, and was set at liberty. He returned to Mâcon, where his son was born in October. In June 1791 the King tried to flee the country, thus precipitating the bloodiest stages of the Revolution. In Mâcon the Lamartine family were arrested as suspect nobles—the patriarch Louis-François, aged over eighty, his wife, his three sons and three daughters. By cart they were carried off (with the exception of the Chevalier, who was incarcerated in Mâcon) to prison in Autun. From prison it was but a step to the scaffold. Distraught, the

Citoyenne Lamartine, with the young Alphonse in her arms, pleaded with the authorities in Lyons and Dijon for the release of her husband and his family. However, it was only after the events of Thermidor 1794, which marked the end of the Terror, with the fall and execution of Robespierre, that the Lamartines were able to return to Mâcon. Late in his life Lamartine was to give a vivid account of these stirring times in his *History of the Girondins*. Meanwhile, Pierre de Lamartine, his military profession closed to him, removed with his family to Milly, to make a new life as a *vigneron*. Henceforth for Lamartine Milly was to become '*la terre natale*'.

Lamartine was just four when, in the autumn of 1794, the family were installed in the modest square house at Milly, with its blue shutters and low roof of sunburnt tiles. There he passed almost uninterruptedly the next six years, he and his three sisters playing with the village children, whose dress and simple manner of life they shared almost completely. The journey from Mâcon to Milly by the road to Cluny was imprinted, perhaps through the eye of the imagination, on his memory, as he later described it in his *Memoires Inédits*. The road passes the avenue of plane trees leading to the seventeenth-century château of Monceau, where lived his 'terrible uncle' François-Louis de Lamartine, since his father's death the head of the family. The house, which today is an old people's home, came afterwards into Lamartine's possession, and it was in a kiosk which he built among the vines, calling it *La Solitude*, that he wrote his *History of the Girondins*. Relating his earliest impressions, Lamartine remembered:

I began to see and understand external things, when my father and mother led us, all their tribe of children, in a long line of bullock carts, to establish us at Milly. Our mother was in the cart which led the procession, with two little girls between her knees, another on her breast. A host of packages filled the cart. My father went on foot, dressed as for shooting, a gun in his hand, supporting with the other hand the carriage at the bad places; his two dogs were on the lead, and two carts, filled with maids, pots and pans and luggage, followed him. All that formed a long column of curious conveyances advancing in the mud. The urging on of the bullock drivers, the lowing and jibbing of the bullocks, the frightened shrieks of the women, the laughter of the children in the carts, made a spectacle at once half picturesque, half touching. . . .

In his *Confidences* Lamartine wrote of his family life and his station in the world 'half-way between nobility and rusticity':

God has given me the grace of being born into one of those families of predilection, which are like a sanctuary of piety, where one breathes only the good air that several generations have exhaled in passing successively through life; a family without great distinction, but without stain, placed by Providence in one of these intermediate ranks in society, where one belongs at the same time to the nobility by name and to the people by the modesty of fortune, by the simplicity of life, and by residence in the country, in the midst of peasants, with the same habits and almost the same occupations. If I had to be born again on this earth, it is there that I should wish to be reborn. One is well placed there for seeing and understanding the diverse conditions of the human race —in the middle. Not high enough to be envied, not low enough to be disdained. The just and precise point where are met and summed up in the human condition the elevation of ideas which produces the elevation of viewpoint, the naturalness of feelings which association with nature preserves.

It could not be better expressed; Lamartine was to need in his tempestuous life all those reserves that such a background ensures. After learning the rudiments of Latin from the curé of the village, the Abbé Dumont, he was sent to a rough school in Lyons, from which he ran away. Placed with the Jesuit fathers near Belley in Franche-Comté, he progressed rapidly, carrying off many school prizes and making some lifelong friends in Louis de Vignet, Prosper Guichard de Bienassis and Aymon de Virieu, all of the provincial nobility like himself. It appears that before he left school at seventeen he had revealed a sexual precocity, his relations with a local girl leading to the birth of a child, an event which was hushed up by the collusion of his mother with the good Fathers of the Spirit. A prey to illnesses of a nervous kind, home at Milly and Mâcon he read widely and deeply between intermittent affairs of the heart. At this period he saw much of the Abbé Dumont, who was to be the hero of his immensely popular poem *Jocelyn*. It was to remove him from what his family considered a social *mésalliance* —he wished to marry Henriette Pommier, the daughter of a judge in Mâcon—that his relations furnished him with the money to go to Italy at the end of 1811. The financial prospects of the family were brightening; by dint of careful husbandry on the part of his parents the property at Milly was extended, the Hôtel d'Ozenay purchased in Mâcon, and a small estate, consisting of vineyards, fields and a ramshackle château was bought not far from Milly, at Saint-Point. An additional reason for allowing him to travel was to avoid the general conscription ordered by the Emperor Napoleon, whom the royalist Lamartines looked on as the 'Usurper'. After visiting Florence and Rome, Lamartine in the following January, having dissipated his resources in gaming and on prostitutes, accepted the invitation of his cousin, M. Dareste de la Chevanne, the director of the Manufacture Royale des Tabacs, to put him up in his house, a disused convent in Naples.

The experiences from which Lamartine distilled the love poems and elegies of the *Méditations Poétiques* centre on two women: Antoniella (*Elvira, Graziella*), the fisherman's daughter from Procida in the Bay of Naples, and Mme Julie Charles, whom he met at Aix-les-Bains in 1816. The end of both women was tragic. It would be quite unjustifiable to deny or to doubt the reality of the feelings—the unburdening of an exacerbated sentiment—of Lamartine as expressed in these poems; the romantics did feel in this way; this was indeed the 'romantic sensibility'. In reaction to all it stood for in literature and in life, Baudelaire and Flaubert were to follow. Reality, too, with Lamartine had at times a different complexion, something more earthy, more robustly Burgundian—a fact too often overlooked. Evidence of this is the birth on 1st March 1813 at the sumptuous château of Cormatin of a son, Léon de Pierreclos, to Nina, the extravagant, flighty wife of his friend Antoine de

Pierreclos, both the real father, Lamartine, and the putative father acknowledging the former's paternity. Furthermore, Lamartine was an excellent parent to his son, who in turn loved him; the death of Léon in 1841 was a bitter blow to his father.

Lamartine's love for Antoniella, however, was purely cerebral, a classic example of sex in the head. We see it beginning in a letter he wrote to his friend Virieu on 27th May 1812, the month in which he returned to Mâcon from Italy: 'I have no news from Naples. I am worried about this poor little Antoniella. I will perhaps never find again a heart like that. Where in the devil is it going to find its nest? All my life I shall regret her, and at times tears come to my eyes, when I think of her.' He was, in truth, to think of her all his life; but the *Elvire* poems and the story, *Graziella*, are true only in the reality of his sentiments, not in the facts. In the meanwhile he found carnal consolation in the ever-open arms of Nina de Pierreclos —and of others. On 6th January 1813, when he had for some time known that Nina was *enceinte* with his child, he wrote again to Virieu: 'I am almost in love with a pretty little actress, who loves me to distraction. I become more stupid every day. I must have a great superfluity of sentiments to cast them away thus like pearls before swine. But I must love no matter who. . . .' In this revealing confession Lamartine was at least honest about himself.

If the love offered so entirely and selflessly by the beautiful young Neapolitan was rejected by Lamartine by reason of the incompatibility of their social class, it was, after her untimely death, a source of constantly nurtured—if unconsciously nurtured—regret. No less ill-fated was the love which sprang up at first sight between him and Mme Jacques-Alexandre Charles (Julie) in the autumn of 1816 at Aix-les-Bains, where they both had gone to take the cure, and where chance found them staying at the same pension. After three weeks in Julie's company, Lamartine was obliged to return to Milly. The parted lovers wrote to each other daily. On 12th December he confessed to Virieu: '. . . And then, and then, I am now in access of a passion the most violent that the heart of a man has ever known. We are two who die literally of despair and of love. . . . What a being! What genius! What a superhuman creature!' Julie was eight years his senior, she was married, and she was, as she rightly suspected, dying. The end came almost exactly a year later, on 18th December 1817. A short time before, once again at Aix-les-Bains, Lamartine had written: 'Seated on the rock of the sporadic fountain, 29th August 1817, thinking of you, Julie; abbey of Hautecombe sheer above the lake. A sojourn so desired, if. . . Memory of our day of the month of September passed on the same lake—four o'clock in the evening.' And he composed the well-known lines:

> *Un soir, t'en souvient-il? nous voguions en silence;*
> *On n'entendait dans l'air, sur l'onde et dans les cieux*
> *Que le bruit des rameurs qui frappaient en cadence*
> *Tes flots harmonieux.*

A cultivated Frenchman, once asked by a foreign critic why the verse of Lamartine was rated so highly in his own country, replied that, whatever value he might have for individual Frenchmen, all had read him—he was an imperishable part of the French literary heritage.

> *Kennst du das Land?* . . .
> *Sur la plage sonore où la mer de Sorrente*
> *Déroule ses flots bleus au pied de l'oranger*
> *Il est, près du sentier, sous la haie odorante*
> *Une pierre petite, étroite, indifférente*
> *Aux pieds distraits de l'étranger.*

However, despite all this poetic soul-searching, the Burgundian in Lamartine constantly asserted its vital presence. In February 1819 he responded warmly to the advances made to him in Mâcon by Mme Lena de Larche, a very beautiful Florentine, married to a captain in the French army. But a crisis of conscience during a serious illness seems to have cut short this connection; or was it some desire to find in the solidity of a career and a family a cure or an alleviation of the neurasthenia which possessed him? His marriage to Mary-Anne (Marianne) Birch, the well-to-do daughter of an English army officer, took place in June 1820. In his wife Lamartine found an educated and sympathetic woman, no great beauty but sufficiently attractive to arouse and maintain his affections, and who in understanding and forgiving him his much-advertised past, was to provide a firm centre around which his life could henceforth revolve. The publication in March 1820 of the first volume of his *Méditations Poétiques*, without the name of the author, was followed by a second signed edition in the following month. His verses, previously only circulated among his friends or in the *salons* of Mâcon and the Faubourg St-Germain, were immediately read and taken to heart by almost the entire French reading public. Victor Hugo has recorded the effect that the poetry of Lamartine had on his generation. Appointed second attaché at the embassy in Naples, in the summer of that year he set himself up with his wife in that enchanting city and on the island of Ischia. Happy in those beautiful surroundings, Lamartine expressed at this time his modest hopes for the future: 'I would like to raise myself in Italy to the rank of secretary . . . and return at length to *finish*, as our fathers said, in some cottage of Burgundy or the Mâconnais, a patriarch pure and simple.'

Once back in France, he began in the winter of 1821–2 the restoration of the château of Saint-Point, parts of which dated from the fifteenth century, the stonework of the whole building having been much damaged by peasants armed with iron bars at the time of the Revolution. The somewhat bizarre, heterogeneous appearance which the château presents today is the result of carrying out the reconstruction in what Lamartine fondly imagined to be the *style anglais*—a Mâconnais Strawberry Hill. Through deaths in his family (the 'terrible uncle' died in Mâcon in 1827, his loved mother succumbed from an accident in 1829, and his father died at the ripe age of eighty-seven in 1840) Lamartine came in the course of time to be a large landowner in Burgundy, remitting to his five sisters their share of the inheritance in the form of annuities. Besides Milly, Monceau, Saint-Point, and the Mâcon town houses, he inherited on the death in 1826 of his somewhat sceptical uncle, the ex-Abbé Jean-Baptiste-François de Lamartine, the château of Montculot. Lamartine had a liking for the ex-Abbé's

company, sharing his difficulties in accepting wholeheartedly
the Catholic faith, and frequently visited him. The château, a
building in the style of Louis Seize, today appears rather run-
down and neglected; it stands in the wooded hills above the
beautiful Canal de Bourgogne, about fifteen miles by road west
of Dijon. The ponds at Montculot were fed by some fourteen
springs; it was seated at their edge or in those woods that
Lamartine wrote several of his *Méditations*, and the poem *La
Source dans les bois*. Here in autumn the woods are brilliant in
their colouring, aflame with burning reds and gold; and in the
ponds the reflections on the enamelled surface of the water
jump up like fish to meet the falling orange-yellow leaves. It
was with sorrow that his crippling financial difficulties compelled Lamartine to sell Montculot in 1831.

   All his life Lamartine looked on his social condition and
principal activity as those of a Burgundian gentleman-farmer,
un bon propriétaire, in his vineyards and farms of the Mâconnais.
Except for the periods when he served as a diplomat in Naples
and Florence, and for his trip to the Middle East, he spent the
winters in Mâcon and the rest of the year on one of his estates,
at Milly, Saint-Point or Monceau. He played an active part in
local administration, sitting on the departmental council for
Saône-et-Loire, where his prominent position in the country
lent weight to his presence there. Even when he was elected to
the Chambre des Députés, and took a lead in the liberal
democratic movement that precipitated the overthrow of
Louis-Philippe, when briefly he became minister of foreign
affairs, he returned to Burgundy each autumn to be present
at the vintage. Following the habits of his childhood, in the
country he rose at five each morning, gave orders to his
vignerons and farmers, received visits from the mayor, whom he
advised on local matters, or the curé, come to solicit his assistance, before settling down to his writing. He loved nothing
better than to ride, mounted on a beautiful Arab or thorough-
bred, accompanied by Marianne or their daughter Julia, while
she lived, or one of his many guests, overseeing the work in the
vineyards. He would be greeted by old peasants, raising their
hats to salute the *grand seigneur*, but addressing a '*Bon jour,
Alphonse*' to the man whom they had known since childhood as

one of themselves and who had grown up into the '*grand diable de Bourgogne*'. His attitude to these tenant *vignerons* and their families had much in it of the old feudal regard of the lord for his vassals and retainers. But this sense of *noblesse oblige* cost him dearly.

Like most contemporary landowners Lamartine ran his estate on the *métayage* system. Further, each year he bought from his *vignerons* their share of the wine harvest, paying them in ready cash, then selling the wine, together with his own half-share, to wine-merchants in gross, often at a price ruinous to himself. In addition to the rebuilding carried out at Saint-Point and to his customary extravagance and generosity, he managed his affairs badly. As early as 1825 his mother, an excellent housekeeper herself, noted sadly: 'He has sold his wine at three-quarters the price he should have. . . .' As a young man he had gambled, and lost heavily. In 1833 he wrote: 'I am a gambler still, but as I am no longer able to yield to my passion after having received the blessings of all the apostolic hands of Europe, I have taken to planting vines. The vines make a vast green cloth. The sun and the snow are its two croupiers, who play to bring you treasure or ruin.' Bad seasons and good alike, his *vignerons* must have their cash without delay. The result was that he had to borrow deeply; ultimately he became so encumbered with debt that he was no longer able to increase the mortgages on his properties and was forced to put them up for sale, to meet his creditors. Nobody would come forward to buy—this may have been out of local loyalty and respect—and he was obliged to go on borrowing to pay interest due, at a rate as high as 26 per cent. In 1852 he wrote to a friend: 'All goes here to supreme misery. Ice, hail yesterday as big as apples. Rain every day, bailiffs every week . . . I pay nevertheless my *vignerons* and after them I will be able to pay nobody. . . .'

One resource open to him was in the great popularity of his writings, both poetry and prose, for which he was paid sums which few authors could command today. Since the vines cost him so much, 'the ink', as he said, 'had to go to pay the wine'. But this ink was but a drop in the ocean of his indebtedness. He wrote incessantly; his output was prodigious, as was his

success. The *History of the Girondins*, which was published in
1847, sold 25,000 copies in a few months. The necessity of
maintaining a house in Paris, and the constant entertainment
at the time when he was among the leaders of the opposition
against King Louis-Philippe, which led to the revolution of
1848 and the foundation of the Second Republic, added greatly
to his financial distress. The sale of Milly was only avoided by
the timely request of a publisher for his *Confidences*. Later the
Emperor Napoleon III, recognizing France's debt to Lamartine, tried in vain to assist him with public funds, but the proud
old man refused, saying, 'I cannot and will not accept at any
price. Rather die than be dishonoured'. In fourteen years he
had earned with his pen seven million francs, from which he
had repaid loans of four and a half millions; the rest had gone
on payment of interest. Nevertheless he could not make ends
meet. At length he was forced to accept a governmental sub-
vention; the day he did so he put all his remaining property
up for sale; he wished, as he put it, 'to go out with his hands
clean'.

Although he had written 'Before having lived, I was wearied
of living', nothing could have been further from the truth. He
had the native-born Burgundian's zest for life, despite the
failure of so much in which he had hoped and the malign
intervention of fatality among those he loved. Besides the deaths
of Antoniella and Julie, he lost his son, while still a baby, and
his adored girl Julia, tragically, at the age of ten. His illegitimate son, Léon de Pierreclos, died in 1841, aged twenty-eight.
His mother scalded herself to death. His father almost alone
lived out his years. When his wife Marianne died on 21st May
1863, Lamartine was in bed completely immobilized with
rheumatism, cared for by his favourite niece, Valentine de
Cessiat. This unselfish young woman, who broke off her
engagement to look after her worshipped uncle, did everything
to protect the failing old man, disbursing what money came in
among the pressing creditors. Then, in September 1867, on
receipt of a telegram from Pope Pius IX, according the special
dispensation necessary, Lamartine went through the religious
ceremony of marriage with Valentine de Cessiat. The civil
ceremony never took place. By an imperial decree of 31st

August 1868 'Mlle de Cessiat, canoness of the chapter of St Anne of Bavaria', was permitted to style herself the Comtesse de Lamartine. The man of peace did not live to witness the war and humiliation of 1870. Lamartine died on 28th February 1869. Refusing, by his wishes, the state funeral offered by the Emperor Napoleon III, the Comtesse de Lamartine buried her uncle and husband in the mausoleum he had built for his family at Saint-Point. As his universal legatee, she took upon herself the liquidation of debts amounting in all to 2,214,838 francs.

Every year many visitors to Mâcon make the *Circuit Lamartinien*, a pleasant short run among hills covered with vines, meadows and crops, best perhaps seen in early October, at the time of the *vendange*. Leaving the town by the N.79, the visitor may turn off after five miles to visit the grounds of the château of Monceau and then continue on, until about a mile past the appropriately named village of La Roche-Vineuse he turns left for the hamlet of Milly, today, in commemoration of the poet, Milly-Lamartine. Closely adjoining Milly are the villages of Bussières and Pierreclos, all three associated in the minds of readers of Lamartine with the enigmatic figure of his first schoolmaster and for long his friend, the Abbé François Dumont. The romantic story of this priest against every inclination, which he idealized in his *Jocelyn*, was told to Lamartine by his mistress Nina de Pierreclos in the days when he visited her at the château of Cormatin. Her sister-in-law, Marguerite de Pierreclos, or Mlle de Milly, as she was known, lived in the château of Pierreclos. She was the original of Lamartine's Laurence in *Jocelyn*. After Thermidor and the end of the Terror, those royalists who had been released from prison or had taken part in and survived the general resistance against the Revolution in the Lyonnais and the Cevennes, gathered at the châteaux of the Pierreclos family. Among them was the handsome, educated, fiercely anti-Jacobin François Dumont who, although in orders, shared fully the life and the tastes of his friends. François and Marguerite fell deeply in love; he was about thirty, she then twenty-three. A child was born to them who, it seems, was

brought up in Lyons. In 1800 Mlle de Milly married a Lyonnais banker, M. Mongez, and the Abbé Dumont was appointed
curé to the parishes of Bussières and Milly. Such were the bare
facts on which Lamartine based his romantic tale in verse,
which was published in 1836. The Abbé Dumont died in 1832
and was buried by the door of the apse of his church at
Bussières, where may be read this memorial to him:

> To the memory
> of F. Dumont, curé of Bussières and Milly
> for nearly forty years
> Born and died poor as his divine
> Master
> Alphonse de Lamartine, his friend,
> has consecrated this stone
> near the church
> to perpetuate among his flock
> the memory
> of the good pastor
> 1832

Saint-Point, which is due west of Bussières, separated by a
high hill (Lamartine's 'mountain'), is reached by two roads:
that from the north, passing Berzé-la-Ville (where a visit may
be made to the Cluniac Chapelle des Moines) and the feudal
castle of Berzé-la-Châtel; or from the south *via* Tramayes. Of all
this Burgundian countryside which figures so largely in the
development of Lamartine's thought and work, perhaps the
village and château of Saint-Point bring the visitor closest to
the poet, who restored the house and church there, and who
rests in the Victorian gothic mausoleum by the park wall. The
twelfth-century parish church, which is of the Cluniac romanesque style, used to contain two paintings of saints by Marianne
de Lamartine, but they were not there on my last visit. In the
château, the drawing-room, study and Lamartine's bedroom
remain much as they were in his lifetime. The bed, that on which
he died, was brought from Paris. On the chimney-piece are the
murals painted by Marianne for her husband; and many me-
mentoes recall moving incidents from his long life, particularly

the crucifix left to him by Julie. If the gothic chapel by the gate, in which were buried beside Lamartine his mother, his son, his daughter Julia, his wife Marianne, and Mme Valentine de Lamartine, breathes an air of somewhat Victorian religiosity, the words of the inscription perhaps suggest the poet's final words on the Christian revelation: 'SPERAVIT ANIMA MEA— My soul has hoped.'

CHAPTER XIII

Premier Duchy of France

WITH THE DEATH of Charles the Rash outside Nancy on 5th January 1477 and the failure of the male Valois line, Burgundy reverted to the throne of France, but only after King Louis XI had sent the Sire de Craon to occupy the duchy with a military force. By the edict of 18th March of that year the King confirmed the privileges of Burgundy and created the Parlement in Dijon to replace the *Jours-Généraux*, which the dukes had formerly held at Autun or at St-Laurent-lès-Chalon. However, it was not until two years later that Louis felt sufficiently secure to brave the antipathies of his reluctant subjects and to come to Dijon, where he swore in the church of St-Bénigne to maintain the franchises of the city and the duchy. Burgundy was to remain a *pays d'états*; its rank as the *premier duché-pairie* of France was likewise retained, and at the coronation of the French kings the senior prince of the royal blood represented the duke of Burgundy as the first peer of the realm, bearing the royal crown and girding on the king's sword. François Ier sought to win the loyalty and affection of the Burgundians, spending much time in the duchy and appointing as its hereditary governor a prince of the house of Guise. In the seventeenth century the Guise were succeeded by princes of the Condé family, who remained at the head of the government of Burgundy until these administrative arrangements of the *ancien régime* were swept away in the Revolution. These first governors presided over the meetings of the Estates of Burgundy to which came representatives of the provincial nobility, the clergy led by the Bishop of Autun, and the third estate, which had as its leader the viscount-mayor of the city of Dijon. The capital of the province took on a new life, the departed splendours of its ducal past being in some way compensated for by the presence in those sumptuous town houses which are still the pride of the city, of a numerous nobility, mostly of the *noblesse de robe*, an educated body of *grands bourgeois* families, from whom were recruited its councillors and advocates, and a well-to-do merchant class, which was based securely on the exploitation of the trade in the wines of the celebrated Côte d'Or.

In the sixteenth century the education of the youth of the province was promoted by the foundation of the Collège de Dijon (Collège des Godrans), established by the President of the Parlement Odinet Godran in 1581, and by the formidable scholastic instruction introduced by members of the Order of Jesus. It was in this ambience that the young Bossuet grew up, his mother, Madame la Conseillère Bossuet, being typical of the cultivated piety of these Dijonnais governing circles. Another woman who made her mark on the religious life of the century was the Blessed Mother Jeanne-Françoise Frémyot, Baroness of Rabutin-Chantal, who was born at Dijon in 1572, and, left a widow, came under the gentle but persuasive influence of François de Sales, in association with whom she founded the Order of the Visitation, with the declared purpose of assisting 'strong souls with weak bodies'. She was the famous 'Sainte Chantal' of the family of Bussy-Rabutin and his cousin Mme de Sévigné. Of Burgundians at the court of the Grand Monarque few could illustrate such dissimilar native characteristics as Comte Roger de Bussy-Rabutin, the very personification of the Gallic spirit, with its courage, panache and verbal raillery, and the sober, weighty Bossuet, whose measured eloquence was a constant panegyric of the natural—and by that he understood the existing—order of things.

Jacques-Bénigne Bossuet was born in Dijon in 1627 of a prosperous legal family, his father being a judge of Parlement, and was educated first among the Jesuits in his native city before being sent to Paris to the Collège de Navarre, there to carry out the wishes of his pious mother by studying theology, to fulfil her desire for him to enter the Church. His studious turn of mind and his assiduous application to his studies earned him the punning nickname among his colleagues of *Bos suetus aratro*—the ox broken to the plough. By his father's influence he obtained a canonry in Metz at the age of thirteen, and subsequently an archdeaconry, but in 1659 he was back in

Paris, where his reputation among the aristocratic circle which frequented the Hôtel de Rambouillet (the original home of the *Précieuses*) gained him the appointment as preacher at the Chapel Royal. His pulpit eloquence was not in the fashionable style of his prominent rival Bourdaloue, and did not appeal to the taste of ladies such as Mme de Sévigné, although it was to win the praise of discriminating critics like La Bruyère and Fénelon. His oratorical qualities were best displayed in those sermons preached at the funerals of highly placed persons, in the presence of the court, and which were subsequently published in the *Oraisons funèbres*—at the obsequies of Henrietta Maria, widow of King Charles I of England (1669), her daughter Henrietta, Duchess of Orléans (1670), and of the great Condé (1687). In 1670 he was appointed by Louis XIV tutor to his only son, the Dauphin, 'that merely genealogical incident at his father's court', and Bossuet then wrote for his pupil's instruction his great trilogy: the *Traité de la connaissance de Dieu et de soi-même*, the *Histoire universelle* and the *Politique tirée de l'Ecriture Sainte*. In the last he is said to have 'hallowed the France of Louis XIV by proving its astonishing likeness to the Israel of Solomon'. No mean feat. If it would do him an injustice to say that his able pen was at the disposal of his king, yet his great controversial powers were used in defence of what he considered the rightful place of the Catholic Church in the monarchical state: against the Huguenots, the Jansenist, quietist and protestant heresies, and in defence of the Gallican Church and the traditional theology—and in his latter years against the views on the love of God of his much younger pupil Fénelon. Over all the work of the Burgundian Bossuet there breathes the spirit of reasonableness; it has been well remarked that Bossuet would 'willingly have undertaken to make an intelligent Chinaman accept all his ideas, if only he could be induced to lend them his attention', that attention which through the ages has been conspicuously lacking.

Perhaps even more remarkable than the career of Bossuet in church and state was that of another Burgundian, his contemporary, who rose from a humble station to become a Maréchal de France—the most celebrated of all military engineers and a clear-sighted economist, Sébastien le Prestre de Vauban. Vauban, who was born at Saint-Léger-Vauban (Yonne) in 1633, was orphaned at the age of ten, and in the wretched circumstances in which he found himself had the good fortune to be befriended by the Prior of the Carmelites at Semur-en-Auxois, who, realizing the boy's capabilities, educated him in mathematics and the sciences. At the time of the Fronde, when he was seventeen, he enlisted in the army of the great Condé, and within a year gave proof of such gallantry that he was offered a commission, which he declined on account of his poverty. Captured by the royal troops, he was well treated by Mazarin, and thenceforth he became a devoted subject of the King, being in 1655 commissioned as an *ingénieur du roi* and quickly advancing in the royal service. He gained fame from his conduct of sieges, several of which he carried out in the presence of Louis XIV; after the capture of Lille he was rewarded with a lieutenancy in the guard (ranking as a colonelcy). Subsequently he was put in charge, as *commissaire-général des fortifications*, of building the fortresses which guarded France's eastern frontiers, and he was the author of several books which became the standard works on fortification. Saint-Simon in his *Memoirs* is not known for the benignity of his judgements, especially on those whom he considered his social inferiors, yet he drew a pleasing portrait of this old soldier, who had the courage to represent to Louis XIV the necessity of reintroducing the Edict of Nantes, and whose heartfelt consideration for the plight of the French peasantry caused him to publish in 1707 his *Projet d'une dixième royale*:

Vauban, surnamed Le Prestre, was a gentleman of Burgundy, no more, but perhaps the most honourable and upright man of his day. What is more, although he had the reputation of being more skilled and learned in the art of siege-warfare than any other engineer, he was the simplest, truest, and most modest of men . . . there never was a man better natured, gentler, nor more obliging. He was courteous without servility, almost miserly with the lives of his soldiers, and possessed the kind of valour that bears every burden and lets others enjoy the credit. When, in 1703, the King informed him of his intention to make him a Maréchal de France,

Vauban begged him first to reflect that that honour was never intended for men of his condition who could not command the King's armies. It might be embarrassing, he said, if the marshal in command at a siege were found to be his junior in rank. This generous objection, supported with many manifestly unselfish arguments, only increased the King's desire to advance him. . . . Vauban received the rank with a modesty equal to his previous unselfishness, and one and all acclaimed a most signal honour to which no other man of his condition was ever raised before or since. Such he was when he was elevated to be a Maréchal de France. You shall now see how he was brought broken-hearted to his grave for the very qualities that had earned him his laurels, and that, in any country but France, would have won for him honours of every other kind.

A patriot in the true sense, he had always been moved by the sufferings of the peasants under the disproportionate burden of taxation. His professional experience had taught him the need for government spending and the little likelihood that the King would consent to retrench in his pleasures or his pomps. He therefore despaired of there being any alleviation of their ever-increasing afflictions. With such considerations in mind he never made a journey (and he continually crossed and recrossed the country from end to end) without making precise records of the values and yield of the land, the trades and industries in the various provinces and towns, the nature of the taxes, and the methods of collection. . . . He devoted at least twenty years to that research and spent on it large sums from his own purse. In the process he gradually became convinced that the only sure source of wealth was the land, and accordingly began to evolve an entirely new system of taxation. . . .

He proposed abolishing levies of every kind and substituting in their place a single tax, divided into two parts, the first part to be on the ownership of land rated at one-tenth of its yield; the second, on a somewhat lower rate, on commerce and industry. . . . This single tax he wished to call the King's tithe. . . . But the plan had one incurable defect. It produced more wealth for the King than he had received by the older methods; it relieved the peasants from ruin and oppression; but at the same time it destroyed an army of financiers, agents, and petty officials of many different kinds, obliging them to live by their own labours and not at the public expense. . . . That in itself was enough to condemn the book. . . .

Thus it came as no surprise when the King, sheltered and prejudiced as he was, gave the maréchal a frigid reception on accepting his book. . . . From that moment onwards Vauban's past services, his military genius, his virtues, and the King's regard counted as nothing, and thenceforward he was viewed as being no better than a lunatic lover of the peasantry, a scoundrel bent on undermining the power of the ministers and consequently the authority of the King himself. King Louis said so much to his face, and he did not mince his words . . . and the unlucky Vauban, who was loved by all right-thinking Frenchmen, did not long survive the loss of his master's favour. He died in solitude a few months' later, wasted by grief and in a distress of mind to which King Louis appeared wholly insensible. . . . Vauban's fame, however, had spread throughout Europe . . . and in France itself he was sincerely mourned by all who were neither tax-farmers nor their agents.

His death took place in March 1709, in his seventy-fifth year.

In 1749 the newly established Académie de Dijon offered as the subject of an essay prize the question: *Whether the progress of the sciences and the arts has contributed to corrupting morals or purifying them.* The winner of this competition was a hitherto little known writer and unsuccessful inventor of a system of musical notation, Jean-Jacques Rousseau. A few years later he again competed, but failed to gain the prize with his *Discours sur inégalité.* These two works established the literary reputation of Rousseau and resounded no less to the fame of the Academy of Dijon. In 1701 the councillor to the Parlement Pierre Fevret had bequeathed his fine library to the Collège des Godrans, stipulating that it should be open to the public on two days of the week. In this way was founded the Bibliothèque Publique

H

de Dijon. The old-established parliamentary family of Bouhier had amassed a splendid collection of books and manuscripts over the generations; in this library the President Jean Bouhier brought together what was in reality an academy, the Literary Society, frequented by scholars whose names were to add lustre to Dijon's reputation for civility and erudition. The Bouhier library has not survived intact, but many of its manuscripts have enriched the Bibliothèque Nationale. Then in 1722 was created the University of Dijon, although in possessing only one faculty, that of law, it disappointed the hopes of the citizens. This failure was made good by a legacy of the Dean of Parlement Hector-Bernard Pouffier by which was instituted an Academy, for the purpose of holding 'learned conferences' in medicine, physics and the moralities. The institution was granted letters patent in 1740, and it was this Academy, which was stoutly supported by the famous naturalist, Buffon, that proposed the essay competition won by Rousseau in 1750. Two years later a Literary Society, the successor to that of Bouhier, was formed by the President Gilles-Germain Richard de Ruffey, which had as members such outstanding spirits as Buffon, Charles de Brosses, the musician Rameau, the dramatist Crébillon and other celebrities. Under the leadership of President Ruffey the Dijon Literary Society became amalgamated with the declining Academy, infusing it with new life, so that Ruffey might be considered the second founder of an institution which contributed so largely to the intellectual life of Burgundy in the latter half of the eighteenth century.

Jean-Philippe Rameau, one of the most distinguished names in French music, was born in Dijon in October 1683, the son of an organist, who with an eye to future security wished his son to follow, like so many of his class, the lucrative and socially accepted profession of the law. In this he was unsuccessful, but it does appear that he imparted to the young Rameau the only formal musical education that he received. Virtually unknown until the age of forty, Rameau was first recognized rather as a theorist, as a *savant* and a *philosophe*, than as a composer—as the learned exponent of musical theory in the famous *Traité de l'harmonie*, published in Paris in 1722, the same year as *The Well-Tempered Clavier* of Johann Sebastian Bach. The music on

which Rameau's fame depends was composed for the most part
between the ages of fifty and fifty-six, after his brilliant talents
for operatic composition had been discovered by the rich patron
La Pouplinière, who arranged for the first performance of his
opera *Hippolyte et Aricie* in Paris in 1733. This success was
followed two years later by the opera-ballet *Les Indes Galantes*,
and again, two years after, by his masterpiece, *Castor et Pollux*.
From the outset, Rameau's work stirred up critical controversy;
his style was found abstruse, forced and difficult by the supporters of Lully, who looked on him as a dangerous innovator,
a subverter of the established French operatic tradition. In
1745 he triumphed with the comedy-ballet *La Princesse de
Navarre*, which was performed at Versailles to celebrate the
marriage of the Dauphin with the Infanta Maria Teresa, and
was rewarded by Louis XV with an annual pension and the
honorary title of Composer of the Royal Chamber Music. In the
'50s he was again the centre of another battle of critics, the
so-called War of the Buffoons, when the man who twenty years
previously had been reviled by the Lullists was now extolled
as the idol of those upholders of the French operatic style as
opposed to the Italian, whose music found favour with Jean-
Jacques Rousseau and the Encyclopaedists. Prominent among
the latter was Denis Diderot, that near-Burgundian from
neighbouring Langres, who was to write a small masterpiece
about the composer's parasitic, malicious, cynical nephew,
Jean-François—*Le Neveu de Rameau*. In his later years Rameau
turned his attention once more to musical theory. A perfection-
ist to the last, he died in 1764, and was reported on his death-
bed to have reproached the attendant priest, come to administer
the last rites, for the incorrectness of his chanting.

Prominent among the members of the Dijon Literary Society
of Ruffey and of the Academy were the two friends and former
school-fellows at the Collège des Godrans who were so typical
of their class and age, George-Louis Leclerc, Comte de Buffon,
and Charles de Brosses, known usually as the President de
Brosses from his presidency of the Parlement de Bourgogne.
The former was born in Montbard on 7th September 1707, son
of a councillor of Parlement; the latter, two years his junior,
coming from a similar family background, was born in Dijon.

These two men, Burgundian to the backbone in their intellectual interests and their style of life—unlike many of their successful contemporaries they made Burgundy their home—reflect the age that produced the Encyclopaedists, de Brosses indeed requesting from his friend Buffon an introduction to Diderot for whom he later contributed articles to the *Encyclopédie*. (Diderot afterwards drew the unkind, but possibly lifelike, portrait of Mme de Buffon: 'She had no neck any more. Her chin made half the journey, her breasts the other half, as a result of which her three chins repose upon two fine soft pillows.') Buffon, like de Brosses, first studied law, but then switched to mathematics and the physical sciences. At twenty-five he inherited the very considerable property of Montbard from his mother, and devoting himself to the study of natural science, at the early age of thirty-two he was appointed keeper of the *Jardin du Roi* and the Royal Museum. His life-work was the great *Histoire naturelle*, the first edition, in forty-four quarto volumes—much prized by collectors for its beautiful plates—being published in Paris from 1749 to 1804. Buffon died in 1788, at the age of eighty-one. His only son, George-Louis-Marie, an officer in the royal army, met his death under the guillotine, aged thirty, in 1793.

Charles de Brosses had at least two points in common with his somewhat older contemporary Alexis Piron (1689–1773), the author of the successful comedy *Métromanie*—both men were the possessors of a sparkling wit and both failed to be elected to a chair in the French Academy. De Brosses was debarred by the personal antipathy of Voltaire; to whatever reason Piron might have attributed his exclusion from a place among the immortals, he has immortalized his rejection in the epigrammatic epitaph;

> *Çi gît Piron qui fut rien.*
> *Pas même académicien.*

De Brosses was one of the most remarkable men in a remarkable age. Besides fulfilling in an exemplary way his duties as first president of the Parlement de Bourgogne, he gave proof of an astonishing range of interests. As a classicist he showed a scholar's regard for the purity of the text in his edition of Sallust, whom he translated, providing commentaries on the historian and his period, and filling in the lacunae in the *mss* in the style of the original author. After his Italian tour, taken in 1739 in the company of his friend, the mediaeval French scholar Lacurne de Sainte-Palaye, he published his *Lettres sur l'état actuel d'Herculée*, the first book describing the excavations of Herculaneum, and left his celebrated *Lettres familières*, an account of his travels written in a graceful style, at once polished, urbane, yet enlivened with an engaging *brio*. He had an eye for the unusual, as in the account he gave of a musical concert provided by the teenage girls of the foundling conservatory of the *Pietà* in Venice. 'They are reared at public expense and trained solely to excel in music. And so they sing like angels, and play the violin, the flute, the organ, the violoncello and the bassoon. . . . Each concert is given by about forty girls. I assure you there is nothing so charming as to see a young and pretty nun in her white robe, with a bouquet of pomegranate flowers in her hair, leading the orchestra and beating time with all the precision imaginable. . . .' (What a wealth of suggestion there is in that word 'solely'.) Persuaded by his friend Buffon, de Brosses turned to the natural sciences and brought out his *Histoire des navigations aux terres australes*, a work that influenced both Cook and Bougainville, and led indirectly to the founding of the penal colony at Botany Bay. His contributions to the nascent science of anthropology were considerable: E. B. Tylor in his *Primitive Culture* praises de Brosses' researches into the origin of language, published in his *Mécanique des langues*; and the same methods he applied to the history of religion, making public his findings in the *Culte des dieux fétiches*, in which he showed how in the evolution of religious ideas the practice of fetishism preceded that of idolatry.

It is clear that in the civilization of the eighteenth century Dijon owed much to its position as capital of Burgundy, the existence of its Parlement demanding an educated class of functionaries, a *noblesse de robe*, which formed an important link between the higher ranks of the bourgeoisie and the territorial nobility. These Burgundian patricians contributed greatly to

the age of the Encyclopaedists—but then so did the essentially
plebeian Rousseau. It is in the light of the influence of Jean-
Jacques that one may perhaps best appreciate the strange
career of another Burgundian, Nicolas-Edme Rétif (or Restif)
de la Bretonne. This prolific author—his published works
numbered something in the region of two hundred volumes—
was born in Sacy (Yonne) in 1734 and, outliving the Revolution,
died in 1806, before he could take up the place offered him by
Napoleon in the ministry of police, an appointment eminently
suited to the exercise of his compendious knowledge of the
seamy side of life. Contemporary taste has found much to
admire in Restif, in his disturbing introspection, arising from
his acute self-analysis and his recognition of the force of human
sensuality and eroticism. Drawing on his own experiences, real
or imagined, Restif, in his very numerous short stories and his
autobiography in fourteen volumes, *Monsieur Nicolas*, has left
an invaluable picture of his times. In a not dissimilar manner,
as a painter of genre scenes, Jean-Baptiste Greuze, a native of
Tournus, where he was born in 1725, has furnished another
commentary on his age—and on its taste. Greuze was much
admired by Diderot, not for his portraits, which still find favour
with the critics, but for reasons which today would appeal
perhaps only to communist advocates of the style of socialist
realism. Although Diderot granted that 'there is no great
painter who has not known how to do portraits'—and he cites
Raphael, Rubens and Van Dyck, among others—yet the
paintings of Greuze that he estimated most highly were those
with such titles as *The Village Bride, The Paralytic, or The Fruits
of a Good Education, The Ungrateful Son or Filial Piety*. 'This
Greuze, truly he's my man. The genre pleases me; it is moral
painting.' And to show what he meant, Diderot praised most
enthusiastically a painting entitled *The Well-loved Mother*, which
showed a large brood of offspring gambolling around their
parent. This work, which Mme Geoffrin described as *'une
fricassée d'enfants'*, drew from Diderot the commendation, 'It is
excellent, both in respect to talent and morals. It preaches
population. . . .'* To us this seems about as relevant to the art

* This view of Diderot's estimate of Greuze's art is based on that of
Professor A. M. Wilson in his excellent *Diderot*.

of the painter as Charles Dickens' remark in the preface to *Martin Chuzzlewit* to the art of the novelist: 'I hope I have taken every available opportunity of showing the want of sanitary improvements in the neglected dwellings of the poor.'

Greuze died in 1805. Another Burgundian who spanned the centuries, carrying with him an enigmatic reputation, which has puzzled both his contemporaries and posterity, was Charles-Geneviève-Louise-Auguste-André-Timothée d'Eon de Beaumont, commonly and more conveniently known as the Chevalier d'Eon. The charming renaissance-style house, the Hôtel d'Uzès, in which the Chevalier was born in 1728 of a family of the Burgundian *noblesse de robe*, still exists in Tonnerre (Yonne). It stands at No. 22 Rue du Pont, and is today occupied as the office of the Caisse d'Epargne. The reason why this active and intelligent man should have wished (if indeed he did wish) to dress and live as a woman for some forty years, after he had lived forty-two years as a man, has never been entirely satisfactorily explained. Recent revelations and confessions of the psychological and social drives that have brought men to seek to change their sex may have some bearing in the case of the Chevalier d'Eon, but still do not completely dispel the ambiguity which surrounds his life. He was a redoubtable swordsman and had served gallantly with the army of Maréchal de Broglie on the Rhine, where he was seriously wounded. D'Eon is said to have first put on female dress when on a diplomatic visit to the court of Elizabeth of Russia. There, acting as the Empress' reader, he spent long periods in her company and successfully accomplished his delicate mission.

Bets on his sex were laid in London, where he had been sent on diplomatic business at the court of St James, and on one occasion he beat up some offensive bookmakers with a stick. In 1777 an action brought before Lord Mansfield for the recovery of one such bet brought the question to a judicial decision—he was adjudged a woman. He had certainly been employed by Louis XV in his secret diplomacy (that is, his negotiations carried on outside official channels)—indeed, for his services he was awarded the Grand Cross of St Louis. After the King's death in 1774 Beaumarchais, the author of *The Barber of Seville* and *The Marriage of Figaro*, was employed to

demand from the Chevalier the return of certain incriminating
documents in his possession. Beaumarchais seems to have
allowed himself (perhaps willingly) to be persuaded of d'Eon's
femininity and described him as a Joan of Arc of the eighteenth
century. 'Our manners are obviously softened,' Voltaire wrote.
'D'Eon is a Pucelle d'Orléans who has not been burned.' In
retirement in London during the Revolution, he took part in
fencing matches, being seriously hurt in one at the age of
sixty-eight. He lived on, dressed as a be-diamonded old lady, at
the house of a Mrs Cole, the recipient in his last years of charity.
He died in London in 1810.

The Revolution destroyed the much that still existed of the
autonomy and independence of the ancient historical province;
the Estates-General of Burgundy, the Parlement and the
Chambre des Comptes were all swept away; even the Academy
of Dijon did not escape the ruthless suppression of all that was
tarnished, in the eyes of earnest republicans and others, by its
aristocratic connection with the *ancien régime*. The Paris of the
States-General, the Legislative Assembly and the Convention
became the capital of France, and the provincial capitals,
among them Dijon, withered away with the loss of effective
political power. Nevertheless, travellers such as the Prussian
J. F. Reichardt attest the general security and material well-
being of Burgundy in 1792. Two years later was completed an
undertaking which had been envisaged as early as the beginning of the seventeenth century—the Canal du Centre, linking
the Saône with the Loire. (The communications of the province
were further improved by the Canal de Bourgogne, which,
joining the Saône with the Yonne, was open for navigation in
1834; and finally by the development of the railways after 1850,
benefiting greatly Dijon.) It is significant that in the revolutionary era it was still the class which provided the members of
the legal profession (not now the patricians of the *noblesse de
robe* but rather notaries and minor magistrates) which for the
most part produced those Burgundians who played a conspicuous role in the events which then shook France, and with it
all Europe.

Saint-Just can hardly be called a Burgundian, although he

was born in 1767 at Decize in the Nivernais, his mother being the daughter of a local notary named Robinot. He lived there for but five years of his boyhood, from the age of four to nine; and his name is associated rather with his father's native Picardy. Another prominent revolutionary figure was born in 1763 also on the borders of Burgundy, at Auxonne; this was Claude-Antoine Prieur-Duvernois, usually known as Prieur de la Côte d'Or, which he represented in the National Assembly, to distinguish him from another member, Pierre-Louis Prieur 'of the Marne'. Like Lazare Carnot, with whom his name will always be joined as his loyal colleague, Prieur of the Côte d'Or was an officer of the engineers in the royal army, and he was already a well-known member of the Academy of Dijon and the Natural History Society of Paris at the outbreak of the Revolution. It was he who promoted the adoption of the metric system of weights and measures; not all the proposals mooted in the first flush of revolutionary innovation were so practical. The best comment made perhaps on the reforming of the calendar and the ridiculous renaming of the months was the contemporary English rendering of *Vendémaire, Brumaire, Frimaire,* and the rest:

> Wheezy, Sneezy, Freezy;
> Slippy, Drippy, Nippy;
> Showery, Flowery, Bowery;
> Wheaty, Heaty, Sweety.

In addition to his work in the government and with the armies, where he energetically supported his great chief, Carnot, on the Committee of Public Safety, Prieur was one of the founders of the Ecole Polytechnique and of the Institut de France. In 1808 Napoleon created him a count of the Empire. He died in Dijon in 1832. Born in the same year as Prieur of the Côte d'Or, in Dijon, was the diplomat, statesman and publicist, Hugues-Bernard Maret. Following his father in the legal profession, he became advocate at the Conseil du Roi in Paris. In 1792 he was sent to London to negotiate with Pitt, and afterwards was appointed ambassador at the court of Naples. His fortunes henceforth became linked with those of the First

Consul; and as editor of the *Moniteur* he was later the official mouthpiece of the Emperor, who created him Duke of Bassano for his loyalty and indefatigable service as his private secretary. On his return from exile after Napoleon's fall Maret again held high office, and was made peer of France by Louis-Philippe. He died in Paris in 1839. But undoubtedly the greatest of all Burgundians in the service of the state under the revolutionary government and the First Empire was Lazare Carnot.

Lazare Nicolas-Marguerite Carnot was born at Nolay (Côte d'Or) in 1753, the second son of a notary and local magistrate. Of the sons of the family the eldest, Joseph-François, followed his father in the legal profession and became a judge of the Court of Appeal, the third Claude-Marie, who was later known as Carnot-Feulint, like his brother Lazare, chose the career of officer in the corps of engineers. The Carnot boys first went to school at the College of Autun, where their schoolfellows included Joseph and Lucien Buonaparte; later, on the recommendation of the Duc d'Aumont, Lazare and Claude-Marie attended the School of Military Engineering at Mézières. In this they were privileged, whereas their somewhat older contemporary, the talented Gaspard Monge of Beaune, afterwards the illustrious scientist and inventor of descriptive geometry, was, as the son of a knife-grinder, rejected on grounds of birth. Lazare Carnot became known to the world beyond the officers of the engineers when in August 1784 he was awarded the prize for an *éloge* on Vauban offered by the Academy of Dijon, receiving his double medal from the Prince de Condé, Governor-General of Burgundy. His intellectual gifts had been already recognized by others than Montalembert at the outbreak of the Revolution. Many years later, Carnot wrote of the political hopes of many in 1789: 'The Revolution was prepared by a mass of purely philosophical writings; hearts lifted high by hope of a happiness hitherto unknown suddenly took a leap into the realms of imagination. We thought we had grasped the shadow of national felicity; we thought that it was possible to obtain a Republic without anarchy, an unbounded liberty without disorder, a perfect system of equality without factions. We were cruelly undeceived by our experience.' In the autumn of 1791 Carnot and his brother Carnot-Feulint, although remaining regular officers, were returned to the Legislative Assembly, as representatives of the Pas-de-Calais. In April 1792 began the long Revolutionary Wars, first against Austria, later against a coalition of European powers; on 11th July the President of the Assembly in solemn session declared, '*La patrie est en danger.*'

Carnot was above all else a patriot in Saint-Simon's sense; as he himself said, '*J'ai idolâté ma Patrie*'; and throughout his life this and his democratic beliefs were the key to all his actions. It was with this overriding aim in mind that he voted for the death of the King, when he believed the latter cherished the hope of the defeat of his country by its enemies. It was this that sustained him, when, as a member of the Committee of Public Safety, combining the offices of chief of staff and adjutant-general, he carried out the prodigious, the unending tasks of planning the campaigns and providing the munitions and men, that earned him the title of the 'Organizer of Victory'. It was the sense of where his duty lay that allowed him to agree in the elimination of Robespierre and Saint-Just but to defend Barère; that supported him in maintaining his republican ideals as a member of the Directorate; that guided him in all his relations with Napoleon—first, to select him for command and then to urge him on in Italy—'*Marchez; pas de repos funeste . . . Frappez et frappez vivement*'; to be the sole vote cast in the Senate against the First Consul's assuming the imperial dignity; to retire from office when he considered the Emperor's wars as wars of aggression; to offer again his services in 1814, when France was in danger; and finally, to serve as minister of the interior during the Hundred Days. Proscribed at the second restoration, Carnot retired to Magdeburg, where he quietly resumed his scientific studies, until death overtook him in August 1823. Few men deserved better of their country's tardy recognition, when in 1889, at the time of the centenary of the Revolution, the remains of Lazare Carnot were brought back to France and interred in the Pantheon.

The words Carnot addressed in a letter to his brother, on hearing the news of Napoleon's death on 6th May 1821, are a judgement not only on the Emperor, but also on himself:

One cannot see the fall of a colossus without emotion. But I
assure you that in politics personalities count little with me.
I only think of them in regard to the good or bad which they
have done to their country; and, without mentioning his
military disasters, few men have exercised a more pernicious
influence on the fate of their country than did Napoleon,
despite his prodigious ability, keen judgement, inflexible
character and a heart that was brave and often kindly. . . .

Few families in modern France have been more distinguished
than that of Carnot, many of whose members over the generations have shown the same disinterested service of the state and
the same outstanding intellectual gifts as their illustrious
Burgundian ancestor. Of the two sons of Lazare Carnot, the
eldest had been born in 1796 and christened Sadi, after the
Persian poet; the second, Hippolyte, was born five years later,
in 1801. Like his father, Sadi was destined for the Engineers,
being educated at the new Ecole Polytechnique. He inherited
from his father a love for music and the arts and a gift for
mathematics; even more so than with his father the width of his
scientific knowledge was astonishing. The writer in the *Encyclo-
paedia Britannica* describes him as 'one of the most original
and profound thinkers who have ever devoted themselves to
science'. In 1824 there appeared his *Reflexions sur la puissance
motrice du feu*, in which he published his researches into thermo-
dynamics, the science with which Sadi Carnot will ever be
associated as the formulator of the famous second law and the
principle which goes by his name. He died in 1832, at the early
age of thirty-six. His younger brother, Hippolyte, had studied
for the law, but from literary beginnings he turned increasingly
his attention to politics, being elected to parliament in 1839.
After the fall of Louis-Philippe, and the inauguration of the
Second Republic, the Burgundian Lamartine called Carnot to
serve as Minister for Education in his provisional government.
In office he sought to fulfil the dream of his father in proposing
a law to establish free and compulsory education for all and to
extend secondary education for girls, but he alienated both the
extremes of Right and Left and was forced to resign. In his
leisure he collected the papers and published a biography of

his father in two volumes in 1861 and 1864. After Louis Napoleon's *coup d'état* Carnot declined to take his seat, in order to avoid swearing the oath of allegiance to the Emperor. He played a prominent part in drawing up the constitution of the Third Republic, and in 1875 he was named Senator for life. Hippolyte Carnot died in March 1888, three months after his eldest son, named Sadi after his uncle, had been elected President of the French Republic.

Marie-François-Sadi Carnot came to the fore after the disaster of 1870, when his hereditary republicanism and his known integrity marked him out for high office at a time when financial and political scandals were threatening the stability, indeed the existence, of democracy in France. The probity of Sadi Carnot's political and personal life was in marked contrast with that of many prominent figures in French governmental and high financial circles, and it was the recognition of this that led to his unexpected election. President Sadi Carnot had indicated his intention to retire from public life, when he was assassinated by an Italian anarchist named Caserio, after delivering a speech at a banquet in Lyons on 24th June 1894. His son François, following the family tradition, was elected deputy for the Côte d'Or in 1902. Today Nolay is a charming small town, typical of many others in Burgundy, with its fourteenth-century covered market and its curious coloured *Jacquemart* in the neighbouring church tower. In the Place Carnot, facing the statue of the Organizer of Victory by Deglane and Roulleau, stands the house where Lazare Carnot was born in 1753. It is still in possession of the Carnot family.

CHAPTER XIV

Un Paradis de la Gastronomie

M. PIERRE POUPON, the writer and *vigneron* from Meursault, in his excellent book on his native Burgundy, *Toute la Bourgogne*, tells of an unexpected visit one day, when he and his wife had just finished luncheon, from a friend, accompanied by a herculean young man, unknown to them, who was returning to Paris from the funeral of the novelist Roger Vailland. Introductions hardly over, the hosts were taken aback when the young man demanded in a loud voice, 'A drink, let me have something to drink!' M. Poupon thought at first that he desired something strong, perhaps to drown his sorrow on the loss of his buried friend; but it appeared that all he wanted was water, a carafe of which he drank on the spot. It was, in fact, a fine compliment to his host, the *vigneron*, a necessary prelude to the two excellent bottles which he was offered, a Meursault '59 and a Volnay '53. Such wines could not be wasted on a commonplace thirst. Furthermore, one of the children was sent out to procure the most fitting adjunct to the wine, in the form of a cheese of neighbouring Cîteaux, made by the monks.

Food and wine, these are naturally associated in Burgundy, where wine finds its way into most of the regional *cuisine*, which is as robust, well-flavoured and full-bodied as the wines of its celebrated *Côte de Nuits*. Unlike some connoisseurs in England, who appear over-delicate in the choice of the food to accompany a superior wine, as if they feared to impair the fineness of their palate, the connoisseur in Burgundy seeks a dish worthy of setting off the excellence of the *grand cru* he is drinking—*escargots à la bourguignonne*, *bœuf bourguignon*, a *coq au Chambertin* or a *râble de lièvre à la Piron*. Or even—although this is not strictly a Burgundian dish—a *lièvre à la royale*, which—we have the word of Colette for it—has no fewer than sixty cloves of garlic to support its 'light and climbing flora of simple, kitchen-garden savours'! This is good bourgeois cooking at its best, with wines appropriate to its excellence. But simpler, more down-to-earth wines need also their suitable companions. It was that Burgundian to her very finger-tips, Colette again, who remembered from her childhood in the Puisaye meals eaten in the fields beneath a hedgerow: 'cheese, hewn in triangles, firmly held on to its slice of bread by a labourer's thumb, followed by a dandelion salad', with its clove of garlic, bathed in walnut oil, the bottle of wine . . . all these 'rustic pleasures'. It was with a similar feeling for the propriety of simplicity that the poet Lamartine recorded in his *Confidences* a supper shared with his friend, the badly-off curé of Bussières, the Abbé Dumont:

It was ordinarily of brown and black bread mixed of rye and bran. Some eggs from the courtyard fried in the pan and seasoned with a touch of vinegar. A salad or asparagus from the garden. Some escargots gathered with the dew on the leaves of the vine, and cooked slowly in a casserole under the ashes. A marrow *au gratin* placed in the oven in an earthenware dish on the days when the bread was baked; and from time to time some old hens, scraggy and yellow, which the poor young wives from the mountains bring as presents to the curés on days of churching, in memory of the doves which the women of Judea brought to the temple on the same occasions. Or some hares or some partridges, the bag of the morning's shooting. One rarely served other dishes. . . . This frugal meal was washed down with a red or white wine of the country; the vignerons gave it to the sacristan, who went in quest of it from wine-press to wine-press at vintage-time. The meal was completed by some fruit from the espaliers in season and by little white goat's cheeses, fresh, sprinkled with grey salt, which gave you a thirst, and which made the wine taste good to the sober peasants of our valleys. . . .

It is this passage from Lamartine that M. Poupon had in mind, when he described a homely country supper, '*une marande*', as it is locally known, partaken on the upper gallery

or balcony of a *vigneron*'s house in the region of the Mâconnais.
It was a summer's evening, when the limestone walls still gave
off the warmth distilled in them by the fierce sun of midday,
and the ruminative eye ranged out over the serried imbrication
of the vines, among which could be discerned the curved back
of some late worker, to where a column of blue smoke from a
fire of vine-cuttings rose in the pale lemon sky, 'as a holocaust
to the happiness of the moment'. On a chequered cloth laid
on the plain wooden table, beside the pots of geraniums,
fuchsias and petunias, were placed a wicker basket, containing
the '*chevrotons*', a bowl of '*pourri*', a *vigneron*'s strong pocket-knife,
some goblets of sturdy glass, a loaf of bread and two bottles of
wine, a Mâcon red and a Mâcon white, 'bedewed with the
emotion of being so quickly passed from the depths of the cellar
to the height of the balcony'. These *chevrotons*, which are small
cylindrical goat's cheeses, are best eaten when they are very dry,
hard and crisp, nutty; in munching them they cling to your
teeth and palate, and require a deep draught of the white
Mâcon to release the full flavour of both cheese and wine. These
are they which Lamartine found 'gave you a thirst'. This is the
right sort of thirst, the *reasoned* thirst which only wine quenches.
As for the *pourri*, which followed after a decent interval and a
glass or two of the white wine, this is a paste of a strong cheese,
or better of two or three different cheeses, well blended, with the
addition of olive oil, white wine, *marc de Bourgogne* and spices.
Spread thickly on a slice of rough bread, the *pourri* makes one's
tastebuds tingle and sets off to perfection the robust male
vigour of the red Mâcon. Over this whole scene, typical of the
Mâconnais, there breathes a Virgilian solemnity, something
of the simplicity which Horace loved, as if labour is sanctified
by a sense of the fitness of things; in this *vigneron*'s meal there
might seem to be symbolized the quality of life in the southern
Burgundian countryside.

The vine appears most likely to have been introduced to Gaul
from Greece and Italy by way of the Greek colonial settlement
of Massilia (Marseilles). At first the growing Gallic market was
exploited by Roman merchants, but the suitability of climate
and soil, especially around the Gironde and in Burgundy, was

early recognized and vineyards planted. A text of the time of Constantine (early fourth century) mentions specifically the wines of Beaune. When the Burgundians established themselves in that part of Roman Gaul that was to perpetuate their name, they took care to preserve the qualities of its wines, as is shown by a provision of the fifth-century code of law, which is known as the *Loi Gombette*. However, it was the monks who took the lead in the cultivation of the wine: the abbey of Cluny was the proprietor of the famous vineyard of Montrachet, and the Cistercians particularly, as leaders in agrarian development, became highly skilled in viticulture, possessing the celebrated Clos de Vougeot and vineyards in the region of Chablis. How extensive was the culture of the vine in Burgundy by the middle of the thirteenth century is seen in the description of the country around Auxerre given by the Italian Franciscan Salimbene. The restriction of wine-production to localities where it can be raised to a high state of excellence came only with the disasters of the last century; the names of two villages to the south of Auxerre, Coulanges-la-Vineuse and St-Bris-le-Vineux, remain as witness of these vintages of former days.

However, it was in the course of the fifteenth century that the *grands crus* of Burgundy became a part of the high politics of Europe, with the accession to power of the Valois dukes, who proudly boasted of being the 'immediate possessors of the finest wine in Christendom'. This was the 'wine-diplomacy' of the Dukes of Burgundy, when white bullock-drays crossed the roads of Europe, laden with tuns of the choicest vintages as presents to Emperors, the Popes of Avignon or the fathers of Basle, to woo these potentates with wine into a state of mind congenial to the far-reaching aspirations of the Grand-Dukes of the West. If the cuisine of *Gallia Lugudunensis*, so praised by Roman gourmets, had never lost its renown, it reached new heights under the Burgundian dukes, when the great kitchens which we admire today in the palace of Dijon served (if we may accept the authority of Mrs Elizabeth David) also as a banqueting-hall—for repasts where the viands rivalled the wines in a studied magnificence hitherto unequalled and possibly never since surpassed. But amid all this splendour the dukes watched over the quality of their *cepage*; as early as 1395 we find Philip the Bold issuing ordinances to improve the stock, and to limit the spread of the *gamay*—a vine that produces more grapes than the *pinot noir* but is very inferior to it in its wine-producing qualities.

The reputation of the wines of Burgundy in more modern times owes much to the recommendation of Fagon, the physician of Louis XIV, who prescribed in 1680 the restorative properties of the noble *crus* of the Côte d'Or, particularly Corton, as a palliative for the debilitated digestive organs of the King. Fagon is said to have personally visited the leading vineyards and to have sampled all of the principal vintages. Fortunate man. When some years later the enterprising M. Claude Brosses of Charnay-lès-Mâcon drove his bullock-wagon of local wines to present them to the King, the court at Versailles developed a pronounced liking for these wines of Burgundy. In the course of the late eighteenth and nineteenth centuries the taste for Burgundy spread from Paris to England, and the great merchant houses of shippers came into being. The Prussian J. F. Reichardt, travelling in France in 1792 during the turmoil of the Revolution, had the highest praise for the *cuisine* of the Rhône and Saône valleys and for the wines, which he coupled with claret in a letter to a German correspondent: '. . . I know nothing so ravishing as this little corner of the earth . . . as for the Burgundy and the Bordeaux that we drink, you have no conception of it in Germany.'

Stendhal was in Dijon in the spring of 1837, and he gives a lively account of his Burgundian tour in his most entertaining *Memoires d'un touriste*. With a developed eye for the beauty of landscape, he was disappointed with 'this famous Côte-d'Or so celebrated in Europe':

> Without its admirable wines, I would find nothing in the world more ugly than this famous Côte-d'Or. According to the system of M. Elie de Beaumont, this was one of the first chains to emerge on our globe, when the crust began to cool.
>
> The Côte-d'Or, then, is only a small mountain, very dry and very ugly; but one distinguishes the vines with their little stakes, and at each instant one finds an immortal name: Chambertin, the Clos-Vougeot, Romanée, Saint-Georges,

Nuits. With the help of so much glory, one finishes by getting used to the Côte-d'Or. . . .

He then tells the story of that General Bisson who, when still a colonel, on his way to the Army of the Rhine, drew up his regiment before the gates of the château of the Clos-Vougeot and solemnly gave the order to his men for a general salute. Whatever his initial disappointment, that evening Stendhal was present in Beaune at a long discussion on the relative merits of planting the vines at the Clos-Vougeot in rows vertical to the road, as compared with arranging them parallel to it. A typical Stendhalist diversion, the reader might think. However, at the end of two hours of this sort of *discussion*, he felt that he was really beginning to appreciate the differences between certain qualities of Burgundy. Later he was to taste and distinguish 'eight or ten different kinds', which he could only compare with 'bouquets of flowers'. Later still, when in Lyons, he was able to confirm: 'I have learned the names of thirty kinds of the wines of Burgundy, the *aristocratic wine par excellence*, as said the excellent Jacquemont.'

Lamartine, the poet and *vigneron* from the Mâconnais, experienced to his cost the vicissitudes of the wine-grower, the power of frost or a hail-storm to ruin in an hour the patient labour of the whole year. He died before the arrival of the phylloxera, the plant louse which, coming from America, devastated the vineyards of Burgundy in the years after 1878. Although the damage was gradually repaired by the grafting of French slips on imported American stock, and although the quality of the wine did not permanently suffer, the post-phylloxera period has been marked by a diminution of the area planted and a concentration on the quality of the smaller quantity produced, especially in those wines of the highest class. The disturbed period between the Wars led to an unhealthy reliance on the export to the English market, where a heavier type of wine, long retained in the cellar, was in demand; this was damaging to the intrinsic quality of Burgundy, which ideally should not be *un vin de longue garde*. In this it is unlike the finest growths of claret. Since the Second World War control of production, and particularly of the *appellation*, has been strictly enforced, with happy results—a refinement in the quality of Burgundy, and a reduction in maturing time, with, as a consequence, a wholly beneficial increase in the lightness and grace, the 'breeding', of the wines. Nowadays, the laying-down usually takes about five to seven years, sometimes more with the heavier growths, sometimes fewer. This, of course, does not apply to many of the freshly drunk wines of Beaujolais; but these are not properly rated as Burgundy, the communes of Saint-Amour, Moulin-à-Vent and Romanèche-Thorins alone being situated in the department of Saône-et-Loire.

For these reasons the distribution of the wine-producing regions of Burgundy has tended to become a concentration of the vineyards in more or less clearly defined areas. In the north of the province, in the district around Auxerre described by Salimbene, there remain today of this once widely planted countryside the rosé-bearing hills of Irancy and St-Bris, and the celebrated vineyards of Chablis. Chablis, producing that excellent dry, light wine, with its exquisite colour of limpid green-gold, which became in England from its popularity almost synonymous with 'the white wine served with oysters or fish', was once the domain worked by the Cistercians of Pontigny and the canons of the collegiate church of St-Martin de Chablis. Only those slopes of these stony hills best exposed to the sun are now planted with the vine by a handful of proprietors, who continue to produce wines of great distinction, with the finest of delicate bouquets, lively and deliciously fresh. South-west of Auxerre, from the region around Pouilly-sur-Loire, in the Nivernais, comes the highly esteemed Pouilly-Fumé, another fresh, light, white wine, whose taste has something of a suggestion of gun-flint. Pouilly-Fumé approximates to the wines of Sancerre from the further bank of the Loire and lying therefore outside Burgundy. Undoubtedly the name 'Burgundy' is most closely associated with the wines produced some seventy miles south-east of Chablis in that extended region which stretches south from almost the gates of Dijon, and down the right bank of the Saône, to where the Beaujolais district begins just south of Mâcon. This is *Burgundy*, and the most celebrated part of all is the world-famous Côte d'Or, a title it has borne since the Revolution. If its appearance so disappointed Stendhal, the recital of its names, that resounding litany of *clos* and *villages*, raised the heart of that connoisseur to a rarely experienced degree of exaltation, almost religious in its intensity.

The Côte d'Or, this pergola of vines, green in the spring, purple, maroon and gold in October, extends from Fixin almost without a break, save where the quarries of Comblanchieu powder its leaves and tendrils with a fine white dust, to south-west of Chagny, a distance of something over thirty miles. Its width varies between two and nearly five miles, from the height of the *côte* itself and its *combes* to the foothills and a short way into the plain of the Saône. The Côte d'Or is divided into the Côte de Nuits in the north and the Côte de Beaune, which begins at Aloxe-Corton. South of this again one comes to the Côte Chalonnaise, which, while not having the prestige of the Côte d'Or, possesses wines of a high quality, grouped in three districts: Rully and Mercurey to the north, Buxy and Montagny to the south, with Givry in the centre. The wine of the Mâconnais is produced in vineyards scattered over a wide area, extending from around Tournus to the south of Mâcon itself. To the south-west of that town, under the rocky grey headland of pre-historic Solutré, come some of the most renowned white wines of southern Burgundy, produced in five little hillside communes under the *appellation* Pouilly-Fuissé— a most distinctive wine, dry, fresh and fragrant.

Of the vines grown in Burgundy (the *cepage*) two kinds hold pride of place—the *pinot noir*, which has the highest reputation and constitutes the stock planted in half the vineyards of the Côtes de Nuits and de Beaune; and the *chardonnay*, from which comes the finest white wine. The *gamay*, which produces double their quantity of grapes, is not regarded so highly as these on the Côte d'Or, constituting only a tenth of the vines, but it comes into its own in the different soils of southern Burgundy. The *aligoté*, a plant producing a good white wine, is grown in about the same proportion as the *gamay* on the Côte d'Or, but has not the quality of the *chardonnay*, which is regarded as the *pinot* of the white. These are the varieties of vine that flourish in the vineyards of Burgundy, the whole area to which the appellation 'Burgundy' is permitted consisting of some 37,000 acres and producing annually something in the region of 17 million gallons of wine. Although there are large proprietors, both private and the long-established merchant houses (*négociants*), by far the greatest number of holdings are of only a few acres, passed on from generation to generation as the precious heirlooms of families. In this Burgundy differs from the great châteaux of Bordeaux. It is said to require about three and a half to five acres to support a family, but the return naturally varies widely from one vineyard to another, or from *climat* to *climat*.

There are three terms commonly met with by the visitor to the vine-growing regions of Burgundy: *clos*, *climats* and the initials AOC (*appellation d'origine contrôlée*). The *clos* is a relic from the middle ages, when it signified those parcels of vines separated from those of the commune and owned by the *seigneur* or a monastery or other private proprietor. Some have survived, such as the famous Clos de Vougeot once worked by the monks of Cîteaux, although even this has not escaped sub-division over the centuries. Today it is the property of the Chevaliers du Tastevin. Another celebrated *clos* was that belonging to the Princes of Conti at Romanée. The term *climat* is applied to parcels of vines which are looked on as homogeneous in respect of quality, the type of vine (*cepage*) and the physical conditions of growth. Thus a larger vineyard may be composed of a mixture of *climats*, only certain of which may be of the highest quality.

The most famous growths, and consequently the dearest, come from certain *clos* or *climats* known by a single name. Of these, Montrachet, which is some seventeen acres in extent, and Romanée-Conti, whose area is a bare four and a half acres, are regarded as the princes of these *grands crus*. But next to them Richebourg (only some two and a half acres), Musigny, Romanée, Chambertin (the largest in extent—some seventy acres), La Tâche, Bonnes-Mares, Clos-Vougeot, Grands-Echézeaux, Corton, La Roche and Saint-Denis, and a few others, must be considered the *grands seigneurs*. Following these noble *crus* are some vineyards of very high quality, which have a communal *appellation*: Pommard, Gevrey, Nuits, Morey and

Vosne; Beaune, Volnay, Aloxe; Vougeot, Monthélie, Auxey, Chassagne, Santenay, Savigny; Meursault, Puligny; Ladois, Pernand, St-Romain, St-Aubin, Chorey, Fixin—giving them in the order as classified by R. Gadille. Similarly, in the Chalonnais come Rully, Mercurey, Givry, Montagny, Buxy; and further south, in the Beaujolais region of Saône-et-Loire there are St-Armour and Moulin-à-Vent. A source of some confusion to the uninitiated arises from the practice of adding to the communal *appellation* the name of a famous *clos* situated within the commune—for example, Gevry-Chambertin, Aloxe-Corton, Chambolle-Musigny, or Puligny-Montrachet. These names have not the *cachet* of the name of the *clos tout court*—a Gevry-Chambertin is not the equal of a Chambertin or an Aloxe-Corton of a Corton, and so on.

Somewhat further down the scale—but what a scale it is— are those communes which do not have the right to be known by an individual communal name but where several are grouped together, with such *appellations* as 'Vins fins de la Côte de Nuits' (five communes), 'Côtes de Beaune-Villages', 'Hautes Côtes de Nuits' and 'Hautes Côtes de Beaune'. The five communes that make up 'Pouilly-Fuissé' come under this category. The use of 'Bourgogne', 'Mâcon', 'Mâcon-Villages' are all controlled, the addition of the 'Villages' being commendatory, as indicating a high quality. Even such names as 'Bourgogne Grand Ordinaire' or 'Bourgogne Ordinaire', represent a classification under the *appellation d'origine contrôlée*.

Beaune is a town whose life depends almost entirely on the trade in wine. There the ancient ramparts and bastions have been converted into cellars for the many *négociants* who have their headquarters in Beaune, so that it has been said that the town is virtually defended by bulwarks of bottles. The *caves* of the wine merchants, growers and shippers are everywhere to be seen: the names stand out of such firms with a world-wide reputation as Bouchard Père et Fils, Calvet, Louis Latour, Drouhin, Geisweiller, Morin, Jadot, Ponelle, and so many others equally distinguished. The visitor is offered the opportunity of a wine-tasting, a *dégustation*, at such famous houses. And for the wine-lover with an antiquarian and historical interest there is the Musée de Vin de Bourgogne, housed in the Hôtel des Ducs de Bourgogne (or Logis du Roi), a building of stone and timber of the fifteenth and sixteenth centuries, with cellars going back to the fourteenth. But pride of place archi- tecturally will go to the Hôtel-Dieu, built by Nicholas Rolin, the chancellor to the Dukes of Burgundy, between 1443 and 1451, and one of the most perfect examples of mediaeval civic building remaining in France. The beauty of the exterior, with its high roof and dormers in the shining colour-patterned tiles of Burgundy, is matched by the beauty of the appointments of the interior—the magnificent hall of the hospital, with the rich crimson hangings and bedspreads of the patients' cubicles, the woodwork, faience and pewter of the pharmacy, and the splendid kitchens. And in the adjoining museum are hung tapestries of Flanders and the great *Last Judgement* of Rogier van der Weyden, commissioned by Rolin in 1443. It is reported that King Louis XI of France, no lover of the Burgundian state, said of this Hôtel-Dieu: 'It is very fit and proper that Rolin, after making so many poor, should build a hospital to house them.' Here on the third Sunday of November is held the auctioning of the celebrated wines of the Hospices de Beaune, which sets the price for the year's vintage, the receipts of the sale continuing the work of charity begun more than five centuries ago by the Chancellor Rolin.

This auction is part of the *Trois Glorieuses de Bourgogne*, those days of celebration in honour of wine which begin on the Saturday with a meeting and dinner (*disnée*) of the Chevaliers du Tastevin in the twelfth-century Cistercian *Grand Cellier* at the château of Clos de Vougeot, when the new chevaliers are enrolled with the now traditional ceremonial. On the Monday the scene shifts to the village of Meursault, the centre of a district whose white wines, together with those of Puligny and Chassagne-Montrachet, have the highest reputation, being dry but at the same time possessing body and an exquisite flavour. Alexandre Dumas considered that Puligny-Montrachet 'should be drunk kneeling with uncovered head'. The '*Paulée de Meursault*', as it is called, consists of a banquet, where around the table foregather all those who live by the vine, and the *vignerons* themselves provide bottles of their own vintages; after which the winner of the literary prize offered receives his reward in a hundred bottles of Meursault. The *Trois Glorieuses* brings to a fitting conclusion the *Foire Gastronomique* of Dijon, which takes place annually in the first fortnight of November.

Robert Carrier has suggested that if the provinces of France were graded for their *cuisine*, after the manner of Michelin, then Burgundy would be awarded three stars. Now this excellence is not to be attributed solely to the perfection and profusion of its wines, since the region of Bordeaux can boast of its fifteen hundred châteaux and its great number of classified first growths, yet has no comparative counterpart in its somewhat undistinguished *cuisine bordelaise*. Nevertheless, wine does play a great part in the success of Burgundian cooking. Perhaps Colette gives a clue to the reason for this superiority: 'Alone in the vegetable kingdom, the vine makes the true savour of the earth intelligible to man.' And Burgundy is peculiarly well placed to catch this savour of the earth; on its doorstep are to be found all the ingredients in abundance and of the highest quality for its renowned cuisine: beef and veal from the famed breed of Charollais; hams and *andouilles* from the Morvan; plentiful game; chickens from nearby Bresse; the white fish of the Saône and Loire, trout and crayfish from the streams and the lakes of the Morvan; world-famous *escargots*; mushrooms of many delicious varieties; vegetables from the valley of the Saône; cheeses; and all manner of fruits, including the famous cherries of Auxerre. With this material to work on, a tradition of cooking that goes back to Roman times (see the bas-reliefs depicting the Gallo-Roman purveyors of food in Dijon's Musée Archéologique), and its wines—Burgundy could hardly fail to be the 'paradise of gastronomy', as has been claimed for it.

Burgundian cooking is large-hearted, abundant (*plantureuse*) richly flavoured, appealing to the *gourmand* that exists in every true *gourmet*. But everything that borrows from the lustre of the name of Burgundy—those *bœufs, poulets, coqs*, to which '*bourguignonne*' is added on the menu—must be regarded with a careful eye, even in Burgundy. For although this provincial cooking has the simplicity of all really good cooking, it requires from the chef or housewife long experience, skill and much care in order to reach perfection in those rich red-wine sauces or *meurettes*, as they are known in Burgundy. For a good *coq au vin à la bourguignonne* it is wise to choose a restaurant where it is one of the specialities—such places as the *Trois Faisans* at Dijon or the *Gourmets* at Marsannay-la-Côte, south of Dijon, or at the *Marché* in Beaune. Very few chefs could cook a cock in Chambertin at the price which that excellent wine fetches today, but a good Burgundy is essential. And the same goes for a *bœuf bourguignon*, with its little glazed onions and firm sliced mushrooms. These restaurants are not cheap and it makes sad reading today to see old pre-war menus and hear accounts of such bygone meals—or to remember back too far.

Stephen Gwynn in his *Burgundy*, published in 1930, writes of three resturants which still exist in Dijon: 'the famous *Hôtel de la Cloche*', 'the *Hôtel du Chapeau Rouge*, largely frequented by commercial travellers, cheap and good', and the *Trois Faisans*, 'one of the best and most characteristic restaurants in Burgundy, or for that matter, in all France', to which has now been joined the *Pré aux Clercs*. At the Chapeau Rouge 'in the ordinary restaurant', we are told, 'you are served *à prix fixe*, and your lunch or dinner will cost you from two shillings to half a crown'. We have paid indeed for our progress. Stephen Gwynn referred approvingly to the *Hôtel de la Poste* at Saulieu, a town praised by Rabelais for its good fare, which later proved something too much for Mme de Sévigné. Today the restaurant in Saulieu for the excellence of its cuisine is undoubtedly the *Hôtel de la Côte d'Or*, which has been written about with such affectionate appreciation—and its renowned chef-proprietor, M. Alexandre Dumaine—by that discriminating *bon viveur* Alexander Watt. Dumaine once confessed to Watt that he had been making a certain sauce, a not very complicated one, for over thirty years, and it was only lately that he thought he was succeeding in achieving 'the right balance'. Another *Hôtel de la Poste* is the coaching inn at Avallon, where the Emperor Napoleon stayed on his return from Elba and from which he went on the next day to meet Maréchal Ney at Auxerre. This is a very beautiful old inn, with a two-star for its food—but it is certainly not cheap. Burgundy, however, is so rich in its inns and so well provided with restaurants of all categories that it would be invidious to single them out for praise here. Perhaps I may be allowed to recall the *Moulin des Ruats* in the verdant valley of the River Cousin, not far from Avallon, for the beauty of its position, delightful in summer, beneath the shade of its trees and beside its stream.

In addition to these ways of serving beef and chicken, which have become part of the repertoire of the western world, and have lost all their peculiar Burgundian *cachet* in becoming so, there are some specialities of the *cuisine* of Burgundy which are perhaps only found in their perfection within the confines of the province. *Jambon persillé à la bourguignonne* is one of these; among others are *pauchouse, saupiquet, queue de bœuf des vignerons, escargots à la bourguignonne,* and *gougère.* *Pauchouse* (also *pochouse* and *pochouze*) is a *matelote* or *bouillabaisse* of freshwater fish, which I must confess never to have tasted (nor, extraordinarily enough, has that incomparable writer on all things culinary, Mrs David, although in her *French Provincial Cooking* she gives a recipe for it from Henri Racouchot, a former proprietor of the *Trois Faisans* at Dijon). It is a speciality of Verdun-sur-le-Doubs, where fish from both the Saône and the Doubs are employed in its making. Stephen Gwynn ate it there and found it 'very, very good (much better than bouillabaisse with its cloying saffron), but what we all smell like after consuming it I can only guess'. This last remark is because of the large amount of garlic used in the preparing of this dish of coarse fish (perch and eel are essential, but also others that may be available—tench, pike and carp), cooked in dry white wine and flambé'ed with a *fine Bourgogne.* Garlic, too, with shallots, parsley and mushrooms, goes to stuff the *escargots.* These edible snails, *hélices vigneronnes,* used to be produced on the Côte d'Or at Chenôve, where may be seen the enormous wine-press of the Dukes of Burgundy—on the outskirts of Dijon. When a lot had been brought into the village for despatch, the snails would be given their food, fresh vine leaves, and the noise of their munching was said to have resembled the rustling of a wind in an autumn wood. *Saupiquet* is a mediaeval dish, going back certainly to the fifteenth century, of slices of Morvan ham, cooked in butter and served with a *sauce piquant à la crème.* With the ox-tail *des vignerons* which is stewed with white grapes, we might imagine ourselves to be eating sheltered from the too-fierce sun, under the covered upper gallery of a vine dresser's house, high among the vine-covered hills of the Mâconnais. The *gougère* would be appropriate on a similar Burgundian occasion, being a kind of Gruyère cheese pastry, eaten hot or cold, and excellent with wine.

'A diversity of wines is the fitting accompaniment to a diversity of cheeses' is the dictum of that most demanding of Burgundian connoisseurs, Colette, who prided herself on her skill in 'feeling the rind, gauging the elasticity of the inside, *divining* a cheese . . .' There was a time, she declared, when a woman could choose a cheese better than a man, but that time has gone. As in Normandy, only a man now has the true nose and touch for a cheese. The Burgundians have not the variety of cheese of Normandy, but they are great cheese-eaters: Epoisses, Chaource, Cîteaux, St-Florentin, Reblechon, Soumaintrain, the goats' cheeses, Rigotte, the *crottins* of Chavignol, those of the Morvan and the Mont d'Or of the Lyonnais—all these go famously with the wines of Burgundy, white and red; and the Burgundians are not too proud to go outside their province in search of the perfect foil to the perfection of their own vintages.

From the days of the Gallo-Romans Dijon, along with Lyons, has enjoyed a reputation for being one of the culinary centres of France. After the passing of the Grand-Dukes of the West this tradition of *bien-manger* and *bien-boire* was maintained in Dijon, with its status as a regional capital, by a numerous *noblesse de robe* and by a rich and highly civilized bourgeoisie—the poet and wit Piron had a classical dish of hare called after him, *le râble de lièvre à la Piron*. The mustard of Dijon was famous very early; when the Duke of Burgundy entertained Philip the Fair of France in 1336 a hogshead of mustard was consumed. On the death of Charles the Rash and the amalgamation of the duchy in the kingdom, King Louis XI tried to soften the blow to the pride of the Dijonnais by granting them a monopoly as purveyors of the royal mustard. Other specialities of Dijon are *pain d'épices* and *cassissines*, sweets made from the blackcurrants grown on the Côte d'Or. From these also is made the *crème de cassis* which, with the addition of a white *aligoté*, forms a popular aperitif. And to complete your meal in one of Dijon's celebrated restaurants, what could be better than a glass or two of the province's *eaux-de-vie*—a *marc* or a *fine* (long matured in oak), or a *prunelle de bourgogne*?

In France the state in various ways has long honoured the fine arts. In February 1975 President Giscard d'Estaing sought to recognize the high place that *gastronomie* holds among the civilized values by awarding the Légion d'Honneur to one of France's leading chefs, M. Paul Bocuse of Collonges-au-Mont d'Or, near Lyons; and in honouring him to honour all those who practise his art. The Lyonnais, situated as it is just to the south of Burgundy and adjoining Bresse and the region around Bugey, where was born the prince of gastronomes, Brillat-Savarin, shares much of the Burgundian culinary tradition. At the luncheon at the Elysée Palace, when M. Bocuse received his award, he and a number of the most celebrated chefs of France prepared and cooked the meal for the President and his guests. The repast was a simple one, but not lacking in elegance and finesse:

Menu
Soupe de truffes
Escalope de saumon de Loire à l'oseille
Canard Claude Jolly
Les Petites salades du Moulin
Fromages
Les deserts

LES VINS
Montrachet 1970
en magnum du Domaine de la Romanée-Conti
Château Margaux 1926
Morey Saint-Denis 1969
Champagne Roederer 1926
Grand Bas-Armagnac Laberdolive
1893
Grande Fine Champagne
(âge et origine inconnus)

It seems that they still order these things better in France.

CHAPTER XV

The Lost Paradise of Colette

IT WAS COLETTE's husband, the charming, talented Maurice
Goudeket, who described her Burgundian childhood, spent
in the village of St Sauveur-en-Puisaye, as 'a lost paradise'.
La Puisaye, the region around St-Sauveur, is a moist
countryside, where among the woods, which predominate,
and the few meadows, lie scattered lakes, ponds and reservoirs,
linked by the innumerable streams which flow into the Rivers
Loing and Vrille. This is the wet Burgundy, very different from
the well-drained, sun-drenched hillsides of the Côte d'Or; a
land of damp and heavy clays mostly, not of dry, light soils,
friable from the presence of gravel. How deep was Colette's
debt to this 'poor Burgundy' of La Puisaye, she herself is the
best witness. The Burgundian countryside and her mother, 'the
incomparable Sido', these were her two uniquely formative
influences. They are there present in the background of so many
of her books—in all the *Claudine* series, in *La Naissance du Jour*,
L'Etoile Vesper, *Mes Apprentissages*—and they overflow on to the
evocative pages of *La Maison de Claudine* and *Sido*.

Neither of her parents was a Burgundian by birth, they were
so only by the adoption; but in their daughter environment
rode triumphant over heredity. As Michelet pointed out, in
Burgundy the nordic meets the meridional, and their marriage
has been singularly fruitful. If we had not so many other
distinguished examples, the case of Colette would go well to
prove the point. Her mother, Adèle-Eugénie-Sidonie Landoy,
was born in Paris, lived as a girl and young woman in Belgium,
and married a moderately well-to-do landowner from the
Yonne, named Robineau. This sojourn in Belgium of Mlle
Landoy is not without its relevance; it brings that robust
Flemish element that has always been so necessary an ingredient
in the true Burgundian. It was M. Robineau's provision that

after his early death, allowed his young widow to marry a handsome but impecunious Provençal, Captain Jules-Joseph Colette, late of the 1st Zouaves, who had been invalided out of the army after losing a leg at the second battle of Melegnano in 1859, during the wars for the unification of Italy. Colette—it is strange to find how awkwardly his famous daughter's name sits on its true owner—had nothing but his small army pension, but with the rents derived from his wife's property, which consisted largely of tenanted farms in La Puisaye, they lived, comfortably at first, in the solid bourgeois house in the Rue des Vignes in St-Sauveur.

This whole countryside of La Puisaye, which centres on St-Fargeau, a small town of some sixteen hundred inhabitants, has long been cleared of the primeval forest that once covered it, yet the effect today to the casual eye is as if those great trees had never been felled, since woods, copses and plantations abound, and the meadows, never of any significant size, seem to have been cut out piecemeal from this fabric of green baize. Colette speaks of these woods, 'the deep, encroaching woods that ripple and wave away into the distance as far as you can see', as contributing much of the charm, the visual delight of this verdant countryside. The woods consist for the most part of oak, but they include an amazing number of other varieties: beech, poplar, plane, ash, acacia, birch (somewhat etiolated, these) cider-apple, chestnut, aspen, hornbeam, wild cherry (in spring their blossom is seen everywhere) and the odd conifer. Beside the roads and narrow overhung lanes grow close thickets of hazel, untidy brambles and matted bracken, beneath trees whose branches and foliage are often lost under a tangled web of old man's beard. In cleared spaces and especially in the pine-plantations the lighter soil allows some heather to grow. Frequently on the larger roads the encompassing woodland has been clipped and cut back to form vertical screens, high impenetrable walls of interlaced leafage. The meadows— there are very few fields—are separated by trees as often as by hedges, and appear isolated—swamped and threatened, menaced by the rapacious vigour of the woods.

As a consequence, and Colette constantly draws our attention to the point, the financial return from the countryside is poor.

Cattle, the statuesque Charollais, standing like ivory chessmen on their green chessboard, are raised on scattered farms, whose roofs of red-brown tiles contrast pleasantly with the prevalent greens. (Colette, as a young woman, married to M. Willy, and living in Paris in a third-floor flat in the Rue Jacob, would look northwards over the courtyards towards the Rue Visconti, her gaze dwelling on the old tiled rooftops, and would see again in her mind's eye these red-brown tiles of her native Puisaye.) Milk, cream, cheese and meat—these most necessary of food-stuffs—and the produce from orchards and gardens, together with the raising of the more domesticated farmyard animals, give a livelihood to the peasantry and provide rents for some larger landowners. Of industry—at least until of recent years—there is little, except that the presence here of clays, both white and red, suitable for pottery, has, as long ago as the middle ages, given rise to the manufacture of faience, mostly of the commoner sort of household crockery and china.

Colette, when she referred to La Puisaye as 'my poor Burgundy', was distinguishing it from the rich, opulent Burgundy of the Côte d'Or. As a girl, she had never visited this prosperous neighbour to the east; and when as a grown woman she first saw it, in the glowing mellow warmth of late September, at the season of its greatest glory, the time of the *vendange*, she was, she declared, 'thunderstruck'. She was unprepared for all this richness, the lavish splendour of its palette—the purple of the pendant grape-clusters among the profusion of tendrils and leaves of the vines, turning from ruddy gold through all shades of crimson to magenta. But with the customary caution of the countrywoman-bred she waited, and withheld her judgement. She returned, she tells us, 'at the ambiguous moment when spring is only a date, a quivering, a brief phrase that the blackbird improvises. The vineyards seemed asleep, bone-like, severely aligned. On the wood the buds had not yet changed their shapes. . . . It appeared to me as gentle, as austere and fore-shortened, this Burgundy of the *grands crus*, resembling from so close at hand, in its hummocked nakedness, the other Burgundy, my well-beloved poor Burgundy.'

A countryside, then, of woodland and water, enclosed

between the Rivers Loire and Yonne, its name La Puisaye
being derived from the conjunction of the Gallic *poel*, a 'lake',
'marsh', 'pond', or 'pool', with *say*, 'forest'. From St-Sauveur,
through St-Fargeau and Blenau, to Rogny stretches a chaplet
of ponds and reservoirs: Moutiers, Chassain, Guedelon,
Bourdon, Lélu, Cahauderie, Blondeau, Gazonne, and 'the
lovely little forest lake of Guillemette', which the Colettes
owned. Mirrors whose enamelled surface reflect the blue of the
sky and the deep brown-greens of the rushes and woods that
approach right to the water's edge. On high days the Colette
family would harness the horse to the victoria and, accompanied
by their dogs, drive out to Guillemette to picnic by the lakeside.
While the captain sang in his deep southern voice of 'dames and
knights who gather within this charming glade

>   To pass their days in tasting the delights (*repeated*)
>   Of sparkling wine and love beneath the shade' (*three times*),

'Sido' would tell the children of bygone wolves which haunted
the Puisaye and of one many years before, a poor starving
summer wolf, who had followed the victoria for five hours. And
the children would wander off, the boys to find their own way
home, where they would arrive, always late, tired and
dishevelled, their clothes betraying their passage through
marshes and streams and sharp, tearing brambles. And 'the
little one, otherwise known as Minet-Chéri', as her parents
called her, would wander away also, to follow 'paths in the
rusty woods that smelt of mushrooms and wet moss, gathering
the yellow chanterelles that go so well with creamy sauces and
veal casserole'; or in the clearings of fine reedy grass to places
in which she knew that 'domes of mushrooms broke through the
light silver-grey soil where the purple heather thrived'. Today
these lakes and ponds are frequented by fishermen; and on the
Reservoir du Bourdon, a resort for bathers, the white sails of
yachts move like moths against the shoreline of woods.

And apart from the natural beauty of its landscape, La
Puisaye reveals the civilizing handiwork of men in its ancient
châteaux and manor houses, its *gentilhommières*: the châteaux of

St-Fargeau, Ratilly, Mézilles, Le Tremblay, Druyes, Grand-
champs, St-Armand and the priory of Boutissaint, among so
many pleasant old manors hidden in the depths of the woods. If
much of the military architecture of the middle ages, the strong-
holds of feudal barons, was demolished by orders of the King
and Richelieu, and some châteaux were destroyed during the
Revolution, yet much remains to link Puisaye with historic
Burgundy. Such are the châteaux of Ratilly and St-Fargeau.
Ratilly stands in a world apart, away from main roads, forgotten
in the heart of the country, obscured from view by the trees
until the visitor is almost upon it. With its deep moat and its
ochre-coloured walls covered with lichen and creepers, Ratilly
seems to have forgotten the harsh clangour and clamour of
horses and armed men; it has gradually fallen asleep, oblivious
of its seven centuries of existence. From the gateway, under
the ancient chestnuts, the straight drive, bordered by low
hedges and walls, leads by a bridge over the moat to the main
entrance, flanked by two huge cylindrical towers, with their
characteristic conical caps. Between them, directly above the
doorway, giving a central focus to the mediaeval façade, is a
high pavilion. Standing somewhat removed from the main block
are two further round towers, the cones of whose roofs are of
disparate height, adding a rather haphazard note to the mass of
buildings. It was at Ratilly that the Jansenists, expelled from
Port-Royal by Louis XIV, sought refuge. They must have
felt safe enough here from ecclesiastical disturbance, since they
installed a printing press and published clandestinely their
forbidden literature. Today the château houses a school for
pottery, and in the summer it is used for exhibitions and
meetings of cultural associations.

Seen from the picturesque mediaeval Tour de l'Horloge
the château dominates the little town of St-Fargeau. From
the town side its huge round towers in time-worn brick
give an impression of formidable strength; but another side,
opening on to a park of lawns and great trees in the English
style, presents a softer, gentler picture, with the pale rose of the
brick reflected in the placid waters of its lake. St-Fargeau will
always be associated with the formidable figure of Mlle de
Montpensier, la Grande Mademoiselle. In 1575 St-Fargeau

had been raised to a duchy in favour of François de Bourbon, and it was through him that it came into the possession of his descendant Mlle de Montpensier, who was exiled here in 1652 for her active participation in the Fronde. At St-Fargeau La Grande Mademoiselle was visited by the amusing Comte Roger de Bussy-Rabutin, also exiled to his Burgundian estates, and her lover Lauzun, not so amusing but still irresistible, to whom she subsequently presented the château.

St-Sauveur, too, has its château, the present sadly neglected house on the hilltop replacing in the seventeenth century a castle built in the twelfth by the Counts of Nevers. Of this earlier building a solitary tower, overgrown with ivy, still remains: the 'Saracen tower', so deeply engraved on the memory of Colette, '. . . the tower, its crumbling, red-brown stone draped with ivy, and the village that cascades below it and looks as if it is pouring out of it'. For Colette the château and its attendant tower on the crest of the hill above the River Loing symbolized the St-Sauveur of her childhood and youth. At the beginning of *Claudine at School*, that most extraordinary, surely, of all books written about schooldays, she describes the 'Montigny' of her girlhood:

> . . . to my mind, the houses just tumble haphazard from the top of the hill to the bottom of the valley. They rise one above the other, like a staircase, leading up to a big château that was built under Louis XV [she is in error here, it was built a century earlier] and is already more dilapidated than the squat, ivy-sheathed Saracen tower that breaks away from the top a trifle more every day. Montigny is a village, not a town; its streets, thank heaven, are not paved; the showers roll down in little torrents that dry up in a couple of hours; it is a village, not even a very pretty village, but I adore it.

Today the steep streets of St-Sauveur are paved; there is about it a prosperous air; it is—very much so—a pretty village. Colette tells us something of the inmates of the château, improvished members of the local nobility, M. and Mme de Bonnardjaud, who struggled to make ends meet, and 'whose demesne after repeated sales was reduced to a walled-in park'.

They had 'no money and three marriageable daughters', and all St-Sauveur watched with fascinated interest their efforts to marry them. One of the luckless girls was seduced in a pavilion of the garden by a local boy of romantic name, Gaillard du Gougier. This 'penniless Lothario' was kicked out of the house 'like a lackey' by the enraged Baron, and the girl was married off quickly to the first taker.

On Wednesdays the sloping *place* in the centre of St-Sauveur is crowded with market stalls of all kinds, of household goods and clothing, but expecially of the local produce, brought in fresh from the countryside around, and laid out on trestled tables—meat, poultry, game, rabbits, fruit, vegetables, butter, cream and the array of countless varieties of cheese, the cheeses Colette so loved, and could judge with the eye, and the nose, of a connoisseur. 'Not far away from my village were made *soumaintrains* and the red *saint-florentains*, which came to our market wrapped in beetroot leaves. I remember that the long, elegant leaves of the sweet chestnut, with their serrated edges, were reserved for the butter. . . .' It is only a short distance from the *place* to the Rue des Vignes. Colette remembered the 'warm terrace beside a ruined château, arches of climbing roses spindly with age, shadow, and scent of flowering ivy falling from the Saracen tower, and stubborn rusty gates that close the Cour du Paté'. In descending the narrow, steep Rue des Vignes, the house is on the left, a large, well-to-do, middle-class house—perhaps 'solemn', but not 'forbidding', as Colette described it—today inhabited by a woman-dentist. The reader of Colette will not need the plaque, informing him that 'Colette, 1873–1954, was born here', to recognize the house. In *Claudine Married* the young heroine brings her newly-married husband Renaud to her native town: 'I remember the clutch to my throat that kept me standing motionless before the double flight of steps with the blackened iron railing that led to the front door. I stared fixedly at the worn copper ring I used to tug at to pull the bell when I came home from school.' The gates of the yard to the right of the house stand open, and the visitor may look in and see the stables, with the loft above, and the garden wall on which the girl Colette lay sunning herself like one of the many family cats. But the visitor today finds difficulty in placing the 'upper' and the 'lower' gardens, and the orchard behind the house, where the young gardener pruned the apricot trees and stole a kiss from the maid, while the cook enfolded the child's head in her voluminous apron. Perhaps a street has, since Colette's day, been cut through, parallel with the Rue des Vignes, although the walls here look too old and long-established for that. . . .

Yet the memories that came flooding back to the mature Colette at the sight of those steps up to the front door in the Rue des Vignes were not all happy ones. As a girl in her late 'teens, she had seen her parents evicted from this house, and had witnessed the distressing sight of the familiar household furniture and objects put up for public auction from these very steps. The ageing couple, taking Colette with them, had then gone to live with her half-brother Achille Robineau, who was a doctor with a practice in Châtillon-Coligny, a small town some twenty miles north-west of St-Sauveur.

Mme Colette had had two children by her first marriage. The elder, a girl, Juliette, who remains more than a little mysterious, in some strange way 'unsatisfactory', married young, impetuously and unhappily. The second child was a boy, Achille, later the doctor. To Captain Collette his wife bore two further children: another son, Léo, four years Achille's junior, and six years later a daughter, Sidonie-Gabrielle, who was born on 28th January 1873. It was this younger child who, becoming a writer, adopted her patronymic as a pseudonym, and although marrying three times, was never known to the world by any other name than 'Colette'.

The childhood and early girlhood of Colette, the youngest, the 'Minet-Chéri', the 'Bel Gazou', of this admirable family, were usually happy ones, eventful in the everyday, humdrum events of village life, carefully watched over and warded, but not cossetted, by the most sympathetic, intelligent and passionately independent of mothers, 'the incomparable Sido'. Independent of everything and everyone, save the welfare of her husband and children. The marriage of Captain and Mme Colette was a romance that ended only with their deaths. Mme Colette loved—no, adored is the fitting word—life in all its aspects, in humans, animals and plants. With her it took the place of religion. An unbeliever in such matters, she was far too well-bred to display her agnosticism. Every Sunday, accompanied by her dog, she shut herself in the family pew beneath the pulpit and buried her head in a black leather-bound volume, with a cross stamped on either side of the binding—her copy of the plays of Corneille. For the rest, she obeyed the proprieties —'The holy water, the sign of the Cross—she forgot nothing, not even the appropriate genuflexions.' She was a provincial by choice, regarding life in the country as superior to life in cities. If anyone deserved the title of honorary Burgundian it was Sidonie Colette—'Sido' as she was known in her lifetime only to her husband and, after her death, with an irreverence which was only the highest form of reverence, by her younger daughter. Later she reproved any suggestion that she should leave her beloved country for Paris, this countryside of which her knowledge, sharpened by her temperament and education, was more embracing than any peasant's, yet no less down-to-earth. 'Leave my village? Why ever should I? You mustn't expect that. . . .' The very suggestion was preposterous. 'She set the provinces above Paris,' her daughter tells us.

Never for a moment idle, Mme Colette filled her days supervising her servants, shopping, cooking, sewing and gardening. In the long sleepless nights she would read—Saint-Simon or Mme de Sévigné. She would rise with the lark. Under her experienced fingers everything would grow, and the garden was filled with flowers, which characteristically she would not give to the church or permit to adorn a hearse. Once every three months she would make an expedition to Auxerre to shop, setting out from St-Sauveur at two in the morning in the family victoria. Frugal by nature, she fed her household imaginatively and well, and for much of her married life the family was affluent enough for her to order up a bottle of Château Larose, if the 'little one' looked ailing. Latterly, after the crash and the move to Châtillon-Coligny, she wrote to Colette in Paris almost daily, wonderful letters in a beautiful limpid style that was typical of her character. But she worried over her husband and her children, and used to hope that she would survive the Captain, whom she could not bear to think of living alone without her loving care. In this her wish was fulfilled, and she lived on with her doctor son in Châtillon, dying in 1912. She was, quite simply, as Colette entitled an article on her, 'A Woman of Distinction'.

Her husband, the Captain, was by worldly standards a failure. Educated, with a fine war record, a member of the Légion d'Honneur, he was sensitive to the handicap of his amputated limb; his efforts to educate the villagers, to enter politics, to manage the estate, to write, were all evidence to this essentially inward-looking man of his own incapacity, which no assumed air of blithe southern spirit could dissimulate. Colette, late in her life, was told by a fortune teller, 'You are exactly what he longed to be and in his lifetime he was never able.' In the library at St-Sauveur on the highest shelf was a row of black spined volumes, with the titles written in Gothic lettering—*My Campaigns, The Lessons of '70, Elegant Algebra, Marshal MacMahon seen by a Fellow-Soldier, From Village to Parliament, Zouave Songs* (in verse). After her father's death, Colette took down the volumes; in the first was the dedication:

> To my dear soul,
> her faithful husband,
> Jules-Joseph Colette.

That was all; the books were unwritten in.

It was the same with the management of the farms, his wife's properties. Gradually they had to be sold off. After a visit to a farmer to collect the long overdue rent, they would hear the Captain's beautiful voice, as he came singing up the street:

> I think of thee, I see thee, I adore thee,
> At every moment, always, everywhere . . .

Or 'Golden sunsets, balmy breezes . . .' These songs were to convince his wife that things had gone all right, that all was well, and to cover the truth that he had been unable to extract the rent.

These foxy peasants of La Puisaye cheated the Captain and finally ruined him and his family. On his visits to the farms he allowed himself to be persuaded that such and such repairs or improvements were imperative, that market prices had fallen, that abject poverty stared the poor peasant in the face— anything that would serve as an excuse for the non-payment of the rents due. To provide money for the household, the Captain was compelled to have recourse to local solicitors who would provide short-term loans at a high rate of interest. Unbeknown to him, it was the same peasants who had withheld the monies owed to the Colettes who were now granting him, through their agents, the necessary loans. In the end the family lost to their former tenants all their farms, and the 'lovely little forest-lake of Guillemette', and suffered the final indignity of having their furniture and household chattels auctioned from the doorstep in Rue des Vignes.

But that was in the future. Colette grew up, playing with her older brothers, with the village children, surrounded by the stray cats and dogs and their everlasting litters, all lovingly cared for by Sido; attending the village school, wandering in the woods and meadows, breathing in and absorbing the country life that went on so pulsatingly all round her. In *My Apprenticeships* she looked back on

... my own native Puisaye. My Puisaye garland is of flowering rushes, the great rose-coloured water lilies rising from the lake, bolt upright upon their reflections in the water, and the berry of the rowan and the sorb-apple of the service-tree, and the medlar, ruddy and tough, that will not ripen in the summer sun but softens and yields to autumn. It is the water-caltrops, with the four sharp horns, its greyish flesh that tastes of tench and lentils; it is the red, the white, the purple heather, growing in a soil as light as birch ashes. It is the bulrush with its brown rat's fur and, to bind my wreath together, the snake that swims across the pool, its little chin just ruffling the water. Nothing, no hand, no storm, can take from me the marshes of my childhood, the fruitful, swampy places by the ponds, where the reeds grow. Every year the harvest of rushes is cut down and roughly plaited into mats, but it is never altogether dry before the plaiting. My bedroom had no other comfort than these rush-carpets, spread over the cold, red tiles, and no other scent. Green scent of earth and water, marsh fever that we brought into our homes like some gentle beast, wild and sweet of breath—it is with me still. I press it close, between my pillow and my cheek, and it breathes as I breathe. . . .

This rich heritage of their Burgundian childhood never faded from the minds of Colette and of her brother, the melancholy, unambitious Léo, with the fine ear of the natural musician, who at his humble clerk's desk in Paris in reality never left his native Puisaye. Maurice Goudeket writes of Colette's 'rolling Burgundian "r's" ', and remarks on the habits she had retained, like that of holding 'a good coin in her left hand when she ate pancakes on Shrove Tuesday, as people did in her part of the country'. Particularly Burgundian is her unrepentant realism, her desire 'to taste things as they really are', her intellect embedded firmly in what comes to her freshly through her fully alert senses. The poetess Lucie Delarue-Mardus once criticized her for her exact use of names, sometimes the old, or even technical names of objects in daily use but often named vaguely or wrongly. But there was nothing pedantic about Colette; she used the correct word because she saw the object clearly, and its true name singled it out in all its parti-cular, peculiar individuality. Goudeket speaks of her producing a kind of poetry 'from the very precision of terms and their homely technicality', citing her descriptions of cheeses. This use of an exact nomenclature is the necessary concomitant of the accuracy of her eye, the precision of her senses. In this realism she is at one with other literary Burgundians; with St Bernard of Clairvaux, Philippe de Commines, Roger de Bussy-Rabutin and his cousin Mme de Sévigné, with—yes, Restif de la Bretonne.

Somewhere in her works Colette writes of her brother Léo— or was it in Maurice Goudeket's book on her?—this strange *revenant* of their Burgundian childhood, this adult who remained a child, his musical gift never fulfilled. When in later life, successful and rich, Colette lived in the flat that became famous, overlooking the trees, children and pigeons of the Palais-Royal, her brother would from time to time drop in unannounced on her in the evening. He would listen to some music, sit down at the piano and pick out with unpractised hand some piece of Mozart or Chopin, smoke a cigarette or two, say little or nothing, and take himself off. One winter's evening he arrived, wet and cold, looking from the back, Colette thought, 'not unlike an empty overcoat'. With hardly a word, he sat down and smoked his cigarette. Colette, who knew him so well, respected his long silences. At last he spoke.

'I have been down *there*', he said, with a shrug of the shoulders vaguely in the direction of St-Sauveur-en-Puisaye.

'Yes?'

Silence. He continued pulling on his cigarette and meditatively exhaling. After a minute Colette resumed her writing. Léo was lost in his, their, private world, and Colette let him remain there undisturbed.

At length, 'Do you know what they have done?' he asked.

'No. What?'

Another long silence; Colette took up her pen. Léo gazed into the distance, far beyond the walls that encompassed them.

'You remember that gate?' he asked eventually. And Colette saw again the gate of the Cour du Paté, the rusty, creaking iron gate to the château.

The silence redescended and enveloped them.

Finally, Léo got up, and stubbed out his cigarette.

'They have oiled it. . . .'

And with this remark, this rebuke to inevitable progress, he took up his hat and left.

Colette retained her memories of Burgundy vivid and intact until the end. Two months before she died on 3rd August 1954, going through some old papers she came upon a photograph, showing herself among some thirty little girls between the ages of twelve and fourteen at the school in St-Sauveur. She named one after the other, without hesitation; she remembered them all. Her last words to her husband were, 'Look, Maurice, look!' Goudeket thought that in dying Colette was rejoining Sido in the Burgundian garden of her childhood, returning to that terrestrial paradise that was her own country.

BIBLIOGRAPHY

ALLSOPP, B., *Romanesque Architecture*, Arthur Barker, London, 1971.

BRANNER, R., *Burgundian Gothic Architecture*, Zwemmer, London, 1960.

BRAUNFELS, W., *Monasteries of Western Europe*, Thames & Hudson, London, 1972.

BROGAN, O., *Roman Gaul*, Bell, 1953.

BRUNET, R. and CLAVAL, F., *Bourgogne*, Larousse, Paris, 1973.

BULLIER, M. and others, *Bourgogne*, Horizons de France, Paris, 1963.

CAESAR, J., *De Bello Gallico*.

CALMETTE, J., *Les Grands Ducs de Bourgogne*, Albin Michel, Paris, 1949.

Cambridge Mediaeval History, vols. IV and V.

CARTELLIERI, O., *The Court of Burgundy*, Kegan Paul, Trench & Trubner, London, 1929.

COLETTE, *Works*, Secker & Warburg, London.

COMMYNES, P. DE, *Memoirs*, ed. Michael Jones, Penguin, London, 1972.

CONANT, K. J., *Carolingian & Romanesque Architecture*, Pelican History of Art series, London, 1959.

Cote d'Or, La, Edition Richesses de France, Paris, 1964.

CURNONSKY and ROUFF, *La France gastronomique, Bourgogne*, Paris, 1923.

EVANS, J., *Cluniac Art in the Romanesque Period*, Cambridge University Press, 1950.

— *Life in Mediaeval France*, Phaidon, London, 3rd ed. 1969.

— *Romanesque Architecture of Cluny*, Cambridge University Press, 1938.

FOCILLON, H., *Art of the West in the Middle Ages*, vol. 2, Phaidon, London, 1963.

GOUDEKET, M., *Close to Colette*, Secker & Warburg, London, 1957.

GRIVOT, D. and ZARNECKI, C., *Gislebertus, Sculpteur d'Autun*, Trianon, Paris.

Le Monde d' Autun, Zodiaque, Weber, Paris.

GROUT, D. J., *History of Western Music*, Dent, 1962.

Guide Bleu, Bourgogne, Morvan, etc., Hachette, Paris.

Guide Vert (Bourgogne et Morvan), Michelin, Paris.

JAMES, BRUNO SCOTT, *St. Bernard of Clairvaux*, Hodder & Stoughton, London, 1937.

LAMARTINE, ALPHONSE DE, *Œuvres*, Paris.

LEMAITRE, H., *French Châteaux*, Batsford, London.

NORTON, L., editor & translator, *Historical Memoirs of the Duke de Saint-Simon*, Hamish Hamilton, London, 1974.

OURSEL, C., *L'Art de Bourgogne*, Arthaud, Paris, 1953.

OURSEL, R., *Bourgogne Romane*, Zodiaque, Weber, Paris, 1974.

POUPON, P., *Toute la Bourgogne*, Presses universitaires de France, Paris, 1970.

— *Vins de Bourgogne*, Forgeot, Beaune.

RABUTIN, R. DE BUSSY, *Correspondence*, 6 vols, Paris, 1858.

— *Histoire amoureuse des Galles*, Paris, 1856.

STENDHAL, *Memoires d'un touriste*, Paris.

VAUGHAN, R., *Charles the Rash*, Longmans, Green, London, 1973.

— *John the Fearless, ibid.*, 1966.

— *Philip the Bold, ibid.*, 1962.

— *Philip the Good, ibid.*, 1970.

WATSON, S. J., *Carnot*, Bodley Head, London, 1954.

WEST, T. W., *History of Architecture in France*, University of London Press, London, 1969.

WILSON, A. M., *Diderot*, Oxford University Press, New York, 1972.

INDEX

Page numbers in bold type indicate important, usually continuous, references. Italics indicate book titles, French or Latin words, and instructions to reader.

Bibracte, 26, 62, 66
Bienassis, Prosper Guichard de, 259
Binchois, Gilles, 43, 142
Bisson, General, 19, 243
Biturgies, 59, 65
Blé, Antoine du, 195
Blenau, 257
Blois, Henry de, Bp. of Winchester, 85, 116–17
Blondeau, 257
Boccaccio, 145
Bocuse, M. Paul, 253
Boichot, 56
Boileau, 185, 190
Bois du Roi, Mont, 23
Bois-Ste-Marie, 99
Boissy, Armand de, Abbot, 86
Bologna, 200
Boniface VIII, Pope, 103
Bonnardjean, M. and Mme de, 259
Bonnes-Mares, 246
Bordeaux, 16, 60, 62, 247, 249
Boso, 28
Bossuet, Jacques-Bénigne, 32, 39, **221–2**
Bossuet, Mme la Conseillère, 221
Bouchard, Père et Fils, 247
Boudrillet, Jean, 46, 47
Bougainville, 229
Bouhier, Bénigne, 51
Bouhier, de Lantenay, President, 51
Bouhier, Etienne, 51
Bouhier, Jean, 226
Boulogne, 69
Bourbon, François de, 259
Bourchard, Henri, 43, 46
Bourdon, 257
Bourg-en-Bresse, 21
Bourges, 65
Bourgogne grand ordinaire, 247
Bourgogne ordinaire, 247
Bouts, Dirk, 141
Bramante, 200
Brancion, 95, 103, 165, 166
Branner, R., 151
Braunfels, W. Prof., 73, 75

Brenne, River, 194
Brennus, 26, 59
Bresse, 253
Bretonne, N.-E. Restif de la, 230, 265
Brillart–Savarin, 253
Brionnais style, **98–105**, 107–8, 150, 152
Britain, 62, 70, 75
Brittany, 62
Broederlam, Melchior, 30, 45, 140
Broglie, Maréchal de, 231
Brosse, Claude, 18, 242
Brosses, President C. de, 32, 39, 56, 226, **227–9**
Brouhée, Hugues, 54
Brulart, Nicholas, 32, 56
Brunhild, 27
Brunhilda, Queen, 153
Brutus, D. J., 68
Buckingham, Duke of, 173
Buffon, G.-L. L. Comte de, 32, 39, 53, 226, **227–9**
Buffon, G.-L. M. de, 228
Buffon, Mme la Comtesse, 228
Buffoons, War of, 227
Bugey, 253
Bulgéville, battle of, 43
Buonaparte, Joseph, 234
Buonaparte, Lucien, 234
Burgundi, 24, 27, 58
Burgundy, Anthony, Grand-Bastard of, 145, 146
Burgundy, Count of, 90
Burgundian school of sculptors, 15, 138–9
Busset, Comtesse de, 175
Bussières, 217–18, 239
Bussières, Jean de, Abbot, 17
Bussy-le-Grand, 167
Bussy-Rabutin, Count Roger de, *v.* Rabutin, Roger de Bussy-
Buxy, 245
Byron, Lord, 137, 205
Byzantine, 88
Byzantium, Emperor of, 85

Givry, 245
Glaber, Radulphus, 82, 89
Gobannitio, 64–5
Gobelins, 50
Godran, President Odinet, 54, 221
Godrans, Collège des, 54, 221, 223, 227
Goes, Hugo van der, 141
Golden Fleece, King-at-Arms, 146, 148
Golden Fleece, Order of the, 35, 43, 46, 132, 146, 160
Gombette, Loi, 15, 27, 241
Goudeket, Maruice, 254, 265–6
Goujon, Jean, 47
Gourdon-en-Charollais, 99
Goya, 39
Grand-Dukes of the West, 18, 35, 43, 69, 132–49, 166, 241, 252
Grands-Echézaux, 246
Grandson, 30, 137, 141
Graziella, 210–11, 216
Greece, 240
Gregory VII, Pope, 80, 83
Gregory, XI, Pope, 17
Gregory of Tours, 34
Grenoble, 27
Greuze, J.-B., 230–1
Grignan, Comtesse de, 187
Grivot, Denis, 111
Grosne, River, 76
Guedelon, 257, 265
Guerric of Chamballe, 17
Guiche, 180
Guienne, 27, 87
Guillemette, 257, 264
Guise, family of, 31, 38, 220
Guitant, Comte de, 18, 199
Gundicar (Gunther, Gundahar, Gunnar), 27, 58
Gundimar, 28
Gunibald, 15, 27, 28
Guntram, 28
Gunzo, Abbot of Baume, 81
Guy, 129
Gwynn, Stephen, 250–1

Haarlem, 138
Habsburgs, 31
Hachette, 11
Hacht, Henniquin de, 141
Haguenau, Haincelin de, 141
Hain, Claus de, 44, 139
Hallstatt, 58, 59
Harding, Stephen, St, 119, 121
Hautes Côtes de Beaune, 247
Hautes Côtes de Nuits, 247
Heidelberg, 129
Heloïse, 84, 190
Helvetii, 26, 61, 62
Hémery, Michel Particelli d', 202
Henrietta, Duchess of Orleans, 222
Henrietta Maria, 222
Henry I, Emperor, 76
Henry II, 77
Henry IV, 80, 83
Henry I, King of England, 81
Henry II, 123
Henry III, 123
Henry V, 135
Henry VI, 135
Henry I, King of France, 28, 35, 133
Henry II, 47, 54, 169, 171
Henry IV, 31, 36, 172, 194
Herculaneum, 229
Hercules, labours of, 148
Hesdin, Jacquemart de, 141
Heurta, Jean de la, 45, 139
Hézelon of Liège, 89
Histoire amoureuse des Galles, 180
Holy See, 76
Honoratius, St, 75
Honorius, Emperor, 58
Honorius, Pope, 115
Horace, 240
Hubert, M. Jean, 89
Hugh of Poitiers, St, 100
Hugh of Semur-en-Brionnais, Abbot of Cluny, 73, 79, 80–3, 89, 95, 96, 97, 101, 102, 106, 107–8
Hugh of Thil, 161
Hugo, Victor, 213
Huguenin, P., 42

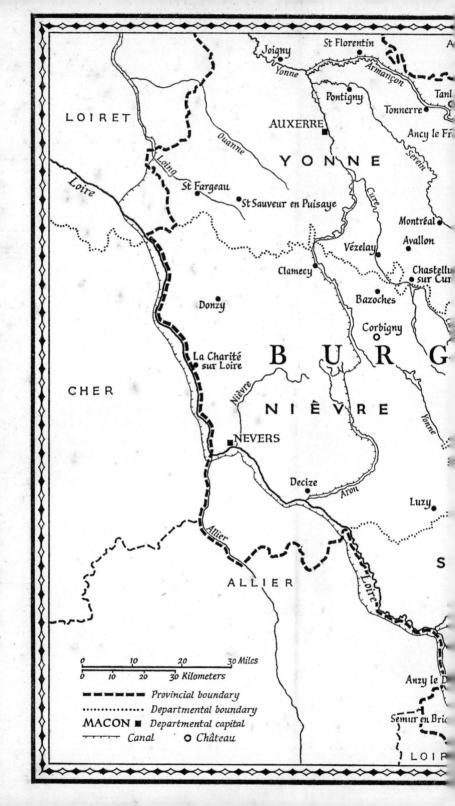